Additional Praise for
Fundraising and the Next Generation

"If you're interested about generational issues in philanthropy and the nonprofit sector, *Fundraising and the Next Generation* is the book for you. Emily combines a wealth of personal experience as a next gen donor and nonprofit leader, the latest in best practices from the field, one-on-one interviews with young donors and fundraisers and more to offer insight into how the shifting generational dynamics of Gen X & Y and Millennials are changing the nonprofit landscape. From engaging younger staff on a fundraising team to engaging young people as donors and volunteers, *Fundraising and the Next Generation* offers a great starting point to explore the compelling issue of generational transition facing every nonprofit around the country."

—Jason Franklin,
Executive Director, Bolder Giving

"Davis captures changes taking place in the fundraising field and encourages the reader to jump right in. She demystifies new approaches to raising money and even makes older readers feel they too can join the next gen revolution."

—Frances Kunreuther,
Director, Building Movement Project

"At a time when every nonprofit needs to spread its arms wide to embrace a diverse world of current and future donors, Emily Davis has given us the tools and strategies to be successful. *Fundraising and the Next Generation* provides a clear plan to attract, engage and motivate the next generation of volunteers and donors. As she so aptly points out, volunteers are donors too and small level donors can be turned into major donors when we have an informed plan. Read this and you will not only be cultivating new donors . . . you will be cultivating new leaders."

—Katie Burnham Laverty,
President, Society for
Nonprofit Organizations and Learning Institute

"*Fundraising and the Next Generation* is the go-to guide for philanthropy in the twenty-first century. Emily Davis has penned a practical, insightful and informed book that everyone engaged in fundraising will find useful. More than ever, the world needs new ways to approach old problems. Davis provides a vision."

—Michael Burke, ChicagoWriter,
(www.ChicagoWriter.blogspot.com),
Author of *What You Don't Know About Men*

"*Fundraising and the Next Generation* offers a great introduction and frame of reference for how to engage the next generation of donors. Davis offers both a research base and tremendous practical tools for effectively engaging the next generation of donors."

—Stephen Bauer,
Director, Strategic Initiatives, Public Allies

"I have been involved in fundraising for nonprofit organizations throughout the United States and internationally for 40 years and this is the first time that I have seen a fundraising professional define the giving patterns across the different generations. Obviously fundraising is a matter of understanding the 'touch points' and interests of donors and this kind of information is critical to successfully raising dollars from donors. The ability to harness and galvanize the power and understanding of both traditional strategies and social media and online approaches, significantly adds to the 'tool kit of success.' Congratulations to Emily Davis for documenting and quantifying this important piece of work."

—Richard Male,
President, Richard Male and Associates

"Emily Davis has put together an incredibly useful compilation of information, analysis and tools for helping your organization successfully engage the next generation of donors. I loved that Davis offers concrete next steps and strategies to take back to the office. Using the voices and opinions of real next gen donors, Davis raises the bar for how, as a nonprofit field, we understand and engage the current landscape of multigenerational philanthropy."

—Mike Gast,
Co-Director, Resource Generation

"Emily Davis does a beautiful job capturing the opportunities and challenges of being a young person involved in philanthropy. She analyzes and synthesizes many of the newest strategies for engaging and supporting young people as they connect with organizations using all of the resources available to them. This is a great book for those wishing to connect with young donors, or for young donors hoping to have a deeper understanding of their role in the broader nonprofit sector."

—Mary Galeti,
Vice-Chair, The Tecovas Foundation

"*Fundraising and the Next Generation* not only informs us of all the changes occurring around us, it provides a road map for the novice as well as the senior development officer on what needs to be done and changed to succeed in a world that has never before existed in its present form."

—Deborah Fugenschuh,
President, Donors Forum of Wisconsin

Fundraising and the
Next Generation

The AFP Fund Development Series

The AFP Fund Development Series is intended to provide fund development professionals and volunteers, including board members (and others interested in the nonprofit sector), with top-quality publications that help advance philanthropy as voluntary action for the public good. Our goal is to provide practical, timely guidance and information on fundraising, charitable giving, and related subjects. The Association of Fundraising Professionals (AFP) and John Wiley & Sons each bring to this innovative collaboration unique and important resources that result in a whole greater than the sum of its parts. For information on other books in the series, please visit:

www.afpnet.org

The Association of Fundraising Professionals

The Association of Fundraising Professionals (AFP) represents more than 30,000 members in more than 207 chapters throughout the United States, Canada, Mexico, and China, working to advance philanthropy through advocacy, research, education, and certification programs.

The association fosters development and growth of fundraising professionals and promotes high ethical standards in the fundraising profession. For more information or to join the world's largest association of fundraising professionals, visit www.afpnet.org.

2010-2011 AFP Publishing Advisory Committee

Chair: D. C. Dreger, ACFRE
Director of Campaigns for the Americas, Habitat for Humanity International
Angela Beers, CFRE
Director of Development, Devereux Pocono Center
Nina P. Berkheiser, CFRE
Principal Consultant, Your Nonprofit Advisor
Linda L. Chew, CFRE
Development Consultant
Stephanie Cory, CFRE, CAP
Director of Development, The Arc of Chester County
Patricia L. Eldred, CFRE
Director of Development, Independent Living Inc.
Samuel N. Gough, CFRE
Principal, The AFRAM Group
Larry Hostetler, CFRE
Director of Marketing and Fund Development, Sierra Vista Child & Family Services
Audrey P. Kintzi, ACFRE
Director of Development, Courage Center
Steven P. Miller, CFRE
Director of Individual Giving, American Kidney Fund
Robert J. Mueller, CFRE
Vice President, Hospice Foundation of Louisville

Maria Elena Noriega
Director, Noriega Malo & Associates
Paula K. Parrish, CFRE
Director of Advancement, Fort Worth Country Day
Michele Pearce
Director of Development, Consumer Credit Counseling Service of Greater Atlanta
Leslie E. Weir, MA, ACFRE
Director of Family Philanthropy, The Winnipeg Foundation
Sharon R. Will, CFRE
Director of Development, South Wind Hospice
Timothy J. Willard, PhD, CFRE
Vice President for Development, Ranken Technical College

John Wiley & Sons:
Susan McDermott
Senior Editor (Professional/Trade Division)

AFP Staff:
Rhonda Starr
Vice President, Education and Training
Reed Stockman
AFP Staff Support

Fundraising and the Next Generation

Tools for Engaging the Next Generation of Philanthropists

Emily Davis, MNM

WILEY

John Wiley & Sons, Inc.

Published by John Wiley & Sons, Inc., Hoboken, New Jersey.

Published simultaneously in Canada.

For general information on our other products and services or for technical support, please contact our Customer Care Department within the United States at (800) 762–2974, outside the United States at (317) 572–3993 or fax (317) 572–4002.

Wiley also publishes its books in a variety of electronic formats. Some content that appears in print may not be available in electronic books. For more information about Wiley products, visit our web site at www.wiley.com.

Library of Congress Cataloging-in-Publication Data:
Davis, Emily, 1978-
    Fundraising and the next generation : tools for engaging the next generation of philanthropists / Emily Davis.
        p. cm. – (The AFP fund development series)
    Includes index.
    ISBN 978-1-118-07702-3 (cloth); 978-1-118-23657-4 (ebk); 978-1-118-22268-3 (ebk); 978-1-118-26150-7 (ebk)
    1. Fund raising. 2. Young adults. 3. Nonprofit organizations-Management.   I. Title.
    HV41.2.D38 2012
    658.15'224–dc23

                                                                    2011050806

Printed in the United States of America

10 9 8 7 6 5 4 3 2 1

*This book is dedicated to all the individuals
who strive to strengthen their organizations and
better serve their missions and the world.*

Thank you.

Contents

Acknowledgments   xv

CHAPTER 1   **Introduction**   1
             Embracing New Approaches   1
             How This Book Is Organized   3
             Getting Started   6

CHAPTER 2   **Generations in Philanthropy**   7
             Setting the Stage   7
             Defining the Generations   8
             Leading Multigen Fundraising Efforts   16
             Conclusion   37
             Notes   40

CHAPTER 3   **Engaging Philanthropy's Next Generation**   43
             The Opportunities of Seeking Funds from Young
                 Philanthropists   43
             Cultivating the Next Generation of Donors   45
             Relationships Don't Change   60
             Conclusion   63
             Notes   70

CHAPTER 4   **Volunteering *Is* Philanthropy**   73
             Creating Volunteer Opportunities Increases
                 Prospective Donors   74
             Committee Participation   80
             Board Service   82
             Conclusion   92
             Notes   93

CHAPTER 5   **The Next Generation of Grant Makers**   **95**
Investing in Professional Development   96
Networking Resources   100
How Social Media Changes Grant Making   101
Understanding Family Philanthropy   102
What Nonprofits Can Do   113
Notes   115

CHAPTER 6   **Harnessing the Power of Online Communications**   **117**
Going Where the Givers Are   117
Social Media Is *a* Tool, Not *the* Tool   119
Listen to Your Fans and Followers   120
Social Media Is a Plant   122
Social Media Is Stewardship   123
Adding Value through Social Media   124
Social Media Is a Two-Way Street   124
Not Everyone "Diggs" Social Media   125
It Ain't Free   126
Build a Social Media Plan   126
Implementing the Social Media Plan   129
Evaluating Social Media Strategies   135
Social Media Policies   135
Conclusion   138
Notes   139

CHAPTER 7   **Conclusion**   **141**
Where to Go from Here   141
Becoming a Learning Organization   143

APPENDIX A   **Worksheets, Plans, and Templates**   **145**
Fundraising and the Next Generation Worksheet   146
Organizational Readiness Assessment   148
Stewardship Plan Worksheet   155
Sample Memorandum of Understanding (MOU)   160
Sample Board Recruitment Plan   162
Social Media Plan Worksheet   165
Social Media Plan Outline   167
Blog Post Template   171
Notes   172

APPENDIX B   **Selected Interviews**   **173**
Next Gen Philanthropist: Mike Gast,
   Resource Generation   174
Next Gen Grant Maker: Jason Franklin,
   Bolder Giving   179

Multigen Family Philanthropy: Sharna
    Goldseker, 21/64   184
Family Philanthropy Consultant: Lisa Parker,
    Family Circle Advisors   190
Family Foundation: Mary Galeti,
    The Tecovas Foundation   193
Giving Circles: Alan Frosh, The Gordian Fund   196
Giving Tiers: Jennie Arbogash, Social Venture
    Partners of Boulder County   202
Notes   206

APPENDIX C   **Survey Summaries**   **207**
Multigenerational Development Office Survey Results   208
Philanthropy's Next Generation Survey Results   230

About the Author   **289**
Index   **291**

Acknowledgments

This book would not be possible without the incredible generosity of a great number of individuals. I have unending appreciation for my writing coach, Amy Rosenblum, for her dynamic insights and unyielding support in the writing process. Thank you for taking the time for honest and constructive feedback, cheerleading, and walks in the park—this would not be possible without you.

Thank you to my dear family and friends for their incredible generosity, patience, and guidance. Countless thanks to all the people who have helped and who continue to help shape my career and knowledge about leading and fundraising in the not-for-profit world. Every success and challenge has taught me so much—each of you plays a critical role in this book.

Many thanks to every individual who donated his or her time in order to be interviewed for the book and to help elevate the conversation about fundraising with and from the next generation. These contributions are invaluable to telling the story of next gen philanthropy. Although not every interview is included in the final book all of them will be posted to the *Fundraising and the Next Generation* blog. Sharing stories of success and hearing from philanthropists themselves is the best way to demonstrate the theories and concepts shared in the pages of this book.

Thank you to the readers who commit to diversifying their resource development efforts and expanding their networks. Although change can be daunting, it provides a platform for creative solutions. It is my hope that *Fundraising and the Next Generation* will inspire new perspective for staff, boards, and volunteers at nonprofit organizations.

Enjoy!

CHAPTER 1

Introduction

Fundraising and the Next Generation provides an introduction to fundraising from multiple generations, in particular the next generation—Generation X and Millennials (also known as Generation Y). As more research is available there will be more data to incorporate into the dialogue. And this truly is a process; it is only the start of the conversation and a jumping-off point for future conversations.

This book is particularly relevant for small- to midsize nonprofits, but nonprofit organizations and foundations of any size can benefit from its content. The most beneficial investment your organization can make is engaging your staff and volunteers in conversations about fundraising across the generations. Ask the hard questions, self-examine, and integrate tools and strategies that will better serve your organization's mission for long-term sustainability. Give everyone in your organization a voice—not only the board and staff leadership. Ask your donors, your "junior" staff, and your volunteers for their feedback. This does not mean that everyone will get what he or she asks for, but at least he or she will have been included in an important conversation. Go on a listening tour to find out where your organizational strengths and weaknesses are.

EMBRACING NEW APPROACHES

Reading blogs and keeping up with research will inspire the creative drive for trying new approaches. There are resources, both print and online, listed at the end of every chapter to help inspire your commitment to fundraising from the next generation. Share your stories of both success and failure. If your organization tries a strategy and it does not work as well as anticipated do not give up. Evaluate what worked and what did not, then try it again. Incorporating new information and adapting to change is a struggle for all organizations, but be open to listening and learning as you go. Alter your approaches to engaging the next generation of philanthropists and be willing to draw outside the lines, knowing that philanthropy is ever evolving. The goal of this book is to help you learn not only how to recruit and retain Gen X and Y, but how to become open to the unexpected changes in the future with Generation Z and more.

In 2011, two surveys were conducted—one focused on multigenerational development offices and one focused on next generation philanthropy—to gather greater insights into fundraising from and with multiple generations. The surveys were conducted in an effort to gain qualitative and quantitative insights into the behaviors both of next gen philanthropists and the multiple generations working in nonprofit fundraising departments. These surveys are not scientific research and the topics require further scrutiny, but what was clear is that the vast majority (more than 85 percent) of development professionals are interested in learning how to recruit and retain the next generation of donors.

The survey on multigenerational development offices was sent out electronically across the United States as a way to gain insights into the internal dynamics among generations at nonprofit organizations. More than 170 individuals from four generations participated in this online survey including executive directors. Anyone involved in a staff capacity as a fundraising professional was encouraged to participate over a two-month period. The questions were designed based on previous multigenerational nonprofit research and simply asked questions that fundraisers often want to know about working in a multigenerational development department. Although there are more and more conversations about multigenerationalism within the nonprofit sector, little has been researched about development departments specifically. Quantitative and qualitative data was gathered and is shared in Appendix C of this book.

The second survey, Philanthropy's Next Generation, was an electronic survey marketed across the country through online and personal networks. Nearly 250 individuals participated in the survey regardless of the amount of money they have donated in the past or current donate financially. This survey focused on donors from Generation X and Y (Millennials) and the intention was to challenge assumptions about giving from these generations. The survey strives to answer questions that fundraisers may have about recruiting funds from these groups of current and future philanthropists. The intention of this survey was to provide a voice and a face to the next generation of philanthropists—to tell a story in a way that would help inform this book further. For the complete survey, see Appendix C. Now more than ever with the financial constraints on the economy, on philanthropy, and on nonprofit organizations' development staff and nonprofit leadership, both staff and volunteers need to open up the possibility of donations from every generation. In truth, there is nothing new here. The trend has been to focus on Boomers and Traditionalists as they age. Traditionalists and Boomers in their thirties were annual givers to begin with and eventually grew into planned giving prospects. The same is true with Gen X and Y. What is unique about the current landscape is that people are simply living longer. Tailoring communications for each of the four generations will help nonprofits to engage and raise funds for years to come. Every donor is influenced by unique experiences and passions—so is each generation. *Fundraising and the Next Generation* provides your organization with ways to engage Generation X and Y to maximize the philanthropic return for your organization.

How This Book Is Organized

Following the quick introduction in Chapter 1, Chapter 2 provides common language used throughout this book about who the generations are and their general characteristics. This does not mean that every donor will demonstrate the characteristics associated with his or her generation, but it does offer a starting point for developing relationships and adjusting communications. In addition, Chapter 2 is focused on a subsector of the conversation happening in nonprofit and philanthropic organizations about recruiting and retaining multigenerational staff members into the development function. There are a growing number of resources on the topic of recruiting and retaining the next generation of staff members. It is important to understand how to work in a multigenerational office setting in order to fundraise from multiple generations. Be willing to be flexible with each generation, but use Chapter 2 as a jumping-off point and a way to set the stage for the remainder of *Fundraising and the Next Generation*. Some comments will shock you and others might be familiar. No matter what your reaction, this is where the conversation begins—at home.

Chapter 3 is all about the next generation of philanthropists and is the heart of this book. It provides you with quotes, stories, and tips for working with and engaging the next generation of donors. Philanthropy and communications have evolved and so have the generations. This chapter begins to outline exactly how your organization can incorporate specific strategies into your existing work. There is no quick fix. Multigenerational prospecting, cultivation, and stewardship is a process; it does not come with the click of a button, conducting a happy hour, or inviting one young person onto your organization's board of directors. As a supplement to the information in this chapter, you can use the worksheets and assessment provided in Appendix A to get an idea of where your organization is and where it can go in the future. Gain insight into the motivations and opinions of many next generation givers to help expand the focus of your fundraising efforts. Of particular interest is GenNext, United Way of Greater St. Louis's outstanding program that has used the best practices to raise dollars and invest in a long-term strategy for relationship building with younger generations.

The next generation of donors sees philanthropy as more than writing a check and volunteerism is a huge part of their contribution to nonprofit organizations. Chapter 4 explores how organizations can better use the next generation of volunteers to support the mission of the organization and leverage future donations to further their cause. Nonprofits need to look beyond administrative work or a junior board to engage younger donors. Board service and committee participation needs to be authentic and rewarding in order to retain quality volunteers as well as spread positive word of mouth about your organization.

Chapter 5 provides an inside look into conversations and activities related to the next generation of grant making. Fundraisers need to know what's happening inside strategic philanthropy in order to be prepared for working with grant makers of all generations. Family philanthropy and young grant-making staff are being significantly impacted on all the generations as well. Understanding family dynamics and multigenerational issues in grant-making organizations provide fundraisers with an inside glimpse into the struggles and changes that could affect how dollars are sought out and distributed. The next generation in grant making refers to not only the individuals involved, but also to the changing approaches in grant making. This book does not address youth philanthropy—philanthropists under the age of 18—although it is an important topic and warrants additional research and discussion.

It would be impossible to talk about fundraising from and with the next generation without incorporating social media. This book is not intended to be a step-by-step workbook on how to use each social media tool, but rather how to apply fundraising concepts to social media in an effective way. In Chapter 6, readers learn that social media is a tool, not the tool in fundraising. Social media can be used as an entry point to new donors and a way to steward anyone in your community. As mentioned, Appendix A has a number of useful tools and templates that your organization can use to begin to incorporate social media into your current efforts. This is not an exhaustive resource on social media, but it will help fundraisers understand many of the basic building blocks in using social media of any kind.

This book's appendices are full of resources including templates, worksheets, and interviews with philanthropists of all kinds. Reading the appendices along with the chapters, or separately, helps illustrate concrete examples and inspires action.

Appendix A includes the following tools, worksheets, and samples:

- Fundraising and the Next Generation Worksheet
- Organizational Readiness Assessment
- Stewardship Plan Worksheet
- Sample Memorandum of Understanding (MOU)
- Sample Board Recruitment Plan
- Social Media Plan Worksheet
- Social Media Plan Outline
- Blog Post Template

Appendix B includes interview material from:

- Mike Gast, Resource Generation
- Jason Franklin, Bolder Giving
- Sharna Goldseker, 21/64
- Lisa Parker, Family Circle Advisors
- Mary Galeti, The Tecovas Foundation
- Alan Frosh, The Gordian Fund

- Jennie Arbogash, Social Venture Partners of Boulder County
- More interviews can be found on the Fundraising and the Next Generation blog (http://edaconsulting.org/category/nextgenfundraising/)

Appendix C includes the results from the two online surveys mentioned earlier in this chapter, conducted to help inform the content in *Fundraising and the Next Generation*:

- Multigenerational Development Office Survey Results
- Philanthropy's Next Generation Survey Results

GETTING STARTED

Fundraising is both an art and a science. This continues to be true in expanding fundraising professionals' focus on Generation X and Millennials. The basic concepts of building relationships and listening to donors' needs are still relevant, but the tools may have changed. Learn how to fully incorporate new strategies into your organization rather than tokenizing or avoiding. Ask everyone in your organization to get involved, engage in discussion, and get your board and staff leadership participating in changes, big or small, happening in your fundraising efforts.

It is certainly not the easiest path to delve into conversations about generational and cultural dynamics as well as change theory, but it can be worth it. Take calculated risks and embrace the entrepreneurial spirit under which so many nonprofits were founded.

Keep in mind that not every strategy will work for your organization and there are plenty of areas of growth in the topic. Customize the ideas, stories, and recommendations in this book to fit your mission—get creative!

CHAPTER 2

Generations in Philanthropy

For the first time in history there are four generations in philanthropy. Fundraisers need to prepare multichannel communications for cultivation, stewardship, and solicitation and need to have knowledge about the generations and any struggles that occur between them. Generational dynamics are equally at play among nonprofit staff and development departments.

The diverse values and work styles across four generations naturally create tension. Nonprofit staff cannot ignore the part sociology takes in the multigenerational nonprofit and development roles. It is important for development staff of all ages to work with awareness about generational differences and similarities among staff and with donors. This will help to raise more dollars and improve the long-term sustainability of organizational missions. Engaging actively with all generations will make an impact in recruiting and retaining staff and donors of all ages.

SETTING THE STAGE

Before identifying strategies and tools for working with multiple generations it is important to set the stage, defining the generations and their basic characteristics. The philanthropic community and the nonprofit community overlap in a number of ways and have distinct definitions in other ways, particularly when talking about "next generation" or "young." Frequently in the philanthropic or grant-making communities, next gen is defined as age 45 or younger. In the nonprofit, or grant-seeking organizations, next gen is defined as age 40 and younger and sometimes age 35 and younger. Next gen philanthropy is not to be confused with youth philanthropy, which refers to philanthropic activities of individuals under the age of 18.

For the purposes of this book, next gen philanthropists are referred to as those individuals under the age of 40. Additionally, throughout *Fundraising and the Next Generation*, there will be references to philanthropic, fundraising, and social media terminology. For definitions of philanthropic and fundraising terms, visit the AFP Fundraising Dictionary Online at www.afpnet.org.[1]

Generational fundraising is a fluid and evolving topic; as more research and trends are available the strategies for fundraising and even the definitions themselves may change. The characteristics and information provided here offers a foundation for conversations about the generations in giving and in organizations.

DEFINING THE GENERATIONS

It is important to define the generations by age and provide general characteristics to help fundraisers understand where to start in approaching and tailoring touch points for next gen donors. Fundraisers need to remember the rule that no two snowflakes are alike just like no two philanthropists are alike. Applying generalities to every donor is risky and it is wise to treat a donor as a unique person, but having some overarching descriptors can be a useful place to start. During surveys and interviews, each philanthropist had his or her preferences on communications and philanthropic inspiration. Although there are common characteristics provided for each generation, be careful not to stereotype. You might risk the donation from an individual or foundation.

When addressing fundraising from multiple generations it is helpful to have common language. Characteristics of and generalities about all generations help staff develop tools and assess existing knowledge and areas for improvement. It is also important for organizations to understand similarities and differences in work styles and values of each generation that affect how organizations manage the resource development function internally. Here is a summary of the four generations and their influential communication platforms as a starting point for how fundraisers conduct their outreach efforts:

- Traditionalists grew up with mail and the nonprofit sector responded with direct mail campaigns.

TABLE 2.1	FUNDRAISING COMMUNICATIONS ACROSS GENERATIONS	

Generation	Influencer	Campaign Communications
Traditionalist	Mail	Direct Mail
Boomers	Television	Television Advertisements
Generation X	E-mail/Internet	Electronic Newsletters and E-mail Campaigns
Millennials	Social Networks	Social Media Campaigns

- Boomers grew up with television and nonprofits responded with television advertisements.

- Generation X grew up with the invention of the Internet and nonprofits responded with e-newsletters and e-mail.

- Millennials grew up with social networking and nonprofits responded with the use of social media platforms like Twestival and Facebook Causes (www.twestival.com).

Table 2.1 offers a breakdown of the four generations and their recommended communication styles.

Communication is not the only aspect of generational change that nonprofit staff needs to explore in order to develop sound and diverse fundraising practices, but it is one of the most important. This chapter covers influencers and features of various generations to learn about fundraising from next gen givers and about working in a multigenerational development office.

Traditionalists

Traditionalists, born between 1900 and 1945, are also referred to as Veterans, the Silent Generation, or the World War II Generation. Traditionalists were influenced by their experiences with the Great Depression and two world wars. The work styles of members of this generation are often described as:

- Loyal.
- Respect for hierarchy and authority.
- Rarely customize.
- Follow traditional models.

- Value of the work they do has more influence than finding personal meaning in work.
- Distinctly separate work and home life.
- Want younger generations to seek more hands-on experience as they did before leading (i.e., "paying their dues").
- Want to be recognized and acknowledged for their contributions to nonprofits and philanthropy.
- Want to be engaged in dialogue and respected for their knowledge.

Traditionalists may be excellent candidates for planned giving and major donations because of their characteristic loyalty to organizations, focus on saving money, and more time to have saved that money compared to younger generations. This is increasingly the focus of fundraising professionals with Traditionalists; their loyalty to an organization is often played out in an estate gift or major donation as part of a legacy. For Traditionalists, direct mail continues to be a strong communication platform for soliciting donations.

In nonprofit organizations, senior staff and board members are often Traditionalists. Traditionalist work styles and values look very different from younger generations, such as Millennials and Gen X, which can have a great impact on the way nonprofits and development departments operate. Traditionalists have a great deal of history of serving in management and leadership roles as well as the history of the nonprofit sector, which can be beneficial to younger staff.

Baby Boomers

With more than 78 million Boomers born between 1946 and 1964, they are considered the largest generation to date, but research is now indicating that the size of the Millennial generation may be rivaling the Boomers. This generation is credited with formalizing the nonprofit sector out of the experiences of the Civil Rights Movement, the Vietnam War, Women's Movement, Chicano Movement, assassinations of President Kennedy and Martin Luther King Jr., and many other events. They challenged the status quo and took action on their ideals by creating grassroots causes and organizations that addressed social ills.

Boomers demonstrate:

- Strong work ethic.
- Optimism.
- Idealism.
- Values of self-improvement and flexibility.
- Seek recognition and respect for their investment and impact on the nonprofit world.

Like Traditionalists, they want to engage in dialogue with younger generations about their experiences in the nonprofit and philanthropic sectors. Their generational values and work styles are often what create tension with younger generations, as there is more emphasis on a "live to work" approach rather than a "work to live approach" that the next gen (Generation X and Millennials) possesses.

In the recent past, nonprofit research such as *Daring to Lead, Ready to Lead*, and *Working Across Generations* has uncovered that there is a perception by the Boomer generation about how knowledge or expertise is acquired in philanthropy and the nonprofit sector. Boomer leaders have had to learn on the job and did not have academic resources to draw on that future generations have had. The new field of academic learning in philanthropy and nonprofit work has come directly as a result of the previous generations' experiential endeavors in developing the nonprofit sector. These experiences provide concrete lessons and tools from which future generations can learn and build.

Many Boomers are founders of nonprofit organizations, executive directors, board leaders, and major donors. Research repeatedly confirms that Boomers prefer that younger counterparts engage in the nonprofit leadership pipeline the same way they did, by spending time within organizations and learning the ropes rather than assuming leadership before they are ready. Nonprofit organizations and philanthropies, including family philanthropy, are increasingly investing in conversations about how four generations can harmoniously work together for the greater good.

Fundraising professionals are looking to Boomers as major donors, planned giving prospects, and board leaders. They are the parents of the next generation of donors that may inherit the Boomers' wealth, foundation organizations, and leadership responsibilities. Because this generation is so substantial in size there is a greater amount of wealth to be distributed to future generations and to nonprofit organizations. It is important for nonprofits to look not only to these individuals as donors, but to their children who are the future of philanthropy and may continue the legacy of giving that their parents started.

Baby Boomers continue to be at the forefront of conversations today because of the size of the generation and their anticipated impact on the global economy as they retire. The nonprofit community has been focusing on pending leadership changes in transfer of wealth and the Boomers' impact on community services including elder care and social security. This generation has had and will continue to have a significant influence on the trajectory of nonprofit services and philanthropic engagement.

Generation X

Generation X-ers were born between 1965 and 1980 and are a little more than half the size of the Boomers at 51 million. Generation X was influenced by the creation of the Internet, MTV, Michael Jordan, Bill Gates, the Clinton years, shows like *Friends*, and were often the children of divorced parents.

Their values and work style include:

- Self-reliance.
- Finding quick fixes.
- Comfort with working both collaboratively with partners and in an independent capacity.
- Direct communication.
- Financially motivated.
- Results-oriented.
- Multitasking.
- Sound-bite communications.
- Like Traditionalists and Boomers, appreciate public recognition for their efforts.

Nonprofits can credit Douglas Coupland with coining the term "Generation X" in his novel, *Generation X*.[2] This generation has consistently fallen under the stereotypes of slackers and misanthropes with little direction or drive compared with their Boomer counter parts. However, research indicates that the motivations for giving to and working for charitable organizations is more often than not, the same as previous generations. Generation X nonprofit staff and philanthropists are seeking out new systems to create change that will make powerful and positive differences in the world.

This generation has started to challenge existing, traditional nonprofit and philanthropic practices and seeking out alternatives. This meant reevaluating everything from work/life balance to hierarchical leadership structures to where work was conducted. For example, the world of cloud computing has completely changed the way business is conducted and how organizations communicate internally and with our current and prospective donors. Generation X-ers have started to use the virtual world in new ways to blend their preferred work styles with the needs of their organizations and senior leadership.

Generation X has been vocal about their frustrations with older generations putting a great deal of emphasis on "paying their dues." From these conversations, research efforts have started about the pending leadership gap, shifts in philanthropy, and changing leadership models. Research from the Annie E. Casey Foundation in 2005 identified "that younger leaders with a more contemporary frame of reference often felt invisible or undervalued by older leaders."[3] Generation X is the first generation enrolling in nonprofit academic programs and shifting leadership styles. Their new approach to leadership focuses on a combination of academic experience, entrepreneurialism, and innovative technology with reduced emphasis on hands-on philanthropic and nonprofit experiences.

Boomer executives and leaders have placed high value on experiential learning rather than academic learning in contrast to younger generations. Types of and lengths of experience in the nonprofit sector have left the generations struggling to find common ground in philanthropy and fundraising because of differences such as these. Differing values on experiential versus academic experience may not change with future generations and are important to identify and consider in generational relationships and communications.

The conversations about leadership transition and values describe not only temporal gaps, but also perceptual gaps in what well-qualified leaders look like. If fundraising professionals are going to work alongside the next generation—staff, volunteers, and donors—it is essential to understand dynamics between generations.

According to Convio's recent research, "The Next Generation of American Giving," lifelong giving begins in the thirties regardless of the generation; it is critical for fundraising professionals to engage Generation X in lifelong giving today for long-term relationships to be possible.[4] Gen X philanthropists are participating in their families' philanthropies, exploring new philanthropic approaches and tools, and are becoming savvier in where and how they give money to organizations. Gen X is challenging traditional models and looking to organizations with whom they have personal connections, getting involved with their time and dollars, and are improving on older strategies for giving.

Millennials

Born between 1980 and 2000, these individuals are coming of age during the turn of the century and are nearly 75 million in size. Millennials (also known as Generation Y) are going to rival the size of the Boomer generation. Combine the Millennial population with Generation X and these generations will play a pivotal role in philanthropy because of their quantitative influence on the world. As a result of their size and participation in service learning, this group is worth significant attention.

These individuals are celebrating diversity in ways that other generations have only paid lip service to and are often engaged in volunteerism and philanthropy in more innovative ways than any other generation. Social media, 9/11, and the global community have all influenced Millennials. They are similar to Generation X in their work styles and communications in that they:

- Desire mutual respect.
- Want to understand why and are challenging the status quo.
- Are independent, but interactive.
- Appreciate transparency.
- Are committed to diversity.

Like Generation X, Millennials are taking on leadership roles wherever and whenever they can. They are not waiting for permission, but taking on new projects with a strong commitment to making the world a better place. They run grassroots organizations and are creating their own organizations as part of their philanthropy and activism. Millienials' approach to social change can challenge traditional models and without any room at the current nonprofit or philanthropic tables they are creating their own new paradigms.

Millennials are questioning the philanthropic status quo through entre-preneurism as well as collaborating across sectors and using new media. They will be savvier as they come into their thirties and forties and get hands-on with the nonprofits they care about, both in terms of volunteer-ism and donating dollars.

Millennials are even challenging the idea of being part of the "next gen-eration." As Rosetta Thurman notes in her *Chronicle of Philanthropy* article "The End of the 'Next' Generation":

> As a young leader, I didn't like how the "next generation" moniker implied that we have to wait for some undetermined time before we can lead. And until then, we have to sit quietly with the other kids and try to catch the crumbs of wisdom and power that fall from the big kid's table. If that's what we meant by saying next-generation leaders, I sure didn't want to be one.[5]

The nonprofit and philanthropic communities are changing as a result of this innovation. Robert Egger writes about Millennials' impact on the nonprofit and philanthropic models that exist and how they will change because of this generation's approach:

> Millennials will be the ones to restore the purpose of nonprofits. There are 70 million people under 30 years old, making you the equivalent of the Boomers in both voting and purchasing power. You are part of the most diverse generation in the history of the country. You have been raised doing community service. You can communicate around the world in seconds. Most importantly, like the boomers before you, you want to change the world; and you will if you don't repeat our mistakes.[6]

Millennials are a powerful generation. Nonprofit organizations need to start using diversified fundraising strategies now to bring these individuals in as donors, staff, volunteers, board members, and more. Fundraising professionals need to be ready to meet Millennials where they are in order to build lifelong donors and keep them.

Table 2.2 outlines a summary on the characteristics and capacity to give by generation.

TABLE 2.2	**SUMMARY OF THE FOUR GENERATIONS**		
Generation	**Born**	**Characteristics**	**Capacity to Give**
Traditionalist	1900–1945	Loyal, respect for authority, separate work and personal life, value work	Planned giving, lifelong donors, major donors
Boomers	1946–1964	Strong work ethic, optimistic, idealistic, self-improvement, flexibility, recognition, respect	Major donors, planned giving, legacy philanthropy through children
Generation X	1965–1980	Self-reliant/independent, quick fix, results-oriented, short and concise communication, direct communication, public recognition	Lifelong givers, annual giving, future major donors
Millennials (Generation Y)	1980–2000	Diverse, networked, entrepreneurial, challenge status quo, look for transparency, service-learning experience	New philanthropists, annual giving, online giving, future donors

LEADING MULTIGEN FUNDRAISING EFFORTS

In the past 10 years multigenerational issues for nonprofits have become a spotlight topic as Boomers prepare for retirement and younger leaders are often looking for significant leadership roles. Many nonprofit leaders, staff and board, have grown professionally alongside their organizations and have long-term investments in the success of their organizations. There are serious concerns about how these leaders, boards, and executives will continue their legacies or be replaced when they transition out of the organization and/or sector.

To raise funds from every generation, particularly younger donors, fundraisers need to understand generational dynamics among their own staff. More research continues to be conducted about working in a multigenerational nonprofit and it is critical that readers understand these dynamics internal to their organization before they can recruit donors from multiple generations. In order to raise funds from the next generation of donors, nonprofits need to understand how generational differences and similarities impact the organizational culture and dynamics and, therefore impact the ability to raise funds.

Finding strategic and attainable solutions that address bridging the gap between generations and the financial questions of leadership are important for sustaining and strengthening the sector. With thousands of new nonprofit organizations emerging every year in the United States, it is essential that the nonprofit sector design steps to engage and retain new leadership.

According to a survey of 174 participants about working in a multigenerational development office, nearly half (43 percent) of participants identified up to three generations working in their development departments and 42 percent thought they had up to four generations working in the overall nonprofit organization. With so many generations represented in these organizations there should be ample opportunity to focus on recruiting and retaining diversity in generational leadership. See Figure 2.1 and Figure 2.2.

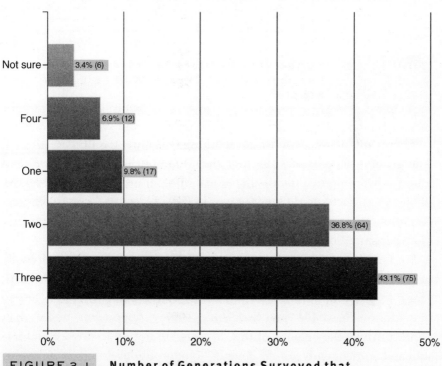

Not sure — 3.4% (6)

Four — 6.9% (12)

One — 9.8% (17)

Two — 36.8% (64)

Three — 43.1% (75)

0%   10%   20%   30%   40%   50%

FIGURE 2.1   Number of Generations Surveyed that Development Staff Thought Worked in Their Nonprofit Development Department

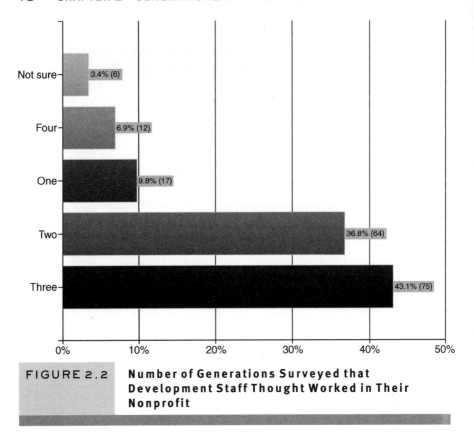

FIGURE 2.2   **Number of Generations Surveyed that Development Staff Thought Worked in Their Nonprofit**

There are many benefits to working with multigenerational staff. The greatest benefits that Boomer and Traditionalist survey respondents found in working in a multigenerational office are diversity of perspective (88 percent); access to different networks (58.5 percent); access to different communication strategies (53.8 percent); and access to a new donors base (44.6 percent). See Figure 2.3.

For Gen X and Millennials, they saw similar benefits including diversity of perspectives (83 percent); access to different networks (66 percent); access to different communication strategies (52 percent); and access to new donors base (44 percent). One survey respondent noted that, "unfortunately the benefits of this diversity are not understood by leadership and consequently are no benefit." Nonprofit development professionals need to not only understand the benefit of working with multiple generations, but also share that information across the organization so everyone on staff values it. See Figure 2.4.

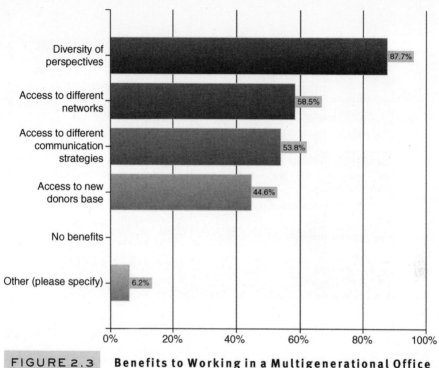

FIGURE 2.3   **Benefits to Working in a Multigenerational Office According to Surveyed Boomers and Traditionalists**

Although these survey results are positive, there still are great challenges in reaching across generations. In researching my paper "Preparing the Path to Leadership," young nonprofit leaders reported that their experiences and strategies for effective leadership often conflict with the values of older leaders. There are nonprofit directors who are committed to preparing and collaborating with the next generation of leaders, but may not see preparation for leadership transition as a priority for sustaining the organization.

During the 1960s and 1970s in the United States, a generation was united by the principles of the Civil Rights Movement.[7] Many of the organizations founded during this time still exist today with Boomers as organizational founders or leaders at the helm. Many directors express concern about who will succeed them and the competency of the next generation

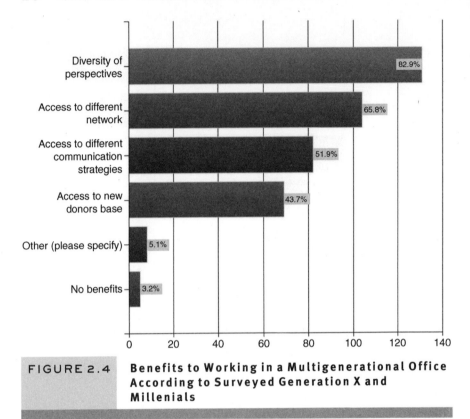

FIGURE 2.4   **Benefits to Working in a Multigenerational Office According to Surveyed Generation X and Millenials**

of leadership. It can be difficult to delegate and share ownership of the mission and vision that they have invested in. These dynamics have a direct impact on the ability to bring the next generation of young nonprofit leaders to the forefront of organizations. One multigenerational development office survey respondent noted, "Sometimes people get stuck on 'how we've always done it' and alternatively 'let's try something new.' It would be better if both groups worked together to make what currently exists better."

Traditionalist and Boomer survey respondents noted that the largest challenges of working in a multigenerational development department are: differences in professional experience (57 percent); communication (48 percent); diversity of perspectives (40 percent); and cultural differences (34 percent). See Figure 2.5.

For Gen X and Y, they perceived challenges of working with multiple generations to be communication (60 percent); differences in professional

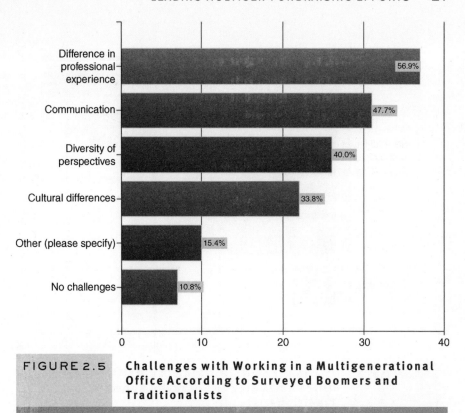

FIGURE 2.5   **Challenges with Working in a Multigenerational Office According to Surveyed Boomers and Traditionalists**

experience (50 percent); diversity of perspectives (44 percent); and cultural differences (35.4 percent). Fundraising professionals need to be aware of these challenges in order to address dynamics and roadblocks to overcoming the tensions. The benefits of these efforts include a better functioning development department, stronger leadership within the organization, and preparation and awareness for succession planning. See Figure 2.6.

The Challenges of Leadership Gaps

There have been countless conversations in the nonprofit world about the pending leadership gap with Boomers leaving leadership roles and challenges of working in a multigenerational office. The leadership gap is defined here as the period of time when Boomer leaders are preparing to leave their roles to when new leadership is installed. It describes not only temporal gaps, but also perceptual gaps in what well-qualified leaders look

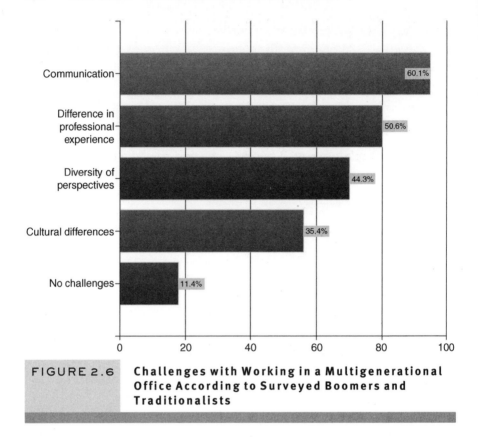

FIGURE 2.6   **Challenges with Working in a Multigenerational Office According to Surveyed Boomers and Traditionalists**

like. Boomer-generation directors and boards often see current and effective leaders as having qualifications that differ from skills that young nonprofit professionals value for excellent leadership. This gap refers to the lack of communication, preparation, and support available to transitioning leaders out of and the next generation of leaders into the sector.

Some young nonprofit professionals feel that older leaders have not adequately prepared them to take over staff roles or that older generations lack the flexibility to adjust to the next generation of emerging leaders. Others believe that young nonprofit professionals have not paid their dues, cannot commit to nonprofit work in a sustainable way, or are too complacent to lead nonprofit organizations.

Articles and research regularly appear in the *Chronicle of Philanthropy*, *Building Movement Project*, Annie E. Casey Foundation, and blogs nationwide about the topic. Frances Kunreuther, Helen Kim, and Robby

Rodriguez have written the most comprehensive source on multigenerational issues in the nonprofit sector in their book, *Working Across Generations*. The authors identify five different theories about the generations working together. They move beyond the quantitative gaps and explore the qualitative gaps in leadership that can be applied to nonprofits and development offices including:

1. **The Replacement Theory**, which is the traditional model of thinking indicating that there are not enough people in line to fill roles and that there is a need to create a pipeline of new staff. This hasn't been a motivating or inspiring reason for nonprofits to recruit and retain emerging leaders.[8]

2. **The Staying on Top Theory** focuses on the lack of leadership opportunities for next gen professionals. The theory surmises that young professionals will go off and start their own organizations if there aren't current spots for them at the nonprofit table. The creation of additional organizations could further saturate the market making funds even less accessible for organizations, and harder for fundraisers to secure. Existing leadership roles and those in them may have to shift to accommodate and prevent further nonprofit creation.[9]

3. **The Redefining the Position Theory** examines the next generation's interests in looking at new leadership models and challenging the traditional hierarchy that many nonprofits operate under. New leadership is looking at ways to distribute the roles of directors through co-directorship and team approaches. These new strategies are becoming increasingly attractive to next gen staff.[10]

4. **The Recognition Problem Theory** addresses the idea that next gen professionals feel invisible to current and tenured leadership. Although the nonprofit sector may talk about the importance of diversity in terms of age and ethnicity, it is not well versed in how to recruit and retain diverse individuals to our organizations. This path requires a paradigm shift in everything from leadership styles to communication to office hours. Next gen professionals want to be recognized for their contributions for the sector as much as older professionals.[11]

5. **The New Structures and Practices Theory** puts a spotlight on the problem from the perspective of organizational structure and

systems. That is, there are new structures to explore that will support the long-term sustainability of organizations, recruit new talent, and disperse power. Organizations that embrace innovation and create fun workspaces may have a better chance at recruiting and retaining talent under this theory.[12]

Development professionals are just as affected by these multigenerational issues as anyone—both inside and outside their organizations. Fundraisers need to leverage every skill and talent in their organization to raise dollars and well-functioning departments that promote leadership rather than simply management.

It is encouraging that more than half (51.9 percent) of next gen respondents noted in the multigenerational development office survey that they did not feel that age was ever an issue in acquiring leadership or advancement opportunities in their organizations. More than half of participants noted that they do receive the support needed from their organization. As the nonprofit sector continues to talk about the resources that individuals need to excel in their jobs, development staff members are showing increased support in their work. Previous research has shown that the kind of support and training has not been available to young nonprofit professionals over the past 10 years. It is important for your organization to continue the trend of recruiting and retaining leaders in fundraising in order to save money and ensure long-term relationships with donors. See Figure 2.7.

To recruit and retain quality young nonprofit professionals and improve organizational dynamics, nonprofit leaders need to encourage intergenerational communication, recognize the value and necessity of young nonprofit professionals in the sector, and consider new leadership and management styles. Leaders at all levels need to expect and facilitate conflict as it arises to generate innovative solutions that will support the long-term health of nonprofit missions.

Successful leaders in development departments and nonprofit organizations strive to:

- Understand unique generational qualities.
- Recognize generational changing work styles.
- Provide financial support and flexibility.
- Consider internships, mentorships, and coaching.

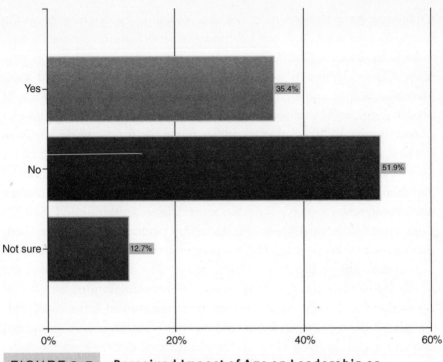

FIGURE 2.7   **Perceived Impact of Age on Leadership or Advancement Opportunities by Next Gen Development Staff**

- Offer professional development opportunities.
- Value academic learning in conjunction with experiential knowledge.
- Share in networking opportunities.
- Focus more on leadership and less on management.
- Embrace qualities of a learning organization.
- Commit to healthy, sustainable communication and transition process.
- Shift to inclusive organizational cultures and dynamics.
- Generate quality leadership opportunities for all ages—both paid and volunteer roles.
- Discuss challenges in shared leadership, executive transition, and communications.

Challenge Assumptions   One of the prevailing experiences of young nonprofit professionals is that of condescension and untrustworthy attitudes from older colleagues and people in leadership roles within organizations. Overt comments concerning employees' young ages and their presumed lack of knowledge, experience, or capability in the shadow of seasoned nonprofit professionals are common.[13] One survey respondent noted, "I recently heard that a number of people from outside NPOs in my field were concerned about my age. They thought it would be best if I didn't participate in my job, but if I just sat back and absorbed more."[14] Another survey respondent shared, "I feel age or perceived age is most challenging when applying for positions within an organization. Given the right mentorship, empowerment, leadership, and team building any staff member who is brought in, who has potential, should be able to thrive."[15]

A common issue that Moore highlights is older professionals' attention to the age of their younger colleagues. "Many young fundraisers say that co-workers or donors often mention their age, and in some cases, colleagues ask them point blank how old they are."[16] If the tables were turned and young people asked older directors, board, or donors the same question, there would most likely be severe consequences. Fundraisers need to be aware of age sensitivities such as these—both on our staff, but also with potential donors. Subtle and overt comments can damage relationships and trust in our offices as well as with donors.

At the same time, younger generations need to be sensitive to the fact that it takes a great deal of time to build relationships with donors—both experience and individual relationships cannot come immediately. There is a great deal for young fundraisers to learn. As one survey respondent noted, "The younger staff would love for me to move over to give them a chance to lead! The competition is not fierce because my experience and relationships with donors trump their eagerness."[17] Competition for jobs is strong as a result of the current economy, but also with the increased interest in working for nonprofits. Collaboration rather than competition should be encouraged within organizations to help leverage all the talents and skills to benefit the mission.

There are numerous resources coming out all the time about learning how to best lead the next generation of employees. Leadership, rather than management, will continue to be essential in developing effective fundraising efforts across generations. Providing opportunities for innovation and enthusiasm, transparent dialogue, and explanations for why certain decisions are made within the organization will continue to make an impact. All fundraising staff needs to be sensitive to assumptions made about any of the generations and to ask questions to learn more about the lenses of other staff.

Changing Work and Leadership Models Traditionally, Boomers have approached nonprofit management with more of a focus on hierarchy while emerging leadership is looking to include more staff and stakeholders in the decision-making processes in an effort toward inclusivity and transparency.[18] Pablo Eisenberg addresses generational leadership fragmentation in the sector in his book *Challenges for Nonprofits and Philanthropy*. He notes that young people are attracted to work environments that are not strongly focused on hierarchy and traditional corporate models, but instead to nonprofit cultures where collaboration and team building are encouraged. Eisenberg argues that young people are interested in participating in the sector as demonstrated by their involvement through internships, Peace Corps, AmeriCorps, and so on, but they are interested in more challenging tasks rather than entry-level opportunities.[19]

The demands on nonprofit executives are changing. There is an increased focus on leadership versus management when working across the generations. Brad Szollose defines his version of the new leadership model in *Liquid Leadership: From Woodstock to Wikipedia*: "The [Liquid Leadership concept] requires adaptability, transparency, and strength, all of what are characteristics of water. Instead of resisting change, aren't we better off adopting a flexible attitude, in which anything is possible?"[20] Szollose goes on to describe what he coins the seven laws of the Liquid Leader:

1. Place People First.
2. Cultivate an Environment Where It Is Free and Safe to Tell the Truth.
3. Nurture a Creative Culture.
4. Support Reinvention of the Organization.
5. Lead by Example.
6. Take Responsibility.
7. Leave a Lasting Legacy.[21]

Development directors, executive directors, and board members need to invest in leadership at every level of their organization and learn about the motivations unique to individuals based on their life experiences including age.

According to Kunreuther, younger leaders are seeking out more inclusive and holistic approaches to leadership that contrast the traditional hierarchical model of leadership employed by previous leaders. It is important to these leaders that all people on staff are able to share their opinions about decisions and are able to simultaneously work collectively on large issues and independently on individual tasks.[22] In *Generational Changes and Leadership: Implications for Social Change Organizations*, Kunreuther also notes the differences between generational leadership and decision-making: "Younger directors were more likely to talk about and try different approaches for decision making. . . . Older directors might have begun their career with similar models and then opted for a more traditional hierarchy with input as time went on."[23]

Cassie J. Moore reports on conflicting work styles between the generations in nonprofit fundraising. "Youthful impatience and a working style that differs from that of older colleagues can also cause trouble, says Chad Linzy, 34, a Kansas City, Mo., fundraising consultant who worked with young fund raisers at the Kansas City Art Institute."[24] The younger generation of nonprofit professionals looks for explanations and history behind courses of action that older professionals can find burdensome. Moore interviewed one individual who commented about the older generation's philosophy, "You do it because I am telling you to do it. You don't question why."[25] This is so important for fundraising professionals to pay attention to in creating learning organizations. Development professionals need to understand that the new generation fundraising staff wants to understand the "why" behind "what" fundraising is. Taking the time to explain the reasons for strategy will be enormously helpful in working with the next generation.

Young nonprofit professionals report being interested in leadership roles within their organizations, but feel they are excluded from leadership opportunities because Boomer executives are filling them or because young people are not valued as leaders. One participant from Indiana University's 2006 Philanthropy Summit noted:

> The Gen-Xers perceive a bottleneck above them, an inability to move into leadership roles. How do we create productive dialogues between

the Baby Boomers and Generation X in the midst of what's being framed as a crisis? . . . It's really a generational question and we're facing a sector-wide founder's syndrome.[26]

Remaining open to dialogue and innovative strategies for leadership will help fundraising offices more effectively work across the generations with not only staff, but also board members and donors.

Young people have evolving strategies for management and leadership that will be unconventional for many organizations. Rather than dismissing new models, executives should objectively consider the benefits and limitations of any new management and leadership style and be willing to take calculated risks. This requires faith and objective examination of the benefits and costs to traditional, hierarchal models of leadership and organizational management. As with any transition, some individuals will not feel comfortable with risk or change despite whatever positive outcomes may result. This is to be expected and open communication about these realities will help better prepare any organization for the future.

Boards, executives, and young professionals need to set a foundation of trust and confidence that all parties have the best intentions for the mission of their organizations and their clients. The perception of limited hands-on experience should not be considered as a deterrent in weighting young peoples' perspectives and talents.

Internships, Mentoring, and Coaching

Internships, mentoring, and coaching are repeatedly coming up as an important tool both for emerging leaders and tenured leaders. These two-way conversations are an excellent way to share organizational and sector history; learn about innovative strategies for fundraising; and sharing ideas on leadership. More nonprofit organizations should consider starting internship programs that are aimed at retaining those interns as staff once their internship is completed. Internships create a learning experience for the intern, staff for the organization, and help to develop consistent staffing within the organization.

Organizations can look to models such as Princeton University and Colorado College who are developing programs where students can apply for paid internships with partnering nonprofit organizations. These universities are making sure that the interns are gaining valuable experience in the nonprofit sector while organizations are receiving quality interns and work. Chapters of the Association of Fundraising Professionals (AFP) often provide a mentorship program for new fundraisers in the field. Young development professionals might also consider looking to professors in certificate and graduate programs who can serve as mentor or coaches.

Nonprofit organizations should encourage young nonprofit professionals to seek out a mentor and support their taking time to meet and consult with them. Nonprofit organizations may wish to consider establishing mentor partnerships within organizations between leaders or former leaders, seasoned nonprofit professionals, volunteers, and young staff.

Continuing Education

Professional development should be a part of any organizational budget. Nonprofits should prioritize ways to encourage staff to participate in ongoing learning and to compensate them in different ways based on financial capacity. Funders need to understand the importance of professional development as a retention strategy for organizations that will help them better serve their mission, serve their stakeholders, and save money by reducing staff turnover.

A host of professional development opportunities are offered locally and nationally for many nonprofits. Organizations like Young Nonprofit Professionals Network (YNPN) are taking the lead in providing mentorship opportunities to emerging leaders. Leaders should work with their boards to create policies that encourage staff to receive academic education wherever possible. Hands-on experience will never be replaced by academic education, but many young nonprofit professionals report that getting access to those hands-on experiences can be harder than enrolling in continuing education opportunities.

Repeatedly, research reveals the importance of experiential knowledge being critical to leadership, secondary to academic learning. Some young nonprofit professionals are pursuing academic education because they feel excluded from other experiential leadership roles. Cassie J. Moore found that her interviewees felt that hands-on experience was still more attractive to older executives than academic experience.[27] This continues to be true according to the multigenerational development office survey,

"The younger generations lack respect for experience. Many of them feel that their educational experience and their new ideas trump years of experience and education of their older counterparts."[28]

Fundraising staff needs to be aware of any stereotypes or behaviors that may demonstrate that negatively affect participation of younger generations. Cassie J. Moore recounts experiences of young people feeling they have limited access to fundraising positions as a result of their lack of hands-on experience: "Young people with limited experience in development have a tough time landing their first fund-raising job, even when they have a college degree that taught them how to manage nonprofit organizations. . . . Would-be fund raisers who earn master's degrees in nonprofit management often face a double challenge from employers: a perceived lack of experience while at the same time being judged as overqualified."[29]

Invite young volunteers to become more active in leadership at your organization through project, committee, and board service. Encouraging an organizational culture where learning and diversity is encouraged will not only support your young volunteers, but will also enhance the leaders who are coaching and developing those leaders. Older leaders will see the direct connection between how their time cultivating these individuals fits with your organization's philosophy and benefitting your goals and bottom line.

Investing in the next generation of development professionals means providing opportunities for these individuals to learn. In order to gain this experience, nonprofit leaders need to encourage their staff and donors to connect to leadership roles. This might not be within your organization either. For example, encouraging staff to sit on committees and boards of other organizations can help the networking for your organization and provide staff with new opportunities to build skills that can be mutually beneficial for your organization as well. Figures 2.8 and 2.9 show survey respondents interest in developing their leadership skills and tools they need to do so.

Promoting a Healthier Balance

In order to retain quality young development professionals and reduce turnover rates, nonprofits should encourage working environments that

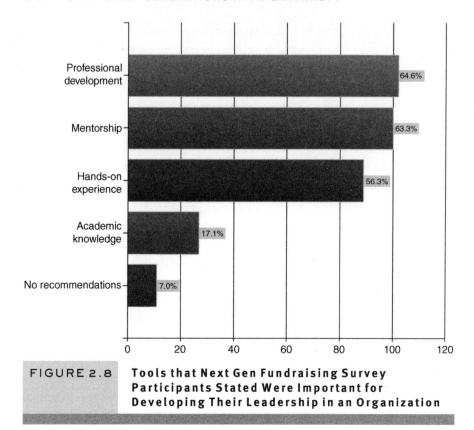

FIGURE 2.8   **Tools that Next Gen Fundraising Survey Participants Stated Were Important for Developing Their Leadership in an Organization**

promote a healthier balance between work and personal life for all staff and encourage to staff to maintain this balance:

> To address this issue, discussions (in organizations and more broadly) are needed to understand how to create manageable jobs that allow for family life, relaxation, and renewal. It is important to acknowledge that staff members derive meaning from their work and at the same time, need to limit the reach work has into every aspect of their lives. Older directors can spend time with young staff and young directors to help them develop ways to stay in the work while maintaining activities outside the office. Finally, funders can help by trying to ensure that organizations set realistic goals rather than encouraging them to do more for less.[30]

In a virtually connected world, many companies are finding that work-hour flexibility is key to recruiting and retaining the next generation of

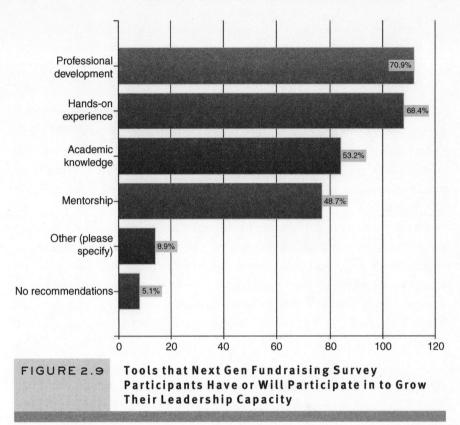

FIGURE 2.9 **Tools that Next Gen Fundraising Survey Participants Have or Will Participate in to Grow Their Leadership Capacity**

leaders. Emerging leaders in nonprofits and development departments are often balancing the demands of a full work schedule with young families, advanced degrees, and more. In a world connected through the Internet it is easier than ever to get tasks completed without sitting at a desk. Organizational leadership would be wise to consider greater flexibility related to work schedules.

The Gap in Communications

Certainly the communication gap between the generations remains an issue in development departments and may impede many recommendations. One Boomer survey respondent noted the biggest challenge that he or she saw in working in a multigenerational development office:

> Younger staff does not understand that donors need to be approached on their terms, not the staffers'. That is, they need to understand and appreciate etiquette that is age-appropriate. Young staff can't expect older donors to follow rules other than those understood by the donors.

One younger survey respondent, also from the 2011 Multigenerational Development Survey, noted, "We prefer connecting electronically, while older clients/colleagues want to talk on the phone. We find it hard to find time to have phone conversations are used to Facebook and e-mail. So, communication can be a struggle . . . it's hard to find time for a phone conversation."

Organizations need to engage in conversations that provide clarification on what communication styles are most effective within the organization and with donors, and why those communication styles are ideal. Be open to dialogue to the preferences of different generations. Often the basic issue is miscommunication. Participate in active listening, take time to ask questions, and be patient in order to generate cross-generational learning. See Table 2.3.

Funders and Financial Solutions

Nonprofit leaders need to prepare to work with a new generation of leaders and simultaneously prepare for the succeeding generation. The sector overall has done little to provide executives with retirement planning or a sense of purpose after their employed activism is completed.[31] Addressing both the financial needs of succeeding executives and young nonprofit professionals will be equally important in preparing for shared leadership and recruiting and retaining the next generation of development professionals.

Boards and nonprofit executives to need to begin planning now for directors' financial retirement needs and should design policies and procedures that will help to support the financial needs of young people without breaking their budgets. It is not necessary to simply increase salaries for young nonprofit professionals, although boards should examine how the cost of living changes on an annual basis. Nonprofit leadership should get involved in advocacy within the philanthropic sector by partnering to create funding specifically for organizational health and sustainability.

Amanda Ballard's advanced policy analysis, "Understanding the Next Generation of Nonprofit Employees: The Impact of Educational Debt,"

TABLE 2.3 PHILANTHROPIC COMMUNICATIONS BY GENERATION

	Understand Their Philanthropy	Frame Your Message	Choose Your Medium	Elicit Their Response	Say Thank You
Pre WWII	Giving is the right thing to do	Traditional organizational message	Traditional org methods	Check in the mail	Send thank you letter or card
Baby Boomers	Giving makes me feel good	Tell a story focusing on impact	Telemarketing	Over the phone	Thank you letter from client or letter illustrating impact of the gift
Gen X	Giving accomplishes my goals	Use formula: $X provides Y well for Z community	Peer-to-peer asks	Online or through payroll deduction	Accounting of how funds were used and results were achieved
Gen Y	Giving is one tool I use to make a difference in the world	Discuss multiple methods of involvement	Build a web presence outlining causes and they will find you	Online gifts and volunteer hours	Interactive thank you that encourages other forms of involvement

Christy Moss, "Generational Philanthropy: Tips for Non-Profits," Thoughtful Philanthropy (blog), February 4, 2009, http://thoughtfulphilanthropy.wordpress.com/2009/02/04/generational-philanthropy-tips-for-non-profits/.

describes the financial dynamics and burdens that young people face in the nonprofit sector and the differences experienced by young professionals in the for-profit and government sectors. She argues that financial burdens are an important cause for high turnover rates in the nonprofit sector for young professionals:

> 74.5% of graduates who enter the nonprofit work force graduated with educational debt. Average salaries for graduates entering the nonprofit workforce were 21.5% lower than those entering the private sector and 10.9% lower than those entering the government. Nonprofit workers tended to pay off debt more slowly, possible delaying other major purchases.[32]

These statistics may encourage young professionals to look to other sectors with higher-paying wages in order to manage their educational debt and to financially prepare for having families and making large purchases. Ballard also highlights that this financial trend is different than previous generations: "trends have shifted some of the burden of paying for higher education from the public sector to individuals. Students and their families now have much more responsibility for the cost of higher education than they did in the past and the majority of the students are using loans [to] meet this increased obligation."[33]

Heather Boushey reinforces this argument in "Debt Explosion Among College Graduates":

> At no point in recent history have we required young people to shoulder so much of the burden for their post-secondary education through a lien on future wages. . . . For many, rising loan burdens will mean abandoning their first career choice or graduate school in favor for more financial stability.[34]

Young nonprofit professionals need to be realistic about nonprofit organizations' capacities to offer staff competitive wages. Young people are looking at getting second and third jobs in order pay off student loans and stay in the nonprofit sector. Young people should be encouraged to get involved with advocacy on a state and national level in order to get the government to consider educational debt forgiveness strategies for those working in the nonprofit field.

Development staff needs to be aware that while younger staff may be committed to the cause and the job, there are financial constraints beyond the work that have a significant impact. Pablo Eisenberg states that while some nonprofits are able to attract young professionals to their organizations through internships, they have not allocated the funding to retain those individuals as employees, and young people move to the for-profit sector, government, or other nonprofit organizations that can afford them.[35]

Nonprofit leaders should institute policies that reward staff members who independently seek out professional development and educational opportunities. Institutional funders should consider funding specifically for developing individuals within organizations through grants aimed at professional development and formal advanced education. Funders need to directly link adequate financial support for recruiting and retaining staff to successful organizational outcomes. An incentive and retention strategy for young professionals might include the organization paying for professional development workshops, allowing time off to meet with a coach, and a flexible work schedule.

Conclusion

As development professionals continue to engage more generations in their fundraising efforts, it is critical to provide clear expectations for staff, interns, and other volunteers. This includes not only job descriptions, but also orientation and feedback. Create work plans, evaluations, and opportunities for two-way feedback and dialogue. Invite staff to board meetings and invite board members into the development office; sharing hands-on experience can help for the generations to understand the expectations in various roles.

In order to identify what the expectations are for nonprofits and what strategies your organization needs to embrace take time to practice activities that will help create a clearer picture for your organization. *Working Across Generations* (Jossey-Bass, 2008) provides a number of worksheets and activities to help your organization participate in conversations about multigenerational leadership.

Current nonprofit leadership from the Boomer generation and young nonprofit professionals can collaboratively leverage skills and experiences to guide and sustain a resilient generation of nonprofit organizations. This collaboration and communication will help to decrease turnover, create innovative strategies for recruiting and retaining staff, and design revolutionary leadership techniques while honoring the history of the sector. This may help to address decreased turnover, innovative strategies for recruiting and retaining staff, and designing revolutionary styles of leadership while maintaining the spirit of the sector. Implementing any combination of the above strategies will help to communicate the value that young nonprofit professionals have in the sector and within specific organizations. Conflict will arise, but with a strategic and flexible approach, organizations will be better prepared for successful executive transition.

Every recommendation provided in this book comes along with challenges and limitations. For many small shops with little to no staff, social media experts or consultants will not be an option until the organization has growth and capacity for external support. Diversifying communication strategies for organization without sophisticated fundraising databases, if any, will prove to be a challenge. The limitations are real and important, but if there is to be long-term, sustainable success at any organization staff needs to get these next gen-ers on their priority lists.

Many changes within your organization will be conducted by trial and error. Experimentation helps to provide your organization with more information on how to reach out. Even failures provide opportunities to learn and tweak your ideas. As new information, research, and recommendations become available, fundraising professionals will be asked to adapt even when the basic concepts of building relationships through "friendraising" still apply. The keys to working with the next generation of philanthropists and development staff is to continue to use the same essential fundraising rules while listening and adapting the platforms and ways in which information is exchanged. In a new world where "friend" is now as much a verb as it is a noun, our vernacular in philanthropy must evolve and adapt in order to welcome a new generation.

As communication was referenced often in this chapter, note that Chapter 6 explores the importance of incorporating online communications (e-mail, social media, and more) into your existing fundraising communication platforms. It answers the questions, "Which communication strategies will be most important"? And, "How can you manage these new multi-channel ways of connecting with current and prospective donors?" Demands for diversified outreach and funding will always be a challenge for fundraising professionals in addition to being asked to be in so many places at one time with limited resources. One of the great things about social media is that it does actually help!

For more research and reading on the topic look at the following resources:

Print Publications

- *Working Across Generations* by Frances Kunreuther, Helen Kim, and Robby Rodriguez
- *Daring to Lead 2011: A National Study of Nonprofit Executive Leadership* by Marla Cornelius, Ricky Myers, and Jeanne Bell
- *Ready to Lead: Next Generation Leaders Speak Out* by Marla Cornelius, Patrick Corvington, and Albert Rusega
- *How to Become a Nonprofit Rockstar* by Trista Harris and Rosetta Thurman
- *Bridging the Generation Gap* by Linda Gravett, Ph.D., SPHR and Robin Throckmorton, MA, SPHR
- *When Generations Collide* by Lynne C. Lancaster and David Stillman
- *Executive Transition Monographs* by Annie E. Casey Foundation
- *The Debt Explosion Among College Graduates* by Heather Boushey
- *Passing the Torch: Summary of the 2006 Philanthropy Summit* by Center on Philanthropy
- *Up Next: Generation Change and the Leadership of Nonprofit Organizations* by Frances Kunreuther
- *Wanted: A Little Respect* by Cassie J. Moore
- *Motivating Young Fund Raisers: Tips for Managers* by Cassie J. Moore
- *Help Wanted: Turnover and Vacancy in Nonprofits* by Compass Point Nonprofit Services
- *Challenges for Nonprofits and Philanthropy: The Courage to Change Society* by Pablo Eisenberg and Stacy Palmer

Websites

- Nonprofit Consulting Café (www.edaconsulting.org/blogs)
- Fundraising and the Next Generation (www.edaconsulting.org/category/nextgenfundraising)
- Young Nonprofit Professionals Network (www.ynpn.org)
- Stanford Social Innovation Review (www.ssireview.org)
- Association of Fundraising Professionals (www.afpnet.org)
- Momentum Consulting (www.makemomentum.com)
- Rosetta Thurman (www.rosettathurman.com)
- Nonprofit Leadership 601 (www.nonprofitalternatives.org/page)
- Idealist Blog (www.idealist.org/blog/en)
- Allison Jones (www.allisonj.org)
- Inside Philanthropy (philanthropyjournal.blogspot.com)
- National Council of Nonprofits (www.councilofnonprofits.org)
- V3 Campaign (www.v3campaign.org)
- Nonprofit Leadership Alliance (www.humanics.org)

Notes

1. www.afpnet.org/ResourceCenter/ArticleDetail.cfm?ItemNumber=3380.
2. Douglas Coupland, *Generation X* (New York: St. Martin's Press, 1991).
3. Frances Kunreuther, "Up Next: Generation Change and the Leadership of Nonprofit Organizations" (Annie E. Casey Foundation, 2005).
4. Vinay Bhagat, Pam Loeb, and Mark Rovner, "Next Generation of American Giving: A Study on Contrasting Charitable Habits of Generation Y, Generation X, Baby Boomers, and Matures" (Convio, March, 2010). www.convio.com/signup/next-generation/next-generation-of-american-giving-whitepaper.html.
5. Rosetta Thurman, "End of the Next Generation," *The Chronicle of Philanthropy* Leading Edge Blog, April 27, 2010, http://philanthropy.com/blogs/leading-edge/the-end-of-the-next-generation/23487.
6. Robert Egger, "Next Generation of Charities," Only Up Blog, January 17, 2011, http://onlyup.org/the-next-generation-of-charities.html.
7. Kunreuther, "Up Next."
8. Frances Kunreuther, Helen Kim, and Robby Rodriguez, *Working Across Generations* (San Francisco: Jossey-Bass, 2008), 9.

9. Ibid., 10.

10. Ibid., 10–11.

11. Ibid., 11–13.

12. Ibid., 14–15.

13. Cassie Moore, "Wanted: A Little Respect," *The Chronicle of Philanthropy*, October 13, 2005, http://philanthropy.com/article/Wanted-a-Little-Respect/58698/.

14. Ibid.

15. Multi-generational Development Office Survey Respondent, July 2011.

16. Cassie Moore, "Motivating Young Fund Raisers: Tips for Managers," *The Chronicle of Philanthropy*, October 13, 2005, http://philanthropy.com/article/Motivating-Young-Fund-Raisers-/58699/.

17. Multi-generational Development Office Survey Respondent, July 2011.

18. Kunreuther, "Up Next."

19. Pablo Eisenberg, *Challenges for Nonprofits and Philanthropy: The Courage to Change* (Medford, MA: Tufts University Press, 2005), 200.

20. Brad Szollose, *Liquid Leadership: From Woodstock to Wikipedia* (Austin, TX: Greenleaf Book Group Press, 2011), 7–8.

21. Ibid., 8–18.

22. Kunreuther, "Up Next," 10–11.

23. Frances Kunreuther, "Generational Changes and Leadership: Implications for Social Change Organizations" (*Nonprofit Quarterly*, 2003), 32.

24. Moore, "Wanted: a Little Respect."

25. Ibid.

26. Center on Philanthropy at Indiana University, "Passing the Torch: A Summary of the 2006 Philanthropy Summit" (McCormick Tribune Foundation, 2006), 11.

27. Moore, "Motivating Young Fund Raisers."

28. Multi-generational Development Office Survey Respondent, July 2011.

29. Moore, "Motivating Young Fund Raisers."

30. Kunreuther, "Up Next," 18.

31. Ibid., 16–19.

32. Kim Klein and Amanda Ballard, "Understanding the Next Generation of Nonprofit Employees: The Impact of Educational Debt" (Building Movement Project, 2005), 2.

33. Ibid., 4.

34. Heather Boushey, "Debt Explosion Among College Graduates" (Center for Economic and Policy Research, 2003).

35. Eisenberg, *Challenges for Nonprofits and Philanthropy*, 200.

CHAPTER 3

Engaging Philanthropy's Next Generation

O ne of the most important reasons for engaging the next generation of philanthropists is that they are rivaling the size of the Boomer generation. They have the greatest and longest capacity for lifelong giving, with so much of their life ahead of them. Resource development professionals would be wise to cultivate them now for long-term benefits in both financial contributions and donations of time and knowledge.[1]

THE OPPORTUNITIES OF SEEKING FUNDS FROM YOUNG PHILANTHROPISTS

There are unique opportunities for nonprofits seeking funding from young philanthropists because of two particular issues: the pending and ongoing transfer of wealth between the generations, and the knowledge that lifelong giving and loyalty to nonprofit organizations of choice start in the thirties regardless of generation. According to the Community Foundation Market Research's study "Family Philanthropy and the Intergenerational Transfer of Wealth":

> American families generated tremendous wealth in the latter part of the 20th century. As a result, America, at the turn of the century, is home to 276 billionaires, 350,000 deca-millionaires and more than 5 million millionaires. In addition to this new pace of wealth creation, a significant transfer of wealth will occur among the generations over the next 50 years. Recent estimates of this transfer range anywhere from $41 trillion to $136 trillion.[2]

Studies and articles began discussing the transfer of wealth in the late 1990s and the conversation continues as to what exactly that transfer of wealth will look like if or when it materializes. The importance of research and statistics from Convio's 2010 study, "The Next Generation of American Giving," and its impact on fundraising from the next generation of givers is cited throughout this book. The general concepts in fundraising do not change, but the importance of bringing strategies, traditional and updated, to the next generation of donors is something that every fundraising professional should have on his or her radar—dismiss no one!

Organizations are being asked to understand and engage in a vast number of communication strategies with young donors and are often not able to create a clear plan on how to execute those strategies effectively. Without understanding the motivations and the ways to engage the next generation, organizations risk losing potential donors of every age.

In 2006, there were more than 50 million Millennials (1981 to present) over the age of 15.[3] Nonprofits should be cultivating Millennials and Generation X because of their sheer size and long-term potential for philanthropy. Wealthy Gen X donors give more and are increasingly aware of charitable causes than earlier generations have when they were the same age.[4] However, they are currently giving less frequently and in smaller amounts than their older counterparts; this is a philanthropic opportunity for nonprofits.[5] Gen X and Millennials are the most educated generations and giving increases as education level increases. In fact, the Center on Philanthropy at Indiana University finds that having a college degree increases annual giving by about $1,900 annually.[6]

This information is enormously helpful when looking at the aging Boomers (1946–1964) and Traditionalists (1925–1945). Traditionalist and Boomer philanthropists will be sharing their philanthropic values and donor dollars with their Gen X and Y children and grandchildren. Boomers are in the peak of their giving years and their philanthropy will change as they age and shift from their peak earning years to retirement and potentially fixed incomes.[7] This means that now, more than ever, nonprofit organizations need to understand the motivations of multiple generations of donors and all the ways that they want to receive communications about the impact of a cause.

It is important to understand who the next generation of philanthropists is and what motivates their giving in order to craft approaches to cultivating their donations. There is much to learn about inspiring philanthropy from and communication styles of Gen X and the Millennials, but "studies on young donors have found that younger donors are more driven by belief in a cause than by a belief in philanthropy itself." Another perspective comes from research out of Indiana University:

> Millennials are much more likely than any other generation to say that they give to "make the world a better place." Whether your organization is an international NGO or a local initiative to a clean watershed in your neighborhood, you're part of a larger global picture. Make that connection clear to donors in your case for support.[8]

Younger donors tend to give to organizations with more of a global focus while individuals from Traditionalists are more likely to give to community organizations and religious groups.[9] In contrast, many Traditionalists feel a deep sense of loyalty to an organization rather than a commitment to see their donations have a distinct and measurable impact.[10]

> According to Sargeant and Woodliffe, members of the Baby Boomer generation often want to know exactly how their donations will be used. Generation X worries about accountability and perceives that marketing is too often targeted toward them. On the other hand, Generation Y tends to be more cause-oriented, ambitious, and empowered with a "passion for social justice and burning desire to make a difference."[11]

Young donors want a connection to the cause through friends, family, or a personal experience; they want to see the impact of their philanthropic contributions of time and money; they want to be at the table making legitimate decisions that benefit the organization; and they want to make a difference on the world stage.

CULTIVATING THE NEXT GENERATION OF DONORS

As a fundraising professional, why focus on cultivating the next generation of donors, especially when next gen donors are currently giving less money than Boomers and Traditionalists? The truth is that age has less of a direct effect on giving than the circumstances of people who are younger. For example, costs of education, marriage, family, and home ownership tend to be higher for those who are younger, therefore, restricting their ability to make large donations.[12]

The study by Campbell and Company, "Generational Difference in Charitable Giving and in Motivations for Giving," provides excellent resources and finding about generations. "When examining the amount contributed by donor households, there are no generational differences in total giving after controls for income, marital status, race, education, region of the country, religious attendance and age of youngest child in household."[13] This tells fundraisers that the differences in giving are more related to lifecycle stage rather than age.

The good news is that with time, these small-level donors can become major donors just like their older counterparts. As in every generation, there are exceptions such as wealthy young philanthropists who can donate outside of their employment income. These individuals are much like the previous generations' donors—lifelong giving for the next generation begins in their thirties.[14]

According to the Philanthropy's Next Generation survey conducted in February 2011, 65.8 percent of respondents began making financial contributions to charitable organizations between the ages of 16 and 30 years old. Ninety-one percent of respondents indicated that they cumulatively donate anywhere between $1 and $5,000 annually to nonprofit organizations. See Figure 3.1 and Figure 3.2.

Where can development professionals find these next gen donors? They are closer than you think.

Prospective next generation donors are already within nonprofit organizations' spheres of influence. They are volunteers, children of existing donors, young professionals connected to or affected by the cause. Essentially, these are the same ways that nonprofit organizations have cultivated donors in the past. Word of mouth was actually the most common way that individuals in our survey found out about nonprofit organization that they donate to at 80.9 percent. See Figure 3.3.

Next gen donors are attracted to causes that demonstrate impact and a direct connection to the cause. Perhaps they become aware of an issue or a cause through a friend or family member or have been directly affected

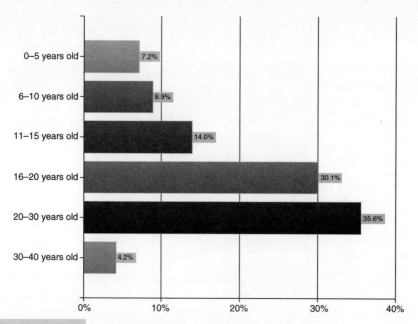

FIGURE 3.1   **Age Next Gen Donors Began Donating**

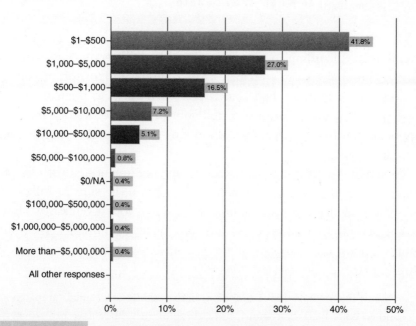

FIGURE 3.2   **Next Gen Donor Annual Giving**

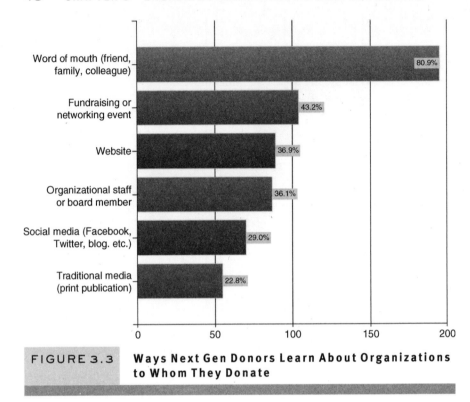

FIGURE 3.3   **Ways Next Gen Donors Learn About Organizations to Whom They Donate**

themselves. According to Convio's "The Next Generation of American Giving" fundraisers can anticipate that "a higher proportion of younger donors plan to increase their charitable contributions to their top charity next year."[15] Now is the time to tell your organization's story and bring opportunities for these younger donors to give philanthropically—both time and money.

Next gen donors want to be included and communicated with like any other donor. If you ask for contact information, be sure to follow up. Never assume that someone cannot participate in your organization's fundraising activities. Without consistent and quality communications, nonprofits can lose out on opportunities to connect with donors of all ages. As this 27-year-old donor states:

> One of the organizations I support is in the middle of a capital campaign and recently held their annual fundraising dinner. They have my e-mail address, but they do not use it to their advantage, I have not received a single e-mail reminding me about the event, updating me on the capital

campaign, or alerting me to a news story about the organization that appeared in a major newspaper. Because I care a great deal about the organization, I would appreciate more frequent communication. If I knew how they would use my donation, I might give more.[16]

Giving Circles

One strategy that next gen donors have been exploring is donor circles. "Giving circles are made up of a group of individuals who pool their resources and decide together how to impact an agreed-upon social problem."[17] This is seen as a powerful way for young donors to collect funds and make a great impact while also exercising leadership in philanthropy. Typically, foundations host giving circles, but any nonprofit can use the power of pooled dollars to benefit a mission, program, or project.

There are young donor circles popping up all over the country including the Gordian Fund, Giving Sum, and the Young Philanthropists Fund. Resource development staff should consider bringing giving circles to their organizations. Using volunteer and board development strategies combined with fundraising basics, organizations can create giving circles within their own organizations.

In one example, youth donors (under the age of 18) have raised up to $200,000 in the last year to grant to selected organizations through the Jewish Community Endowment Fund's (JCEF) Peninsula Community Jewish Teen Foundation. The youth philanthropists operate under fundraising principles that they have been taught to expand into bigger and better ideas. They host events, conduct letter-writing campaigns, and use social media. Some of the participants come from families of wealth and others do not—everyone is able to participate. Any organization can employ a strategy like this to help raise money for various programs.

Provide the young philanthropists' giving circle with the framework and the best practices for fundraising while also letting them lead the effort and explore. Use the opportunity of the giving circle to provide an infrastructure for the donors to make key decisions such as how much money will be granted out annually and how the money will be raised. The giving circle can become much like a learning circle where individuals will not only practice fundraising and philanthropy, but will also learn more about how to best raise money for causes that they care about.

PRACTICAL TIPS

A sample giving circle creation process looks like this:

- **Send** out a request for help from young philanthropists or volunteers to participate in the organization's new philanthropic giving circle.
- **Gather** the interested individuals together and support them in formulating the structure, giving circle name, and other components to critical fundraising and program creation.
- **Ask** the circle member to identify a funding priority or program within your organization. Take time to orient these individuals to your organization through open houses and more.
- **Identify** a minimum amount each young person must contribute annually like a typical giving circle. To raise funds for the circle, provide giving circle members with fundraising tools such as training, online resources, and discussion.
- **Develop** structure in collaboration with the giving circle members for implementation through meetings, events, and more.
- **Evaluate**, celebrate, and capture the history of the giving circle. Your organization may see natural leaders come out of an organizational giving circle that can serve your organization in other ways in the future.

Make sure that one or two representatives from the giving circle present or report to the board or fundraising committee on a regular basis as other committees do. As the organization builds ambassadors for the organization and raises money, watch for particular participants who may be good leaders and representatives for the organization as community speakers, volunteers, or future board and committee members.

The philanthropy of next gen donors in a giving circle can have a ripple effect beyond their circle of friends and expose the organization to more supporters. Many parents are so inspired by the efforts of their children that they may become involved with the organization as well. The network can become vast.

Another strategy that is increasing popularity is creating donor tiers based on age for existing donor circles. Women Give San Diego, a donor circle of the Women's Foundation of California, recognizes the importance of engaging the multiple generations of women in philanthropy. They offer tiered membership prices so that women of all ages can be involved with philanthropy resulting in nearly 40 percent of members under the age of 40. Members in their twenties donate a minimum gift of $250 per year; members in their thirties donate a minimum gift of $300 annually; and Founding Members donate anywhere between $1,000 and $10,000 per year.

They also provide scholarship and matching donation opportunities to include the voices of potential grantees in their decision-making efforts. This has been a successful way to bring in new, talented voices to the organization in increase their ability to serve the San Diego community.

See Appendix B for the interview with Alan Frosh from the Gordian Fund about his experiences with various giving circles.

Events

Next generation donors like a good event—whether it is virtual or in-person. In fact, 56 percent of survey respondents indicated that they made financial contributions to organizations through special event attendance and a fundraising or networking event comprised 43.1 percent of the votes for how individuals learned about organizations to whom they donate. Additionally, next gen philanthropists want to be contacted about their donating to the organization through fundraising (46.1 percent) and networking (24.7 percent) events.

Many young people are taking it upon themselves to organize fundraising events to raise money for nonprofit organizations. Sites such as StayClassy.org, Jumo, and Razoo are great tools for people to do this; these sites combine fundraising for causes with social media. StayClassy in particular provides a social networking platform for fundraising events. Many of the next gen folks may not have the money to write a large check right now, but can serve as an ambassador to raise funds and let others know about the cause. In many ways this is even better because these efforts will spread the word beyond the usual suspects and leverage time for fundraising that your organization might otherwise pay for.

Fundraising professionals understand the time commitment of holding events and potential slow return on investment, but consider providing young people with the tools and let them take on the effort. Delegate the opportunity to raise funds to trusted volunteers—help them learn and expand the organization's network. In fact, nearly 55 percent of all survey respondents indicated that serving as an event volunteer was one of the most rewarding types of volunteer activities. Events can be labor-intensive and having volunteers to help with these activities can be enormously beneficial.

You never know if today's event organizer might be tomorrow's great board member or major donor. Making an investment in these individuals and strategies will help set up the organization for long-term organizational success by applying that approach to the individual. Their total lifelong giving—if cultivated well—can have an unparalleled impact on the cause.

One young donor noted that many young people like a good happy hour, but there should be alternatives to getting young people drunk and then asking them for money. That approach seems to only solicit a one-time donation rather than a long-term relationship.

This is consistent with fundraising practices across the board—events are a great way to cultivate new interest, but the relationship must go beyond a social event and create value, demonstrate impact, and advance the relationship for a great financial impact. Your organization can recruit a lifelong donor by bringing them closer into the inner circle of the organization, teaching them skills while yielding financial support and a larger sphere of influence.

As Trista Harris, executive director at the Headwaters Foundation, notes, "If there's only one person under fifty at an event, the young professional probably won't come back next time. So build a space where young people can learn about your organization and have fun with their peers. Special events should be a starting point, not a substitute for real engagement."[18]

If you are planning on coordinating an event specifically for young professionals, be sure that there is a stewardship plan after the event and begin to foster new relationships. A sample stewardship plan is included at the end of this chapter.

In terms of the kinds of events your organization hosts, consider moving beyond the typical happy hour and try volunteer activities, showcase your organization's programs, and successes. If you have an annual event to

PRACTICAL TIPS

Here are steps your organization can take to develop a fundraising event for young professionals. There are five easy steps to creating a young professionals' event:

1. **Recruit** existing next gen volunteers and/or donors to organize a fundraising event. Your organization will need at least three individuals to start the planning committee. Be prepared to use staff time to support the group before recruitment starts.

2. **Develop** the planning committee by organizing fun and interactive meetings. Ask the founding committee members to recruit one or two of their peers onto the committee. Provide training about fundraising and orient these individuals to your organization by hosting site visits and more.

3. **Set** clear expectations and include goals and parameters including budget. Position the planning committee for success and ask what they need from staff and others to support their efforts. Provide examples of other successful events and be willing to take innovative strides.

4. **Enjoy** a great event and collect contact information from attendees. Be sure to demonstrate the value of getting involved with your organization. Ask that at least one board member and/or the executive director attend and possibly welcome attendees.

5. **Evaluate** the event and process. Learn what worked and what didn't work in executing the fundraising event and in the planning. There will always be mistakes to learn from so be prepared for that experience. If it doesn't help you raise your fundraising goal, don't be discouraged. It typically takes several tries to get the system to help you reach your goals.

honor major donors, consider adding an award for a top young philanthropist as a way to bring awareness and recognition to these individuals.

Regardless of the event, ask attendees for their feedback about the event through social media and invite them to participate in planning future events. Let go of control of all the outcomes particularly because these events will take time to build trust and reputation in the community. The payoff will not come immediately, but the rewards can be wonderful.

Partner with Young Professionals Groups

Look to other organizations that work with young people, like Young Nonprofit Professionals Network (YNPN), which have local chapters throughout the country, or youth groups within community foundations. Sororities and fraternities are great places to find partnerships with young people committed to philanthropy. The young professionals giving circles are a great group as well. Once you have identified those groups, consider hosting a joint event or sponsor an event that is already in place. At that event, share your materials, share a compelling story about your organization, and market your work to this new community.

Boulder 2140 is a group of young professionals created by the Boulder Chamber of Commerce that regularly holds happy hours and professional development opportunities.[19] Each month, the group selects a nonprofit that will benefit from the happy hours. The charity is allowed to have a representative speak and get people to sign up for their programs. Boulder 2140 also opens up sponsorship opportunities to nonprofits for their professional development activities. For example, they host quarterly luncheons on various topics such as fundraising and marketing. They are able to ask well-known and credible speakers from the community to discuss these various topics. It is an outstanding way for next gen professionals not only to learn about a subject, but also to network with leaders from the larger community.

In many community foundations and family foundations there are youth philanthropy groups that are looking for organizations to conduct site visits in order to teach their young participants about philanthropy. Youth donors engaged in the site visits often make donations to the charities that engage with the youth. Build relationships with key decision makers so that your organization can be on their short list of contacts for these purposes.

Reach out to local universities and colleges. Some organizations like Colorado College's Public Interest Fellowship Program work closely with nonprofits to create internship opportunities and connect students with nonprofit causes. Sororities and fraternities are tasked with the responsibility of raising money for charitable causes. V-Day Global and Students for a Free Tibet, among many others, have set up chapters on college campuses to help raise awareness and dollars for their missions. Even if your organization doesn't have the capacity to set up a chapter or program, networking with individuals on the campus—students, professors, deans—can help you get your message across to recruit new dollars and volunteers.[20]

Partnership is a great alternative to starting independent efforts to reach out to the next generation of donors. For example, if you are a staff member at an institutional organization, consider partnering with an organization that might have a younger demographic. This may be particularly relevant for arts organizations like a ballet, theater, or arts museum that might connect with a young theater company. Be sure to be clear about the parameters of the partnership or collaboration, as it can be a pitfall for any good partnership. It is helpful to have a Memorandum of Understanding in place (MOU); a sample MOU can be found in Appendix A. As always, be sure to debrief and evaluate your efforts to learn what should stay the same and what could have been done differently.

In addition to hosting events specifically for young professionals, consider using current organizational events and providing alternative pricing for young professionals. Creating fun and accessible events for young donors is an excellent way to recruit the next generation into the multigenerational organization.[21]

Walk-a-Thons

Events such as walks and races are becoming an increasingly great way to get people of all ages involved in donating to nonprofit organizations. Team in Training for Leukemia and Lymphoma Society and the Susan G. Komen Walk for a Cure are excellent examples. More and more young people are engaging in this kind of fundraising to combine their physical activities and goals with a cause. They are able to fundraise from their network to support them personally and financially support outstanding organizations.

Participants are responsible for achieving their own fundraising goal by soliciting donations from contacts in their network of friends, family, and colleagues. In addition to raising money, they are physically invested in the event by training for the day-of walk or run.

Create events that help young donors set goals, both monetary and physical, and allow them to involve their friends and family in their efforts. Let them share their story with your organization to help serve as an example for others. Be sure to share and celebrate their successes by asking individuals to share their stories about fundraising or host a fundraiser thank-you party and celebration. Give them information about the organization that will help them fundraise on behalf of your cause. Like training for a marathon, good fundraisers for your organization will need training; provide them with the tools to help you.

Young participants are likely to solicit gifts utilizing online tools and social media to meet their fundraising goal. In cases like these nonprofit organizations it would be wise to make sure there is a "what's in it for me" element to help incentivize the fundraising activities. Often this can be physical prizes or you can demonstrate how their involvement can have a positive impact in their professional lives. Provide your young fundraisers with tips and tools for raising money, sample solicitation letters and thank-you letters, individual online fundraising pages, and one-on-one training in fundraising. Your investment in their efforts will pay off in the long run and will establish your organization as a leader in hosting events such as these.

Events are an effective entry point not only for new donors and for visibility, but also for young people who may not be able to write a big check, but have the energy and networks to organize a fundraising event and bring money into the organization. Provide these individuals with all the resources they need while letting them lead the process as much as possible. Make events fun and ask for engagement from young people to coordinate these efforts and programs. Creating opportunities for instant gratification can be a good tool for your organization's young ambassadors.[22]

Peer-to-Peer Networks

Younger donors do like to give more money through spreading the word about the cause, volunteering, through peer recommendations, and emotional connections. They are more open to new organizations compared to older donors that are focused on planning their giving and loyalty to certain organizations or causes.[23] In fact, family and friends were equally cited (about 25 percent each) as the top categories of influencers where next gen philanthropists make donations (Figure 3.4) and 75.5 percent of respondents indicated that they ask friends, family, and colleagues to financially support causes in which they are committed to. With 99.2 percent of

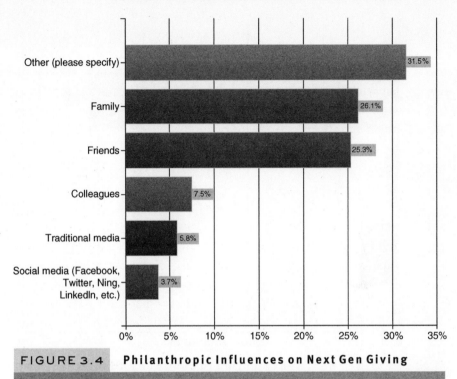

FIGURE 3.4   **Philanthropic Influences on Next Gen Giving**

survey respondents indicating that they plan to continue their philanthropy (Figure 3.5) and 85.4 percent sure that they will increase their philanthropic dollars in the future, their peer-to-peer networks become an even more powerful force as the next gen ages. See Figures 3.4 and 3.5.

Word-of-mouth marketing is just as important as ever and now there are new ways to share the message of your organization quickly and easily. Social media is increasingly popular for peer-to-peer recommendations in the twenty-first century. Becoming a Fan ("like") on Facebook, advocating for a Cause on Facebook, and participating in Twestival are all ways that donors can recommend an organization to their peer group easily about the causes they care about.

Young people have access to networks beyond the online community that can benefit your organization. For example, student networks on college campuses or in graduate school can be a great benefit. Consider partnering with fraternities and sororities to help raise funds and spread the word about your mission. The sheer numbers of people to whom young people have access can be a useful place to look for supporters.

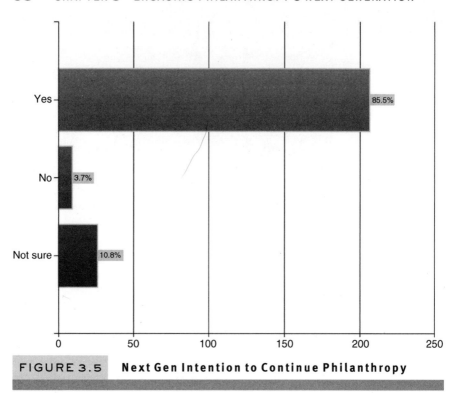

FIGURE 3.5   **Next Gen Intention to Continue Philanthropy**

The same goes for young people in a professional setting. With more and more companies focusing on the importance of corporate social responsibility, finding young people to advance this effort can be mutually beneficial for your organization and the young professional heading up the effort.

Do not forget about the families of young professionals. Young people may have family members whose experience with the cause will inspire them to give; or perhaps they have been personally affected by the issue and are advocating for other family members to get involved. Young donors enjoy being involved in nonprofit activities that are family-focused and fun; do what you can in your organization to open up those opportunities.

Planned Giving

It will be important for nonprofit fundraising staff to learn about planned giving programs for not only the aging Traditionalists and Boomers, but for the generations that follow. With four generations in the philanthropic landscape, now is the perfect time for nonprofits to consider planned giving programs.

The next gen philanthropists are also thinking about their charity after they pass away; 67 percent of survey respondents say that they had already considered leaving money to a charity or charities on their death. Planned giving strategies are not something that the majority of nonprofit organizations consider in their fundraising plans for targeting younger donors, but it continues to grow in importance. "Gen X households, in keeping with their strong interest in philanthropy, are more likely to have established a charitable trust than their older counterparts. Of Gen X trust households, 27 percent have established a charitable trust, compared with 10% percent of Baby Boomers and 9% of the Silent Generation."[24] Even if your nonprofit does not have an extensive planned giving program, it is easy and simple to include information in your fundraising materials that encourage people to list your charity in your will. See Figure 3.6.

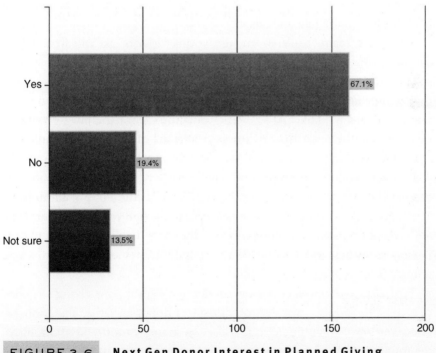

FIGURE 3.6   Next Gen Donor Interest in Planned Giving

The importance of planned giving goes beyond the existing millionaires. The next generation is looking at ways they can contribute in the future, not just in the present. "Gen X households are more generous in their intended charitable bequests than older generations: Gen Xers plan to give 22% of their estate to charity, compared to 16% of Boomers and 14% of the Silent Generation."[25]

RELATIONSHIPS DON'T CHANGE

The same philosophy for cultivating, stewarding, and soliciting donors is useful for donors of all ages: It is all about building relationships. However, the tools and the platforms, like social media versus direct mail, for initiating and developing relationships may be different for each generation and each individual.

Although the avenues for engaging new donors may be evolving, the basic principles and activities related to fundraising and philanthropy haven't changed much.[26] To understand how to raise money from the next generation of philanthropists fundraisers need to understand strategies that have worked in the past and adapt.[27]

There are many tools to engage young donors, so the first step is for nonprofit development professionals to begin to consider young people as prospective donors. "Many nonprofits immediately assume that young people with an interest in their organization are good volunteer prospects. That may be true, but don't immediately write them off as annual or even major donors. Cultivate them as you would any contributor."[28]

Fundraisers need to employ all the tools they have at their disposal to engage the next generation of donors. This is at the core of fundraising across generations. Use multichannel tools to engage younger donors who are civically minded and philanthropically savvy, but continue to use in-person meetings and traditional fundraising strategies to deepen those connections.

Typically, with younger donors (under age 40) they are giving after one or two cultivation steps and through a direct donation rather than donated goods, events, and volunteering.[29] Use the strategies outlined in this chapter for multifaceted cultivation (e.g., events, giving circles). Ultimately, fundraisers need to make a direct solicitation for their funds for the organization. This tells fundraisers that they still very much need to directly solicit donors in the next generation and not completely rely on new strategies like online solicitation.

The top ways that the Philanthropy's Next Generation survey respondents shared that they wanted nonprofit organizations to contact them about donating to the organization were e-mail (50.2 percent), fundraising event (46.1 percent), e-newsletter (32.4 percent), Facebook Page or Cause (25.7 percent), and networking event (24.9 percent). Here there is a good mix of preferred in-person and online solicitation strategies. It is also worth noting that 20.3 percent of next gen philanthropists preferred in-person solicitation and 19.1 percent wanted to be contacted about donations through a board member. See Figure 3.7.

Social media is a way to develop stewardship and stay in touch with young donors, but it in no way replaces one-on-one asks or in-person connections. There is even speculation that social media will replace direct

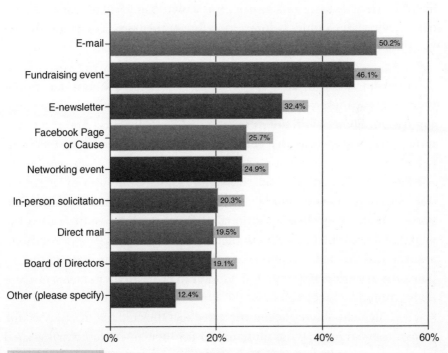

FIGURE 3.7   **How Next Gen Donors Prefer Organizations Contact Them About Donating**

mail, but recent research from Convio suggests that this may not be true. For example, there are young donors who may respond to a direct mail campaign by donating online through the organization's website. On the other hand, other donors may see direct mail as a complete waste of time and money in the face of the new online world.[30]

"The younger the donor, the greater the number of ways they give."[31] Development professionals should consider reaching out in as many ways as possible to increase their chances of bringing in new donors; fundraisers cannot forget that once they open the door to new donors that cultivation is still important to move the individual up the giving pyramid. Of course, having a multichannel approach changes the way organizations evaluate their return on investment (ROI)—new databases will help track this multichannel behavior, but it can't happen effectively without nonprofits investing in donor databases that have this capacity.[32]

It falls on the shoulders of nonprofit organizations to determine the appropriate strategies for the appropriate donors. With the Internet and tools like Facebook, Razoo, and Twitter, it is easier than ever to thank a donor the necessary seven times before asking for another gift. Nonprofits should share their stories online through a blog or Twitter without having to mail out newsletter after newsletter.

The truth is that there is always more to learn. "Ultimately, some of these efforts to improve will turn out to be no more effective than past approaches. Some will result in unintended consequences. And some will result in lasting changes that make a real difference. It's still too early to know."[33]

Like other stewardship and cultivation strategies, nonprofit organizations and fundraisers should be aware that young donors want to feel important, heard, and valuable. Although these younger generations are more viral, still make time to meet with them one-on-one to build a relationship, as this is still the best way to engage donors of all ages. It is interesting to point out that while next gen donors want to be heard they are not primarily motivated by recognition. In the Philanthropy's Next Generation survey, 41.1 percent of respondents indicated that they did not have a need for recognition (beyond IRS requirements) for their financial contributions. The preferences for recognition included a hand-written thank-you letter, an e-mailed thank-you letter, and a printed thank-you letter. See Figure 3.8.

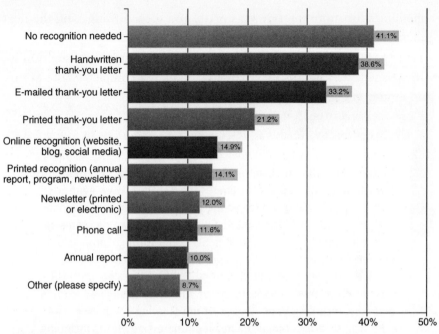

FIGURE 3.8 **Preferred Recognition Types by Next Gen Donors (not including IRS requirements to recognize a financial contribution)**

To find out more about how next gen donors want to interact, ask your current younger donors to participate in an assessment of your organization and provide feedback—this gives them a valuable voice in your organization, increases their investment in the mission, and gives your organization feedback on strategy. Using online assessment tools like Survey Monkey can be a low-cost way to gather information and engage younger people's opinions.[34]

CONCLUSION

There are both traditional and innovative ways to engage the next generation of philanthropists, including through volunteerism, but none is possible without an organizational commitment and focus to diversifying cultivation of donors from every generation. Investment from staff and volunteer leadership will be critical for fundraising success and for long-term funding relationships with the next generation of donors. Visit the appendixes for more interviews, stories, and tools for engaging the next generation of donors.

| ORGANIZATIONAL SPOTLIGHT | GENNEXT AT UNITED WAY OF GREATER ST. LOUIS[35] |

United Way (UW) of Greater St. Louis' Resource Development Associate, Ellen Cooper, coordinates the GenNext (www.gennextstl.org/) program designed for young professionals in their twenties and thirties. United Way wanted a way to engage young professionals with United Way of Greater St. Louis through professional development, volunteer and networking opportunities.

Vice President of Development David Gonzalez and Ellen Cooper have been deliberate about who they choose as leaders and why, including various ages of the steering committee members. The steering committee has led fundraising efforts including the Young Leaders Giving Society.[36] The Young Leaders Giving Society includes young professionals in their twenties, thirties, and forties who participate in fewer activities, but donate more than $1,000 annually. GenNext has had 10 to 15 young professionals who became involved in leadership with the GenNext program and had no giving history prior to their involvement that now give more than $1,000 annually through the Young Leaders Giving Society.

Launching GenNext

David Gonzalez launched GenNext in 2005 when it became obvious that UW had an aging donor base and a board consisting of only individuals over the age of 50. He wondered how he could begin to engage younger donors. He had read research and he knew that next gen professionals wanted more personal engagement and to see the impact of their gifts. The trends indicated that younger donors wanted to be connected rather than feeling removed and making larger donations. Essentially, they needed different messaging and to have more "skin in the game." Out of this information, David created the Young Leaders Giving Society and GenNext.

For David, the concept was a tough sell to the board and staff. The projects would take time and money and any payoff on those efforts wouldn't come for three to five years. David realized that if the organization waited for next gen-ers to naturally gravitate toward UW, it would never happen. He understood that young donors don't necessarily stick with traditions in their giving. He convinced UW that it would take time, but be worth the investment.

In the beginning of the program, it was really based on trial and error. The steering committee needed greater empowerment from UW staff to make decisions. Originally, David was attending every single volunteer project that was rewarding, but not sustainable. By creating project leadership opportunities and training, other volunteers could take leadership roles and share consistent messaging for UW and GenNext at every project.

GenNext wasn't an immediate success, but developed over time. The service projects are led very well despite challenges with retention. The individuals involved in GenNext are a dynamic group with significant life changes, which often includes a lot of geographic movement. To date, there are approximately 750 people who participate annually in GenNext. It can be difficult to connect with every person and get him or her to continue with the organization and GenNext. The retention rate for GenNext is slightly below 50 percent after initially becoming involved. David has learned to accept and understand that GenNext simply wasn't providing what those individuals were looking for.

The GenNext program is unique from other programs and it is especially important to be clear about the UW mission and have those involved in GenNext be educated about the program so they can serve as ambassadors. There are many nonprofits that will invite younger donors to participate for their name or associations in the community. The difference with GenNext is that it is a more open platform where volunteers are asked to invest time and work with the program. Asking individuals to participate in this way has been enormously successful; only about five people in the last five years have not committed fully to the program. By setting a higher standard, GenNext has been able to attract a higher caliber of volunteers, which translates into a better understanding of what they are contributing.

In the end, the programs are an opportunity to have a lot of fun, not just join a professional group. Amazing kinship and friendships have developed and volunteers will interact beyond the service projects. These service projects are an incredible way to strike up conversations and make connections with others; those kinds of outcomes cannot be planned.

Service Learning

GenNext hosts four or five volunteer projects monthly with local health and human service organizations that are vetted by the UW staff. These are unique and rewarding opportunities for young professionals to become involved in hands-on experiences as well as learn about the GenNext program. A project leader leads every service-learning project and is oriented and trained by UW staff about how to serve as an ambassador to the organization and to support other volunteers. The training is one hour that teaches the about GenNext and UW messaging and how to empower volunteers in their service-learning projects. This is a simple, but important role in the GenNext program, because the project leaders are the primary contact for volunteer projects and are the faces of the GenNext program.

Regular Professional Development

The monthly executive professional development luncheons are an informal conversation led by an individual already involved in UW in some capacity. Leaders who facilitate the conversation discuss their journey into their current leadership role, how they are currently involved with UW, how they engage in philanthropy, and why their work, including giving back, is important to them.

Unique Networking Events

The quarterly networking events kick off with a welcome event at the beginning of the year where volunteer prospects come together to learn about GenNext. UW selects a local restaurant or bar and includes door prizes to host the event. In 2011, UW doubled its participation numbers from 75 to 150 attendees.

The next networking event is an annual meeting, which is a bit more formal. The annual meeting is an opportunity to discuss what has been happening at GenNext, where the program is headed, and its connection with UW. Members set the strategic plan for GenNext and encourage as many people to participate as possible. This is another opportunity for people to sign up for additional projects including becoming a project leader.

There is a volunteer recognition event in the third quarter where UW gets donated items to share with volunteers who are recognized for their contributions. The volunteer recognition event is an important opportunity to thank people for their time, but also for networking between GenNext participants.

The final networking event is the annual holiday party, which is really a year-end celebration to reflect on the accomplishments and experiences of all the volunteers. No one is solicited in any way at this event.

GenNext has found that the social component to these activities is critical for building relationships with younger professionals. There is an overwhelming number of nonprofits and nonprofit events, so GenNext wants to provide unique opportunities from other organizations. They realize that it is unnecessary to participate in another happy hour, but need ways to engage young professionals in valuable experiences with UW. Still, GenNext is selective in where they put their time and efforts; if GenNext or UW cannot brand the event to inform participants about the value of the program or share experiences of participating in GenNext, then they will not pursue the event. The key to GenNext success is to keep the conversation going and asking individuals how they want to stay involved.

GenNext Communications

GenNext has a unique web page that allows people to see upcoming events, sign up for programs, monthly e-newsletters (1,500 subscribers), and learn about other GenNext members. Additionally, GenNext has a custom application on the UW of Greater St. Louis' Facebook Page.[37] It keeps all of its social media links, including Twitter, under the larger UW of Greater St. Louis umbrella.

Still, the biggest and best communication vehicle is word of mouth. Although social media is helpful, it is not as effective as peer recommendations. David and Ellen would like to see their core participants use their website more and drive more content. The marketing department currently manages the information distribution, but the resource development associate and volunteer provide the content for their communications.

GenNext Leadership

The GenNext steering committee coordinates all activities and sets the direction for all the GenNext programming. At any given time it has 8 to 10 steering committee members who sign on for a two-year term, with the option of serving an additional two years. The application process includes an actual application followed by an informal interview. Individuals are selected because they have demonstrated outstanding leadership as volunteers in some way. The UW resource development associate serves as the staff liaison for the steering committee, vets projects, answers questions, and so on. UW has shared that the steering committee demonstrates great value for the direction of the programming in addition to the many subcommittees that work on a variety of issues.

The GenNext program has created a unique pipeline to philanthropic giving to UW as well as board leadership. It has more than one young leader who has played an important role in GenNext who later served on the larger UW board of directors.

Staff Support

The volunteers become the ambassadors to the program and although they are empowered to do many things, there are also limitations to what they can do, so Ellen Cooper facilitates the planning for the volunteer service activities. The staff at UW serves as gatekeepers for GenNext leadership and vet partnerships. Staff really provides behind-the-scenes support for the volunteers, but for the majority of the time volunteer leadership manages the program.

Print Resources

- *Engaging Tomorrow's Donors Today* by Sarah Fischler and Alyssa Kopf
- *The Next Generation of American Giving* by Convio
- *Charitable Giving and the Millennial Generation* by Giving USA
- *Generational Differences in Charitable Giving and in Motivations for Giving* by the Center on Philanthropy at Indiana University
- *What's Next for Philanthropy* by Monitor Institute
- *Millennial Donors: A Study of Millennial Giving and Engagement Habits* by Achieve and Johnson Grossnickle and Associates
- *The Impact of Giving Together: Giving Circle's Influence on Members' Philanthropic and Civic Behaviors, Knowledge, and Attitudes* by Angela M. Eikenberry and Jessica Bearman
- *Trading Power: 18 Interviews with Philanthropic Leaders Who Talk about What the Next Generation Has to Offer in Exchange for Seasoned Leaders Can Provide* by Ambrose Clancy
- *Wealth in America 2008: Findings from a Survey of Millionaire Households* by Northern Trust.

Websites

- Young Nonprofit Professionals Network (www.ynpn.org)
- Women Give San Diego (www.womengivesd.org)
- The Gordian Fund (www.gordianfund.org)
- Social Venture Partners of Boulder County (www.svpboulder county.org/partner-experience)
- Boulder 2140 (www.boulderchamber.com/pages/Boulder2140/)
- Colorado College Public Interest Fellowship Program (www2 .coloradocollege.edu/publicinterest/index.asp)
- Young Philanthropists Foundation (www.ypfoundation.org)
- StayClassy.org
- Razoo.com

Notes

1. Trista Harris, "How to Engage the Next Generation of Donors Now" (*Nonprofit World*, 2011), 6.
2. Community Foundation R&D Incubator, "Family Philanthropy and the Intergenerational Transfer of Wealth: Tapping into the Power of Family Philanthropy in the 21st Century" (2010), 1.
3. Center on Philanthropy at Indiana University, "Charitable Giving and the Millennial Generation" (Giving USA Foundation Spotlight, 2010), 4.
4. Ibid., 5.
5. Center on Philanthropy at Indiana University, "Generational Differences in Charitable Giving and in Motivations for Giving" (Campbell and Company, May 2008), 3.
6. Center on Philanthropy at Indiana University, "Charitable Giving," 6.
7. Ibid., 5.
8. Trista Harris, "How to Engage," 6.
9. Center on Philanthropy at Indiana University, "Generational Differences," 3.
10. Vinay Bhagat, Pam Loeb, and Mark Rovner, "Next Generation of American Giving: A Study on Contrasting Charitable Habits of Generation Y, Generation X, Baby Boomers, and Matures" (Convio, March, 2010), 10.
11. Center on Philanthropy at Indiana University, "Generational Differences,"
12. Center on Philanthropy at Indiana University, "Charitable Giving," 3.
13. Center on Philanthropy at Indiana University, "Generational Differences," 5.
14. Bhagat, Loeb, and Rovner, "Next Generation of American Giving," 4.
15. Ibid.
16. Sarah Fischler and Alyssa Kopf, "Engaging Tomorrow's Donors Today: A Toolkit for Success" (Community Shares of Colorado, 2007), 15, www.cshares.org/publications.
17. Angela M. Eikenberry and Jessica Bearman, "The Impact of Giving Together: Giving Circles' Influence on Members' Philanthropic and Civic Behaviors Knowledge and Attitudes" (Forum of Regional Associations of Grantmakers, The Center on Philanthropy at Indiana University, and University of Nebraska at Omaha, 2009), 4.
18. Trista Harris, "How to Engage," 7.
19. Boulder 2140 web page, accessed September 24, 2011, www.boulderchamber.com/pages/Boulder2140/.
20. Center on Philanthropy at Indiana University, "Charitable Giving," 7.
21. Fischler and Kopf, "Engaging Tomorrow's Donors Today," 6.
22. Katherine Fulton, Gabriel Kasper, and Barbara Kibbe, "What's Next for Philanthropy" (Monitor Institute, July 2010), 2.
23. Bhagat, Loeb, and Rovner, "Next Generation of American Giving," 10.
24. Phoenix Marketing International, "Wealth in America 2008: Findings from a Survey of Millionaire Households" (Northern Trust, January 2008), 47.
25. Ibid., 44.

26. Fulton, Kasper, and Kibbe, "What's Next for Philanthropy," 2.
27. Ibid., 3.
28. Trista Harris, "How to Engage," 6.
29. Bhagat, Loeb, and Rovner, "Next Generation of American Giving," 9.
30. Ibid., 10.
31. Ibid., 11.
32. Ibid.
33. Fulton, Kasper, and Kibbe, "What's Next for Philanthropy," 2.
34. Fischler and Kopf, "Engaging Tomorrow's Donors Today," 13.
35. Interview with David Gonzales and Ellen Cooper, United Way of Greater St. Louis, conducted by Emily Davis on August 18, 2011.
36. GenNext web page, accessed September 24, 2011, www.stl.unitedway.org/templates/uw_leadership_aspx/5442.aspx?id=5442&LangType=1033.
37. GenNext Facebook page, accessed September 24, 2011, www.facebook.com/unitedwaystl?sk=app_132776606803042.

CHAPTER 4

Volunteering *Is* Philanthropy

Generation X and Millennial philanthropists are broadening the definition of philanthropy not only to financial contributions, but also to contributions of time—both skilled and unskilled hours. Nearly three quarters of the Philanthropy's Next Generation survey participants' shared skilled volunteer opportunities as being the most rewarding types of volunteer activities in contrast to 4.3 percent enjoying administrative volunteer roles. As one survey participant noted, "[I am inspired to volunteer by a] desire to get more deeply involved with an organization and see more directly the impact that is made. It's an opportunity for me to share some of my talents and skills that I don't get to utilize in my current job."[1]

The Association of Fundraising Professionals defines philanthropy as the:

1. love of humankind, usually expressed by an effort to enhance the well-being of humanity through personal acts of practical kindness or by financial support of a cause or causes, such as a charity (for example, the Red Cross), mutual aid or assistance (service clubs, youth groups), quality of life (arts, education, environment), and religion.

2. any effort to relieve human misery or suffering, improve the quality of life, encourage aid or assistance, or foster the preservation of values through gifts, service, or other voluntary activity, any and all of which are external to government involvement or marketplace exchange.[2]

Next generation philanthropists are using any tools they have to make a difference in the world whether it is through direct dollars, time, or both. See Figure 4.1.

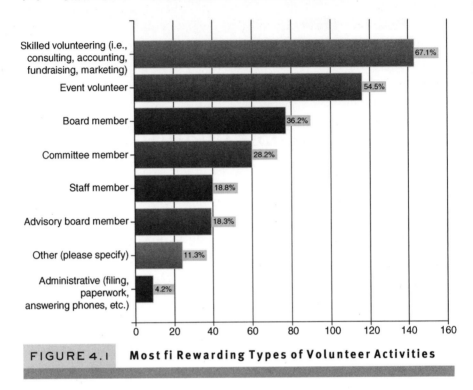

FIGURE 4.1 **Most fi Rewarding Types of Volunteer Activities**

Creating Volunteer Opportunities Increases Prospective Donors

More than half of Next Gen Philanthropist survey respondents began their volunteer activities under the age of 15 and 71.6 percent are currently serving as volunteers for organizations with the majority of those individuals donating time on a monthly or weekly basis. Millennials want to be linked to the cause. "Younger and older donors most likely have more time to be more involved with charitable organizations, whereas middle-aged donors are more likely to have children at home and more demanding jobs."[3]

Individuals who volunteer at an organization are more likely to donate to that organization. Slightly less than 63 percent of survey respondents shared that their financial contributions are affected by where they volunteer.[4] Volunteering is a great strategy for bringing stakeholders into the inner circle of your organization and there are more volunteers than ever coming from the next generation. In 2010, 11.6 million Millennials dedicated 1.2 billion hours of service to communities across the country.[5]

For these reasons fundraisers need to keep their sights on current or prospective volunteers as current and future donors. If your organization has a volunteer development coordinator, work closely with him or her to identify prospects. In the past, nonprofit organizations have folded marketing responsibilities into the fundraising role; in the future development staff may be asked to participate more in the volunteer development function. Fundraising staff should spend more time with younger volunteers to cultivate long-term donor relationships.

Creating volunteer leadership opportunities for the next generation is important for long-term organizational success. Watch for young people connected to your organization who have great potential to be long-term leaders within your nonprofit and for your cause. Thirty-six percent of survey respondents referenced their connections with organizational staff or board members as to how they learned about the nonprofit organization(s) to which they are now donors. Your organization will want to identify young business professionals who are well known in your community for their networks and business expertise. Perhaps these individuals are already volunteering at yours or other nonprofits and have networks that they are willing to open up to your organization. Develop their leadership skills and be willing to listen in an effort to create a lifelong relationship.

It will be important to look at your volunteers as prospective donors, if they are not already, from the small- to major-size gifts. Remember, you never know where the "millionaire next door" will appear. "Give younger constituents an opportunity to tell your organization how they can help you, rather than expecting volunteers to do only tasks that you assign."[6] There are a number of ways in which organizations can use these stories both internally and externally. Externally, your organization can develop a blog that features the stories of your volunteers of all ages, as well as your donors. Ask volunteers to serve as guest speakers at programs or with appropriate funders. Place the stories in your annual reports as a way to put a story to numbers and statistics. When there is negative feedback, leverage that information to improve your services and experiences for others.

Outreach

Internally, ask volunteers to share their stories with your staff in debriefing sessions after programs and events. Invite volunteers to share those firsthand experiences to boards and committees. Your organization can use these stories as "mission moments" to help inspire others in your organization, especially at the board level. Whether your organization is gathering stories for internal or external purposes, remember to ask. Volunteers will not spontaneously arrive at your desk to share their experiences. Gather this information through online evaluations, committee debriefing sessions, informal conversations, and one-on-one interactions.

Ask volunteers about the experience that they are looking for, listen to their interests, and match their skills to your needs rather than simply assuming the best roles for those individuals. This can increase the investment of volunteers and potential dollars donated in the future by these volunteers. Experiences connect volunteers to your mission. Use those experiences and stories to inspire financial contributions and ambassadors for your organization. Social media is an excellent platform for these conversations—use your Facebook page, Twitter, blogs, and other social media to tell the stories of your volunteers and ask about their experiences. Use pictures, the written word, and any other creative tools you can think of to share experiences.

Volunteers for your organization, whether they have a positive or negative experience with your nonprofit, will spread their experience by word of mouth in the community. Volunteers are a great way to reach out in the community and leverage peer networks. See Figures 4.2 and 4.3.

The top five ways survey respondents learned about volunteer opportunities include:

1. Word of mouth (friend, family, colleague).
2. Organizational website.
3. E-mail.
4. Social media.
5. Online search.

Orient your volunteers accurately to your organization. This orientation is critical for consistent messaging and ambassadorship. Your organization wants to have volunteers who are knowledgeable about your programs, missions, and more so that they can both effectively serve your organization as well as communicate these messages to the larger community. Whether you have a skilled volunteer, committee member, or board

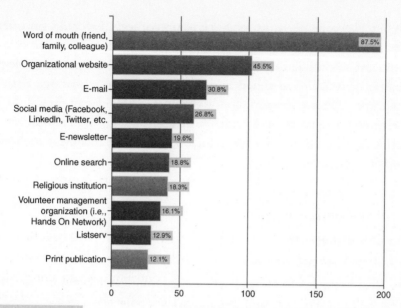

FIGURE 4.2 **How Next Gen Individuals Learn about Volunteer Opportunities**

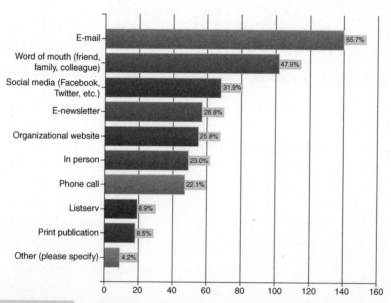

FIGURE 4.3 **How Next Gen Individuals Would Like Nonprofit Organizations to Contact Them about Volunteering**

member, everyone needs a strong orientation process. Record your orientation process and identify who will conduct orientations for different volunteers. At YNPN San Diego, existing board members are responsible for orienting new board members and are given a checklist for orientation. This happens through a board buddy system and provides an excellent way for existing board members to practice their knowledge of the organization and share it with others. Here are sample steps you can include in an orientation process:

- Organizational history.
- Philosophy and values.
- Programs and events.
- Organizational structure.
- Board information (e.g., board and committee descriptions, meeting schedules, letter of commitment, bylaws, policies).
- Committees (e.g., committee descriptions, commitment length).
- Communications (e.g., message map, case statement, summary page).
- Site visits.

If your organization has a message map, share that information with all of your volunteers. A message map is a tool that provides a central message and other messages that connect back to the central message. A message map's central message is different from the organization mission statement, but keeps everyone connected to your organization using clear and consistent information. Find a sample of a message map from MediaMasters.[7] Getting all your stakeholders on the same page with your messaging will allow clear and consistent word of mouth to permeate through the community—whether that is local, regional, national, or global. With the popularity of peer-to-peer recommendations being so popular among the next generation, especially through online platforms, providing these volunteers with the tools they need to succeed and promote your cause is critical.

Event Planning

Many Gen X and Millennial philanthropists are interested in contributing more money to your organization than they are able and, like many individuals new to the nonprofit sector, they are often interested in raising money through events. This is a great strategy for engaging volunteers in fundraising, promoting your cause to new donors, marketing your organization, and saving staff time. Provide your volunteers who want to fundraise with the tools to do so—it will make their job easier and yours as well.

Letting volunteers engage in event planning and fundraising for your organization can be simultaneously valuable and challenging. Do not be afraid to let volunteer fundraisers take some calculated risks. Create structure for volunteer fundraisers to be successful. Start by brainstorming ideas for events and ask to have individuals step up for specific roles. In other words, delegate what you can and start small, growing over time. Provide training on effective fundraising and event creation, thereby deepening the knowledge and investment of fundraising volunteers.

Be aware that a fundraising event of any kind takes time to build and will falter along the way. Patience and investment in long-term strategies for engaging the next generation at every level will help down the road. Expect to have challenges and learning opportunities. Always conduct debriefing meetings to review those experiences and consider implementing evaluations wherever possible including for event participants, planning participants, staff, and funders. Gather information to learn what could be improved on for the future. Do not give up when the first event is not the success your organization had hoped—improvement takes time. Think about the value of the volunteer time and the time saved for staff members who can rely on volunteers for this work.

ORGANIZATIONAL SPOTLIGHT
STAYCLASSY.ORG

Platforms such as StayClassy.org and Razoo.com are new tools that connect fundraising with social media. StayClassy.org started in San Diego and provided a consistent platform for individuals to host fundraising events for organizations. The original idea started with a pub-crawl and grew across the country. The social fundraising concept is similar to fundraising services that support organizations with walk-a-thons and similar events.

From StayClassy.org: "StayClassy provides social fundraising software for nonprofits & their supporters. Their web-based platform allows nonprofits to receive online donations, organize fundraising events and campaigns, manage donors across social media, and access our real-time reporting and analytics engine.

"The company was founded in 2006 by a couple of friends who were looking to fundraise for charity, but didn't know how to get started. They envisioned a platform that made it easy for nonprofits to turn their supporters into fundraisers; and so, they set off to build one. After years of testing their concept with dozens of nonprofits, their initial idea has evolved into what is now an industry-leading online fundraising solution for charities, foundations, churches, schools, clubs and more. . . . The company is also the host of the Classy Awards, the largest philanthropic awards show in the Country."[8]

COMMITTEE PARTICIPATION

Inviting next gen volunteers to serve on committees is an excellent way to create a pipeline from unskilled volunteerism to grooming for board leadership. Committees often require skilled volunteer activities with a longer-term commitment than single-day volunteering, but less than board service. Committee work can provide a way for volunteers and organizations to "try each other on" and find out if there is a good fit for advanced leadership roles. It is critical to recruit and retain quality board and committee members who are younger. With an increased focus on diversity, it is important for nonprofits to work with diverse age groups. Additionally, Gen X and Millienals have a greater focus on the value of inclusiveness than any other generation. The tools and strategies are available for organizations to pursue volunteers of all ages, opening up an entry point for long-term engagement.

Set all your committee volunteers up for success with clear expectations. Before launching a new committee or recruiting new members consider the following important details:

- Committee description.
- Minimum length of commitment.
- Meeting frequency.
- Meeting notes or minutes.
- Skills needed on the committee.
- Orientation to the organization.
- Celebration and evaluation of committee accomplishments (e.g., volunteer appreciation event, annual self assessment and social gathering).

Many organizations have started exploring the concept of a young professionals or next gen committee. The idea is to create a space for young people to gather to do committee work that serves the organization and their age demographic. By creating an isolated committee for a specific age group your organization may not be fully invested in integrating young professionals throughout your organization. Proceed with caution if you are creating a young professionals committee. Read about the United Way of Greater St. Louis and their success with the GenNext program at the end of Chapter 3.

Although nearly 30 percent of Multigenerational Development Office survey respondents did not have a specific plan for engaging younger donors in boards and committees, one survey respondent shared the importance of these volunteer roles in organizations: "Find volunteer opportunities that next gens are interested in to keep them engaged and active with the organization outside of meetings and events. This will better connect them to the mission and help ensure they become future cash donors." Another survey respondent shared the value of having staff connect to volunteer opportunities, personally and with peers. "Continue empowering staff members who themselves are all next gen to assist in recruitment of peers to assist in volunteer fundraising positions and committees that serve as pipelines for hire."

Nonprofit leaders should encourage their staff to participate as volunteers in outside organization's committee and leadership opportunities as a way for these individuals to gain additional experiences that can benefit their employing organization. Be flexible and allow time off for meetings and encourage their participation; the benefits may come back to your organization in ways you might not expect.

Rather than create a separate committee for an age group, unless it is for a specific event or program or requested by individuals in your organization, consider incorporating diverse age groups into current committees and your board. Provide resources and dialogue about your organizational culture and leadership. Be prepared for constructive criticism if your organization is new to bringing young people onto your committees. Consider a focus group to find out how your organization can work better with young professionals across your committees. Finally, encourage young committee members to take calculated risks and explore new ideas that benefit your mission.

Skilled volunteering provided through the committee function can be mutually beneficial for the organization and the committee volunteers. One survey participant shared an inspiration for volunteering as the "desire to get more deeply involved with an organization and see more directly the impact that is made. It's an opportunity for me to share some of my talents and skills that I don't get to utilize in my current job."[9] Committee work may lead to board service as well.

BOARD SERVICE

In 2007, BoardSource began the Next Generation and Governance project to look at how nonprofits were engaging the next generation in board service. According to "results from BoardSource's *Nonprofit Governance Index 2007* survey, [it showed] that only two percent of nonprofit organizations have board members under 30 years of age, and 36 percent of organizations have board members between the ages of 30 and 49."[10] As older board members begin to leave their board leadership roles (or remain in board roles leaving less space for new board members), now more than ever nonprofit organizations need to be doing all they can to recruit and retain younger board members to serve their missions.

Some foundations and nonprofits are using junior boards as a way to train and include the next generation of donors, but nonprofits should engage in young professional boards or committees carefully. Your organization will want to ensure that young people are participating in real decision-making efforts and that their opinions are considered and valued. A number of negative experiences can have a significant impact on the long-term health of your board and your organization's reputation. For a sample board recruitment plan, see Appendix A.

Board Diversity and Tokenism

There is an increasing focus on the importance of diversity on nonprofits boards of directors, but more often than not nonprofit staff and volunteers consider ethnicity rather than age as diversity. The reason for diversity in board leadership is to engage a number of perspectives that will help to better serve the mission and the stakeholders. Any nonprofit board needs to be careful not to create a homogenous leadership team unwilling to challenge one another; divergent opinions are critical in board decision making. These opinions will help the organization look at any issue from a variety of perspectives, and strengthen the mission, programs, and better serve stakeholders.

> Nonprofits must . . . include more young people on their boards and in other positions of power. A nonprofit with mostly white or male staff and board will have trouble cultivating black or female donors; age is no different . . . If your organizational culture is not open to allowing younger people to participate at all levels, a younger donor program is unlikely to be successful.[11]

Look to recruit board members in their twenties and thirties as a way to gain insight into other perspectives, fresh ideas, and experiences that can help shape the programming, leadership, and future of the organization. Whether you are recruiting young people for committees or board service, do not tokenize them. As Mike Gast notes in an interview in Appendix B,[12] avoid identifying one young person to serve in a leadership role as a representative of all young people—organizations should not do that for people of color and it is no different with the younger generations. Trista Harris, in an article in *Nonprofit World*, wrote:

> If you really want a multi-generational perspective in your organization, you must have young people at the table where the real decisions are being made. If you're changing the diversity of your organization's board, you need to have three people from that group represented rather than being a token. . . . Don't have one lone voice that's expected to represent all young people.[13]

Bringing on at least two young people to the board will provide your organization with a good framework for beginning to incorporate new perspectives. It will also help to bring in current or potential donors especially if your organization has a give-or-get policy for serving on the board. Be flexible and evaluate the process by conducting a board self-evaluation annually to ensure that you include and *listen* to the perspectives of those young individuals on committees or the board.

Watch for negative attitudes related to age on your boards. As one young nonprofit professional participating in Frances Kunreuther's research notes:

> I'm not on the board of one organization anymore because a lot of older people came and told us we're doing it wrong. Because I didn't live through the '60s and struggle the same way, our legitimacy as leaders is questioned, or not understood, or challenged because we haven't had the same life experiences.[14]

Board member diversity includes gender, stakeholder, and constituent representation, skills and expertise, and ethnicity just to name a few. Engaging the next generation in board leadership is a great way to bring in new networks and fresh perspectives. It is a fair assumption that many Gen X and Millennial individuals may not have the years of experience that other board members may have, but that can provide an advantage in terms of sharing new concepts—moving away from the "this is how we have always done it" kind of attitude and opening up new ideas and access to donors.

Evaluate your organization's current strengths and weaknesses at the board level to evaluate what skills, talents, and perspectives are needed on your board. Take time to complete a board matrix that will help you to identify what kind of representation, skills, and more that you have on your board. Great examples of board matrices are available from Board-Source (www.boardsource.org). Make sure your board development plan and bylaws clearly reflect the makeup of the board. For example, a minimum of one-third and no more than three-fourths of the board should be comprised of community members directly affected by the mission. Look for board members who are willing to learn about the business of running a nonprofit specifically—not only programs. There are board members who may have extensive experience in nonprofit leadership, but it is important that board members, no matter what their experiences, are willing to continue to learn for the benefit of the organization.

If your organization serves a large number of young people such as at-risk youth or educational programs at the college or postcollege level it is important to have board members reflect the values of those you serve, especially as it related to age. Be sure to understand the legal implications of board leadership for individuals under the age of 18 before considering bringing youth leaders onto your board. Provide next gen leaders with positive experiences so they can boast about everything your organization provides. In other words, create a mutually beneficial relationship. At each board meeting, ask your board members to share a "mission moment"; an experience they had with the organization that helped them stay connected to or inspired by the organization.

Invest in Board Leadership

Many boards operate under the assumption that Gen X and Y board candidates do not have enough life or leadership experience to serve on boards and set the direction for the organization as well as serve in a position of fiscal responsibility. Often nonprofit boards—unless they are more established at an institutional level—are comprised of community members who have been directly affected by the mission, and have less representation of people with extensive knowledge in board best practices. It is not uncommon for board members not to have nonprofit management or leadership background regardless of age—they learn over time or not at all. These are resources that the organization can provide regardless of age to build the capacity and knowledge of their board members that will, in turn, better serve the organization.

Provide board trainings as part of orientation and as ongoing professional development for all board members, new and tenured. Schedule annual board in-services, especially before critical times in your organization. For example, bring in a consultant to conduct training on fundraising before your annual fundraiser to provide your board with tools and ideas for fundraising. Have an outside expert or trainer offer these opportunities.

If your organization is not comfortable bringing young people onto the board right away, encourage more participation from them on committees as a way to give them an orientation to the organization and for you to learn if they might be a better fit for the board in the future.

Critical components to strong board development include: clear roles and expectations, well-defined recruitment process, board orientation (both related to board leadership and the organization), and continued professional development through in-services or other resources like your local consultants or nonprofit associations. Developing the knowledge and the capacity of the board in this way will serve your organization for the long term. Said another way, investing in your board leadership will allow them to more effectively invest in you.

Board Buddies

A great way to provide support to new board members, especially those who are younger, is to create a board buddy system for the first few months of new board service. Pairing up older and younger or existing and new board members as buddies will be a great way to orient new board members and for current board members to share knowledge with others on the board.

Encourage communication and professional relationships between board buddies by asking them to meet in person once per month for the first three months. Consider asking board buddies to take on the role of orientation for new board members. This is a platform to create conversations about the experience of serving on your organization's board, answer any questions, and cultivate the capacity of the board.

If your organization has an especially small board, the board buddy system may be difficult to implement. Continue to evaluate, as your board develops and grows, when and if you can use board buddies. Look at what other organizations are doing to create healthy and welcoming spaces for younger, as well as new board members.

100% Board Giving

Your board should be in engaged in 100 percent giving—whether through "give or get." Inviting, training, and stewarding next gen board members will open up networks to their family members, peers, and other networks that are likely to include other next gen givers. There are a number of print and online resources about board fundraising. Consider bringing in a consultant for an annual in-service about fundraising for your organization.

This can be especially helpful to annual giving time. Share your fundraising plan with your board through the orientation process to help them to understand how the organization fundraises and organizes the moving parts of fundraising. Let your board understand all the work that happens behind the scenes of the organization.

In the case of younger board members, they may or may not have the ability to write a check directly for the organization. Their ability to raise money from their personal networks may be of even greater benefit because they can serve as ambassadors for your organization by sharing the mission and successes of the organization with more people and engaging many donors at lower dollar amounts. It will be important for the fundraising staff to make sure that these smaller donations from younger donors are valued not for their dollar amount alone, but also for the current effort and future potential donors.

One board member who was part of a chapter of Young Nonprofit Professionals Network (YNPN) could not commit personally to donate her board dues, but attended a professional development workshop on fundraising and learned how to apply those skills through YNPN's Facebook Cause. In a matter of two weeks she was able to raise her board dues and spread the word about the organization. She exceeded the amount of money she needed to raise, brought attention to the cause and their online communications platform, expanded the reach of the organization, and developed her knowledge and experience with fundraising.

In many ways, fundraising for board dues rather than making a direct donation can have an even greater long-term impact. Consider asking your board members to split their board dues into "give" and "get." Finally, be sure to have your board president or board development committee chair hold board members accountable for their fundraising efforts. These individuals can check in at the beginning of meetings or contact individuals one-on-one to determine what support they might need to be successful in their fundraising efforts.

Where to Find Next Gen Board Members

Where can your organization find these mysterious Gen X and Y board members? Before you start looking, be clear about what you are looking for in board members by creating board member responsibility descriptions. When approaching a potential next gen board member, make sure to communicate that serving as a board member in itself provides professional development opportunities and that there is learning about board leadership that will happen within the board and through external workshop opportunities. Many young people will automatically assume that they are not qualified as well and you will want to reassure them that there will be support and opportunities to develop their knowledge.

After you have created a board description, reach out to your existing organizational networks in the larger nonprofit community. Communicate your need for board recruitment and specific skills (legal, age diversity, marketing, etc.) in all of your interactions with prospective board members including organizational events, communications with existing volunteers, and in all of your electronic communications (e.g., e-newsletters, e-mail, social media).

Then, expand beyond those networks to your nonprofit associations, professional groups, and other infrastructure organizations. Whenever recruiting for boards, post to local nonprofit job boards, your local YNPN chapter, graduate programs focusing on nonprofit management and leadership or public administration, and any volunteer development organization that is part of the Hands On Network. Idealist.org has a platform to share volunteer opportunities as well. Often these groups will have an e-mail distribution list such as a listserv (e.g., Google group, Yahoo group) and/or other social media platforms like LinkedIn to distribute your request for new board members.

Ask your current board members to help identify individuals that they think would be good candidates for these new recruitment activities. Attend next gen events such as YNPN mixers to meet potential new board members in person. Look to other nonprofits' annual reports for the up-and-coming next gen leaders. Many communities now have news publications, magazines and newspapers, that identify the top 40 under 40 or similar lists. Keep your eyes open for these individuals and reach out to them.

Whenever possible, have stakeholders, past clients, and others impacted by your organization serve in leadership roles. Often these can be young people who would make great board candidates. Intentionally reach out to individuals who are enthusiastic about your organization, committed to leadership, and interested in learning. Invest in them by developing leadership skills through board service as they are investing their time, talent and treasure in your organization. Together you are creating the potential for lifelong ambassadors and donors to your organization.

Onboarding

Once your organization has recruited new board members of any age you will want to ensure that you retain them; retention begins with recruitment. Make sure that your current board is prepared for and invested in diversifying the board's existing demographics. If current board members are resistant to engaging younger board members, your organization is less likely to have a successful, multigenerational board with long-term success. BoardSource's interviewees noted that past barriers to adding younger board members include:

- Skepticism about the need to have younger generations on boards.
- Uncertainty of where to find younger board members.
- Preference for a "C-Suite" or corporate officer type profile on the board.
- Concerns of isolation including minority status as the only young member and lack of social connection or mentor.[15]

To recruit and retain quality board members and promote healthy organizational dynamics, board members need to encourage multigenerational communication, recognize the value and necessity of young professionals' representation on the board, and consider new board development styles. Young people have evolving strategies for management and leadership that will be unconventional for many boards. Rather than dismissing new models, boards should objectively consider the benefits and limitations of any new management and leadership style and be willing to take calculated risks. This requires faith and objective examination of the benefits and costs to traditional, hierarchal models of leadership and organizational management. As with any transition, there will be individuals who are not comfortable with risk or change despite whatever positive outcomes may result; these individuals and the organization will need to weigh the costs versus the benefits of changes in leadership styles as they relate to the mission. Resistance is to be expected and open communication about these realities will help better prepare any organization for the future.

Leaders at all levels need to anticipate and address conflict as it arises to generate innovative solutions that will support the long-term health of nonprofit missions. Boards should set a standard for their organizations by using resources such as facilitators when conflicts become problematic. The board and executive staff should be transparent and share their plans and concerns for executive succession planning with the entire staff and begin to have a genuine discussion about their anticipated steps for the future. This kind of transparency further serves the values of a learning organization while also sending the message that the change and diversity is important for organizational growth.

Adequately prepare your board for an intentional change in engaging in multiple generations in board service. Acknowledging the challenges rather than ignoring them will help to create open dialogue and orientation to multigenerational issues. BoardSource's research identified qualities or skills that board members would need in order to work well with younger board members:

- Training on how to work with younger generations.
- Building respect and trust.
- View Generations X and Y as leaders today.
- Remember what it was like when you joined a board.
- View younger leaders as assets rather than threats.[16]

Orienting your board to multigenerational issues in the nonprofit sector and preparing them for working with younger and older generations will be critical for healthy board service. It is important to note that it is not only Boomers and Traditionalists who should learn about Gen X and Millennials. Also, Gen X and Y must be willing to invest in learning about older generations and their significant experiences in the sector; ask questions, listen, and understand that there are historical and experiential reasons for why organizations do what they do. Change comes slowly—be patient. Cross-generational and peer-learning can be an enormous asset in this setting, but not without road bumps along the way.

VOLUNTEERISM AS A GATEWAY TO PHILANTHROPY

A young, Gen X, hotline volunteer named Erin had been serving as a local hotline counselor for years and excelling in her role at the organization because of its investment in volunteer training and building relationships with its volunteers. Quickly, Erin was "promoted" to a supervisory counselor who supported and led other counselors in the organization's program. Her experience volunteering for the organization was such a powerful one that she wanted to offer more time and talents to the organization. Hearing the stories of those people the organization served inspired her to share her experiences with others.

Later, she eagerly served as the volunteer coordinator for their annual fundraising event, not an easy task for a young person new to volunteer development and to fundraising. Erin combined her newly acquired skills with volunteer development and experiences with the organization to create strategies and systems for the organization's fundraising efforts. A rewarding but challenging experience, Erin became even more engaged and motivated by the organization's cause and impact in the community.

Erin collaborated with her network of friends and contacts locally to organize an annual fundraising event that brought in a small profit for the organization that she herself matched. The organization gained greater exposure in the community that became critical in the coming months as they became involved with public client cases.

Although Erin eventually moved away from volunteering with the organization on a regular basis, she became a sponsor of events in which she had provided a leadership role in the past, an annual giver, and even planned on including the organization in her estate planning. Erin's connection to the cause remained. Her positive experience as a volunteer directly connected to dollars in funding for the nonprofit.

As Erin decreased her day-to-day volunteer involvement so did the communications she received from the nonprofit. There was a great deal of staff turnover, which could have affected the limited communications, but whatever the reason, Erin felt she was less and less important to the organization. Over time, Erin stopped fundraising on behalf of the organization, removed them from her annual giving plan, and took them out of her will. She knew little about what happened in the organization unless she was asked for money. She felt devalued as a donor and decided that the organization wasn't in need of her funding; she would look elsewhere to contribute.

(continued)

> This is a common example that fundraisers hear about; the capacity, interest, strategy, or communication tools are not in place to leverage a new generation of donors. In this case, and many others like it, the organization would have benefited from a database where staff could track both the volunteer hours and dollars donated from this individual as well as to provide resources on planned giving and maintain regular communications with the donor throughout staffing changes. Examples like this demonstrate the need to avoid undervaluing donors who are younger and learn that the possibility for gifts of all kinds is possible.

Conclusion

In order to bring in more volunteers into skilled positions or at the board and committee levels, encourage training on multigenerational philanthropy and nonprofit leadership at your organization. There are so many resources available for nonprofits about healthy board governance. Every individual board member has the potential to bring something unique to your organization's board leadership. Remember to ask why you want to diversify the generations and perspectives in your volunteer base, especially on the board. BoardSource heard from research participants what next gen-ers add in value to their boards:

- Passion for the mission.
- Results-oriented thinking.
- Access to new networks and donors.
- Fresh perspective on old problems.[17]

These characteristics actually appear less to be about the generations as they do about perspectives that new board members bring to an organization. Conduct annual self-evaluations of your board including the recruitment process, orientation, and more. There are a number of resources from BoardSource and on IdeaEncore.com that provide samples of board evaluation, policies, processes, and research.

Recruiting diverse ages onto your organizational committees and board can be an incredibly rewarding way to develop your organization and engage with the next generation of philanthropists. Through some simple planning and investment your organization can create a mutually beneficial experience in skilled volunteering across all generations.

RESOURCES

Print Resources

- *Next Generation and Governance*: *Report on Findings* by Alexis Terry
- *Nonprofit Governance in the United States* by Francie Ostrower
- *Creating Caring and Capable Boards: Reclaiming the Passion for Active Trusteeship* by Katherine Tyler Scott

Websites

- GenNext (www.gennextstl.org)
- BoardSource (www.boardsource.org)
- Board Life Matters (www.boardlifematters.org)
- Carter McNamara (www.authenticityconsulting.com)
- Free Management Library (www.managementhelp.org)
- Foundation Center (www.foundationcenter.org)
- Hands On Network (www.handsonnetwork.org)
- Idealist (www.idealist.org)
- Volunteer Match (www.volunteermatch.org)

Notes

1. Next Generation Philanthropists' Survey, January 2011.
2. The AFP Fundraising Dictionary Online document, accessed September 24, 2011, www.afpnet.org/files/.../AFP_Dictionary_A-Z_final_6-9-03.pdf.
3. Sarah Fischler and Alyssa Kopf, "Engaging Tomorrow's Donors Today: A Toolkit for Success" (Community Shares of Colorado, 2007), 5, (www.cshares.org/publications).
4. Next Generation Philanthropists' Survey, January 2011.
5. Volunteering in America: Information on Volunteering and Civic Engagement web page, accessed September 24, 2009, www.volunteeringinamerica.gov/special/Millennials-%28born-1982-or-after%29.
6. Center on Philanthropy at Indiana University, "Charitable Giving and the Millennial Generation" (Giving USA Foundation Spotlight, 2010), 7.
7. Media Masters web page, accessed September 24, 2009, www.mediamasterstraining.com/messagemap.html.
8. StayClassy.org web page, accessed September 24, 2009, www.stayclassy.org.

9. Next Generation Philanthropists' Survey, January 2011.

10. Alexis Terry, "Next Generation and Governance Report on Findings" (Board-Source, 2009), 1, www.boardsource.org/UserFiles/nextgeneration.pdf.

11. Fischler and Kopf, "Engaging Tomorrow's Donors Today," 14.

12. Interview conducted by Emily Davis on April 1, 2011.

13. Trista Harris, "How to Engage the Next Generation of Donors Now" (*Nonprofit World*, 2011), 7.

14. Frances Kunreuther, "Up Next: Generation Change and the Leadership of Non-profit Organizations" (Annie E. Casey Foundation, 2005), 7.

15. Terry, "Next Generation," 1.

16. Ibid., 9–10.

17. Ibid., 2–3.

CHAPTER 5

The Next Generation of Grant Makers

Nonprofits need to remember that foundations are nonprofits, too; this is a fact many nonprofit staff tend to forget or ignore. Foundations—whether they are private, corporate, community, or family foundations—are facing challenges related to multigenerational leadership and fundraising from the next generation. Foundations also need to fundraise for money or manage the dollars that they have in order to effectively continue their grant-making efforts. As such, those who run or manage foundations struggle with similar as well as unique experiences in working with multiple generations in grant making.

Foundations are equally impacted by the diversity in generations' experiences, work styles, and communication methods. Community foundations are experiencing many of the same challenges as nonprofit organizations face with relationships to multigenerational staff and fundraising from the next generation.

Generations engaged in their families' philanthropy—whether in the form of a foundation, fund, or unstructured family giving—are especially affected by the experience of making grant making meaningful to every generation while continuing a family legacy. There can be up to four generations that are involved with their family's philanthropy; family dynamics can impact the grant-making process as much as anything else. Fundraisers that solicit grants or funds from foundations need an inside perspective on these dynamics in order to engage family members of every generation, and cultivate and recognize these donors.

Organizations like the Council on Foundations, 21/64 and Emerging Practitioners in Philanthropy (EPIP) are prioritizing multigenerational dialogue to improve the quality of philanthropy. In this chapter, learn how foundations are investing in professional development, networking resources, and conversations to leverage every generation in the grant-making process and what this means for development professionals.

INVESTING IN PROFESSIONAL DEVELOPMENT

Senior leaders in foundations are seeing the benefits of investing in professional development opportunities for next gen grant-making staff, both academic and experiential. According to Emerging Practitioners in Philanthropy's (EPIP) Impact Assessment, younger foundation staff members are taking on more leadership responsibilities, finding more confidence in their philanthropic roles, and proactively advancing the foundation's mission.[1] As leaders of today and tomorrow's grant-making institutions, these individuals need support in becoming successful leaders.

Philanthropy is slowly formalizing its field through academic resources including Indiana University's Center on Philanthropy, the grant-making school at University of Michigan, and New York University's grant-making certificate. Through these resources, individuals can learn about the history of philanthropy, trends, best practices, and more. This also means that new models of philanthropy are being developed in the process. Philanthropic leaders are becoming savvier in their approaches to giving and are increasing the transparency they provide and require from grantees.

Much like the nonprofit community with its nonprofit management and leadership programs, philanthropy is developing academic programs that will expand philanthropic knowledge and capture valuable information to share across generations. Both nonprofits and grant makers are increasing the value placed on academic and experiential learning as a way to invest in, develop, and strengthen their staff and missions. In response to this need for professional development and networking, Rusty Stahl created EPIP to respond to these needs and advance the conversation.

Similar to Young Nonprofit Professionals Network (YNPN), EPIP provides emerging foundation professionals with opportunities for leadership development through conferences, workshops, planning and leading events, coordinating chapters, and joining boards. EPIP provides a platform for next gen philanthropy staff to practice and learn leadership in a hands-on way. By embracing the conversation about formalizing the field as a career, professional development has become a priority for career growth in the philanthropic world.[2] Jasmine Hall Ratliff, Program Officer for the Robert Wood Johnson Foundation says,

> EPIP was another avenue for me to connect with other young professionals. I was in a phase where I was trying to decide whether to stay in philanthropy or leave the field. So to meet other young people who were possibly in the same mindset or who were devoting their careers to the field, it really helped to talk to them. It helped me learn more about the field, what they liked about philanthropy, and their career paths.[3]

EPIP is most widely known for its conversations about multigenerationalism in philanthropy. The intention in these exchanges is to connect experiences and learning between tenured and emerging leaders in philanthropy. By providing a platform for senior leaders to reflect, share, and learn from their experiences with younger leaders EPIP is able to create a foundation for conversation around effective philanthropy and capture historical information for future generations. Through these conversations, the next generation of foundation staff and philanthropists are advancing and innovating their philanthropic impact. Mike Gast of Resource Generation explained that it is important that foundation staff are trained in how best to support social change through philanthropy, such as by providing general operating support, mission-related investing of foundation assets, and even through streamlined grant making processes.[4] Conversations about unrestricted grants for nonprofits, transparency, and collaboration have the power to change traditional methods in which strategic philanthropy is conducted.

EPIP has continued to expand its focus on marginalized demographic communities within philanthropy, beyond age, including providing services specifically for young people of color. EPIP's intentional focus on multiculturalism reflects this value in Millennials. EPIP provides young leaders of color with access to previously limited networks through grants to attend conferences and with workshops and networks specifically designed for this even further marginalized group of individuals.[5]

EMERGING PRACTITIONERS IN PHILANTHROPY (EPIP)[6]

No organization has been at the forefront of multigenerational grant making quite the way that Emerging Practitioners in Philanthropy (EPIP) has. In the past 10 years, EPIP has been the leader that brought the conversation about philanthropy as a career and engaging multiple generations in grant making to the table.

"EPIP's mission is to develop extraordinary new leaders to enhance organized philanthropy and its impact on communities. EPIP envisions a day when all generations of practitioners in philanthropy collaborate effectively to build better foundations for a better world. EPIP focuses its efforts in three impact areas:

- Generational Change and Multigenerationalism: Foundations should integrate the experience of senior leaders with the innovation of emerging leaders.

- Professionalism & Effectiveness in Philanthropy: Practitioners in philanthropy should be educated and trained to act according to the highest ethical and professional standards.

- Social Impact to Build a Better World: Philanthropy should endeavor to create a more just, equitable, and sustainable society."[7]

Founder and executive director Rusty Stahl tells the story of how EPIP started. A small group of students at Indiana University's Center of Philanthropy graduate program received funding from the Mott Foundation to attend the Council on Foundations (COF) Annual Conference more than 10 years ago. At the conference, Stahl's professor, Robert Payton, took the time and care to introduce the grad students to the attendees. The grad students noticed what seemed to be a 30- to 40-year age difference and a resistance toward this next generation entering philanthropy as a career. Stahl and other attendees organized an informal dinner for the next gen attendees at the next COF conference and EPIP's network started. Rusty then took EPIP on as a project at the Ford Foundation and developed a network for young professionals in grant making to connect, learn from one another, and learn how to elevate and innovate strategic philanthropy.

Grant making is a powerful experience, but it can also be isolating because of the inherent power differentials between those who provide grants and those who seek grants along with age and experience within the grant-making organizations. Stahl wanted EPIP to develop a safe space for young staff to share their experiences and connect with one another. As "gate keepers" to philanthropy, these individuals need a platform to connect, reflect, and learn. Young people on staff at foundations felt isolated, invisible, and unneeded. Stahl wanted EPIP to develop as a voice for young people in foundations.

While business, government, and nonprofits were beginning to have conversations about intentional recruitment and retention of next gen staff and volunteers, philanthropies did not see this as a priority in the same way. Even orientation into strategic philanthropy meant learning about philanthropy as it was specifically conducted in one foundation, not around best practices in philanthropy throughout the field. Philanthropic leadership assumed that young people didn't have enough experience in life, fundraising, and leadership to serve as grant makers, and that philanthropy should not be considered a career.

Since philanthropy has not historically been considered a career, there has been little, if any, focus on professional development and ongoing learning. Regional associations of grant makers might have provided grant-making 101 training or workshops, but only the basics about the process were covered. Stahl wanted to see education about the broader context of philanthropy—to take a liberal arts education approach to orientation for strategic philanthropy. Without support and education on how to effectively engage in philanthropy, it is difficult to leverage any role and innovate philanthropic activities.

Stahl is quick to note that his knowledge and experience in philanthropy would not be possible without the unyielding support and mentorship of Robert Payton. He credits Payton with opening up the doors to philanthropy for many next gen-ers. Stahl's own experience with dialogue and information exchange across generations provided a platform for multigenerational learning within philanthropy. Ten years later, EPIP is seeing the impact of their efforts and how Boomers and Traditionalists like Robert Payton are opening up to conversations around multigenerationalism.

EPIP has been able to capture and share its impact on philanthropy in its 2011 Impact Assessment.

The full report and executive summary can be found on the EPIP website: www.epip.org.

Networking Resources

Carly Hare, Executive Director of Native Americans in Philanthropy says:

> There are challenges in being new to philanthropy, whether because of age or experience. You need help getting questions answered, dispelling concerns, and talking about valid conflicts. Sometimes a more seasoned mentor might not be the right person to help you. There is value in being able to find and identify with people who are at the same trajectory of professional and career growth.[8]

Like the nonprofit community, emerging philanthropists are experiencing the importance of networking as part of their professional development and education about the sector. Organizations like EPIP provide important networking connections for emerging leaders, whether they are in person or virtual. These networks provide a safe space for emerging leaders to ask questions of their peers that they might not be able to ask of their employers. EPIP partners with groups like Resource Generation and 21/64 to provide opportunities within conferences like Council on Foundations to have unique sessions or tracks designed specifically to next gen grantmaking staff. In this way they provide platforms for both networking and professional development.

The vast majority of foundations provide little orientation to the field of philanthropy outside of their specific organizational culture. Networking can serve as an informal coaching resource, which is particularly valuable when formal coaching is limited in a region or organization.[9] Emerging philanthropic leaders are engaging in dialogue specifically to create an orientation process and an understanding of what philanthropy looks like in a broader context.[10]

Connecting grant makers together and knowing what will help them better serve their goals, visions, and missions could have a positive effect on relationships with nonprofits and save time on the entire process. In addition to networking within the grant-making community, next gen grant makers want to be more connected to the organizations that they support through volunteerism, site visits, and leadership opportunities. Provide opportunities to connect with these individuals in formal and informal ways.

How Social Media Changes Grant Making

Foundation staff members struggle with how to best bridge the online communication gaps the same way that nonprofits are challenged by new communication platforms. Millennials see social media as an everyday part of life, but Boomers and Traditionalists are working to identify what is appropriate to share online, especially as it comes to grant-making decisions. Opening up the grant-making process too much can result in an overwhelming amount of information for staff or family members to manage. On the other hand, having a completely closed-off process is becoming less attractive to next gen grant makers. The various perspectives about using online communications can cause tension and misunderstandings between the generations.

Many foundations ban the use of social media networks within their organizations, limiting the transparency that many next gen philanthropic staff members desire. On the other end of the spectrum, organizations like the Case Foundation and Foundation Center are embracing social media as a way to expose the "glass pockets" within strategic philanthropy.[11] The Case Foundation (AOL co-founders) has gone so far as to open up their grant-making process to the public by using social media. The founders of eBay are looking at similar strategies. The Foundation Center has moved from a print publication of foundation resources to an online directory. Researching foundation grant opportunities may change forever because of these types of shifts in transparency with the use of online communications.

Younger staff may not fully understand the historical context or even policies around sharing protected information online. There has been good reason for grant makers to put up boundaries to protect themselves including the intentional decision to not have a foundation website.

Managing the volume of grant requests is a significant concern for grant makers.[12] Having open dialogue to explain online communications policies is helpful for staff to support executive decisions and communicate those reasons with grantees. Development professionals need to be aware of the broad continuum of grant makers' use of social media so they can tailor their approaches appropriately.

Lisa Parker, from Full Circle Advisors, said that she is seeing e-mail as passé with her younger philanthropists. Younger philanthropists want to do things that are fun—they'll plan an event and send out a text message two days before the event telling everyone to come out and join them. Crowd sourcing is becoming increasingly important in philanthropy as well.[13]

If nonprofits are struggling with multigenerational communications in nonprofits so are families in their philanthropy. Be sensitive to the fact that one communication style may not work for all the individuals in the family foundation. Be accessible and flexible for the different communication needs. Watching these changes may provide greater access to and dialogue with family funders.

Foundations continue to navigate the best way to manage online communications as the generations start to engage in conversation about strategic effectiveness and transparency while balancing the capacity of the grant-making organization. Understanding what roles social media plays in the internal and external decision making for awarding grants will aid fundraisers in their prospecting, cultivation, and stewardship of foundation staff.

UNDERSTANDING FAMILY PHILANTHROPY

One specific section of strategic philanthropy that fundraisers need to be aware of is multigenerational family philanthropy including "kitchen table" philanthropy, donor-advised funds, charitable trusts, and family foundations. Family foundations gained popularity in the early 1900s and initially served as tax shelters for wealthy families until family foundations were required to start disseminating at least 5 percent of their assets annually in the 1960s. According to the Foundation Center, in 2009 nearly 40,000 family foundations contributed more than $20 billion to the nonprofit sector.[14] If fundraisers are going to raise dollars from family funders they need to learn more about how family funders are navigating multigenerational issues as they prepare for wealth and leadership transitions.

With the pending transfer of wealth anticipated, family philanthropies are exploring how to inspire future generations' philanthropy and experiencing new paradigms in philanthropic work.[15] "American families generated tremendous wealth in the latter part of the 20th century. As a result, America, at the turn of the century, is home to 276 billionaires, 350,000 decamillionaires and more than 5 million millionaires. In addition to this new pace of wealth creation, a significant transfer of wealth will occur among the generations over the next 50 years. Recent estimates of this transfer range anywhere from $41 trillion to $136 trillion."[16] If and how this transfer of wealth actually occurs remains to be seen, but the potential for multiple generations of family members engaged in conversations about philanthropy could have a great impact on nonprofit funding cultivation.

Family philanthropies are often caught between maintaining a family legacy while embracing new philanthropic interests and practices across generations; these conversations could shift the way grants are made to charitable organizations as the lead decision-makers in these organizations evolve and bring new ideas to the table.

The original family foundations established in the early 1900s were established to exist in perpetuity and may never sunset, leaving future generations responsible for learning about philanthropy in general and sharing their family's legacy for years to come.[17] For some next gen foundation trustees this is an exciting prospect and for others it can be an undesirable burden.

New models of family philanthropy are emerging as well, including consensus decision making; matching gift programs; and next gen or junior boards developing as a way to explore and learn about philanthropy. In addition to internal structures expanding, the way grants are made is changing also. New generations of philanthropists are challenging traditional models, asking grantees to sit on foundation boards, exploring a new kind of transparency, and asking to be more involved with the grantees they fund. Although every venture in flattened hierarchy may not survive, these are potential opportunities for nonprofits and fundraisers to have a voice in the grant-making and grant-seeking processes. Cultivating relationships with philanthropists across generations in one family can have wonderful outcomes for your organization.

It is important to remember that no two stories, families, or individuals are alike. How younger generations learn about and engage in their family's funding is never the same. Some young philanthropists are aware of and asked to participate in their family's philanthropy from an early age; others may not become aware of any kind of family wealth until much later; some young people may play a critical role in their family foundation, but may not personally have access to wealth. As Sharna Goldseker at 21/64 frequently reminds consultants, the dynamics of one family foundation does not apply to ALL family foundations.[18] In fact, no two foundations, like philanthropists, are alike.

Shifting Family Dynamics

Unlike community foundations or corporate foundations, family dynamics play a powerful role in family foundations. It is important to understand family dynamics so that development professionals can understand the psychology of multigenerational grant making. Family dynamics are discussed frequently in popular culture, but the authors of *Creating Change Through Family Philanthropy* have broken down just what these dynamics might be within family philanthropy:[19]

- Sibling rivalries.
- Family hierarchies and "adultism."
- Gender dynamics and outright sexism.
- Allegiances.
- Conflicts.
- Power struggles.

As fundraisers interact with individuals in philanthropic families, it is important to be sensitive to obvious or subtle dynamics that can exist out of view of the grant-making process, or blatantly in the middle of the grant-making process.

Books such as *Creating Change Through Family Philanthropy* encourage next gen givers to engage in their families' philanthropies and advocate for older generations to open up to the possibilities of younger donors' involvement and philanthropic recommendations.[20] For older family members this means being flexible and patient, taking time to explain the history and legacy of the funding while also being open to new ideas. These new approaches can be everything from when foundation meetings are scheduled to the process for allocating grant funding to how the foundation started and why.

Family foundations that include college-age family members in the decision-making process may have to change their grant-making or meeting schedule when younger members can meet during semester breaks or when their school schedule allows. For foundation families they are learning quickly that is more to consider than just adding children onto the roster of decision makers. Schedules, geographic location, and more can make a significant impact on how grant making is managed. These challenges in inclusiveness may affect nonprofit funding by shifting deadlines and responsiveness.

For many families talking about money, even without the burden of being a public philanthropy, can be challenging and confusing. For philanthropic families, it is important for every generation to understand individuals' values related to money and the foundation's legacy. Shifting values among generations can create sensitivity and tension between family members, affecting grant making and nonprofits. Organizations like 21/64 use strategies to help clarify confusing values and priorities.

Family philanthropies are constantly revisiting the legacy they want to leave with their philanthropy in different ways. 21/64, part of the Charles and Andrea Brofman philanthropies, works with philanthropists to proactively identify their values and desired impact and how they can achieve that in their legacy with engagement from every generation. Sharna Goldseker describes the 21/64 mission:

> Three years ago, at the Andrea and Charles Brofman Philanthropies, we created a division called 21/64 (www.2164.net) to specializing in preparing for this intergenerational transfer, or what we call a *multigenerational* approach to philanthropy. The 21/64 symbolizes our multigenerational approach to philanthropy, as 21 often connotes a young person coming of age and 64 a seasoned person considering his or her legacy. In this era, multiple generations must learn to work together to understand each other's values and visions in life let along in philanthropy. We provide philanthropic tools to facilitate the process of values clarification, strategic visioning, and communicating to help families, foundations, and communities to achieve their goals.[21]

21/64 leads families through the subtle and overt issues related to money, philanthropy, and influence. Through a thoughtfully designed process they can facilitate transformative experiences for families and their philanthropy. Family members use the 21/64 processes with help from tools such as the Motivational Values' cards, Picture Your Legacy cards, and the new Family Quest Giving Deck to help visually identify the differences and similarities in generational philanthropic values. 21/64 spends time identifying the family's philanthropic history about why and how family members engage in the grant-making process, communication with grantees, and more.

ORGANIZATIONAL
SPOTLIGHT

21/64

At 21/64, staff members understand the unique skills and perspectives the next generation can bring to the philanthropic community. However, the prospect of engaging the next generation can be daunting. Next-generation family members have grown up with access to broader opportunities fueled by information technology, increased diversity, and global connectedness. The questions they ask, language they use, and even their values and priorities change the way the family communicates. The more a family is able to see that "involving the kids" does not only mean adding children to an existing system, but rather shifting the family paradigm to become multigenerational—embracing what each generation brings to the table—the better prepared they will be for the next phase of the foundation's evolution, and for meeting the needs of the twenty-first century.

21/64 offers two-day training for professionals interested in incorporating the multigenerational lens into their consulting. The training they offer is not a quick fix or silver bullet, but rather incorporates how cultural understanding and changes can happen across generations involved in family philanthropy.

To read more about 21/64 and an interview summary with Sharna Goldseker, see Appendix B.[22]

Lisa Parker from Family Circle Advisors notes that for young people in their teens and twenties, it's not philanthropy as usual. They want to dig in and get their hands dirty; they want the experience of learning about the organization inside and out. Having meetings about meetings just will not engage younger generations in the philanthropic process the way real experiences can. She has seen the most transformational experiences in philanthropy from young people who have had the opportunity for meaningful volunteer work within an organization and has seen the impact of their work.[23]

She has served as a consultant for a number of families entering into philanthropy at all different stages. Many times the families will partner with nonprofits to actually show younger generations the impact of charitable work. The families or their foundations will frequently compensate the nonprofits for the time they dedicate to their family's learning about giving. In the case of one family foundation, these interactive experiences take the place of traditional site visits and the younger generations have an opportunity to grant funds from the foundation and their personal savings in addition to the nonprofits being compensated for the time they dedicate to the learning process.[24] It can be a beneficial collaboration or partnership for both nonprofits and family members to participate in this type of interaction.

Parker emphasizes connecting philanthropy with issues and activities that younger generations love. She shared one story of a young girl, Amy, who had saved her allowance to give to something she loved on Valentine's Day. On Valentine's Day she decided she would give her money to Archie, the deer at the local petting zoo. She and her mother walked up to the ticket counter and gave the money to the ticket agent. She then went into the petting zoo, sat down with Archie, and told him all about what she had done with her money.

Parker shares that the donation could not have been more than $20, certainly not worth much time to the zoo, but not long after their visit, Amy received a signed photo of all the zoo staff with Archie. As a result of this thoughtful recognition, Amy's family foundation donated to the zoo.[25] For more information, see Appendix B.[26]

Philanthropists in the family may be learning about philanthropy for the first time and only beginning to identify their own values related to money and philanthropy. "Whether it is in how they learn to save, spend, or give their resources, kids are learning to see money as a means toward their goals and values—not as a goal unto itself."[27] Next gen donors getting involved in their family's philanthropy have a lot to learn. They may begin to:

- Understand just what philanthropy is and how they relate to philanthropy individually and within their family.
- Learn about their family's history with philanthropy.
- Engage in soul searching to identify where their passions are and how those fit with other family members.
- Challenge existing organizational cultures.
- Vie for a seat at the decision-making table with their families.
- Reconcile challenging family dynamics and history.
- Investigate new models of investing such as socially responsible investing and how they compare with traditional models.
- Figure out how to be heard by other family members to share new ideas.

New generations of family funders committed to social change are investigating how power and privilege play roles within the family and between the grantee and grantor. Because they have been exposed to philanthropy through their family, they may have more interest in philanthropy than other young people and they have creative strategies for engaging other philanthropists to benefit your organization. Internal to the family, next gen givers are looking at ways to flatten hierarchies in board leadership, shifting the proposal process, and seeking more involved evaluation from grantees on the grant making process.

The vast majorities of family foundations are not only led by family members, but also are not racially, ethnically, or generationally diverse.[28] In addition to age diversification on family foundation boards and committees representation, next gen family funders are investigating the idea of bringing grantees into leadership roles in the foundation or funding platform. Millennials are a generation who value and reflect diversity—they are often challenging the status quo and opening up participation in new ways. How new diversity will alter families' philanthropies will evolve over time and development professionals need to be aware of any changing roles for fundraisers.

With Gen X and Millennials positioning themselves for more leadership roles within family funds are bound to begin using more transparency in how they communicate. Few foundations have a website with organizational information yet require a great deal of information from current and prospective grantees; some next gen philanthropists are viewing this as double standard and are discussing how greater transparency on the philanthropy side can be achieved. Next gen family philanthropists are beginning to use online tools such as social media, websites, and even in-person invitations for grantees to become involved with the grant-making process. Some social justice philanthropists are actually seeking ways to collaborate with organizations on everything from press releases to op-eds to conferences and programs.[29]

Young donors may struggle with the responsibility of being part of a family of philanthropists. Nonprofits need to be sensitive to the fact that young people who are connected to family wealth and philanthropy hold the responsibility of being seen by the community in a certain light; philanthropy can be equally empowering and isolating. Many are learning to identify where their comfort levels lie related to family philanthropy and visibility. Melanie (age 30) explained her experience:

> A lot of times I was really turned off because I felt like program officers at great big foundations were up in an ivory tower and almost condescending to the people they were making grants to. I wanted to be much closer to our grantees. But then as soon as somebody finds out you have access to capital, it's like, "I have this friend who's heading this organization and there's this organization and there's this organization." That's really awkward as well.[30]

On the other hand, serving in a leadership role in a family's philanthropy can be a positive experience—opening up seats at exclusive philanthropic conversation tables. Christopher (age 25) explained his positive experience of being involved and the doors it has opened:

> I'm getting the benefits that go beyond the family foundation itself. It is a personal springboard to get involved in the wider field of philanthropy in a way that I couldn't if I didn't have some role within my own family foundation. It's like the key to entry into a different world that otherwise you're not allowed in.[31]

Resource Generation has become an important player in these conversations by providing literature, facilitating conversations, and even providing retreats such as Make Money Make Change and the Creating Change Through Family Philanthropy retreats. Since 1998, Resource Generation has organized more than 1,400 young people across the United States with access to financial wealth to leverage resources and privilege for social change. Through community building, education, and organizing, it helps young people with wealth bring all they have and all they are to the social change movements and issues they care about. They organize to transform philanthropy, policy, and institutions, and leverage your collective power to make lasting structural change. "Questioning how power is held in family philanthropy has the potential to completely transform or funds—and the field."[32] For a complete interview with Mike Gast, next gen philanthropist and co-director of Resource Generation, see Appendix B.[33]

Individuals and family foundations are both moved by personal connections to missions and nonprofit stories as well as causes that are related to their personal networks. In the social media age, nonprofits should diversify their connections to young donors online in addition to print and in-person connections—fundraisers never know when there might be a young donor who sits on a family foundation board or is slated to be the next staffer running the foundation. Ask these individuals how they want to receive communications and respect that preference; do not apply a one-size-fits-all-approach.

Engaging Family Philanthropists

Fundraisers, like any individual, will have assumptions about family, money, and philanthropy that influence your attitudes and behaviors; be aware and sensitive to yours and your donors' experiences related to money. Many individuals are often eager to problem solve for people, but the best thing to do is to listen first. This means truly engaging in active listening and being 100 percent present in what you are hearing from the philanthropist. Listen for more than the content of what is being said, but for the underlying reason that a next gen philanthropist might be sharing the information. Maybe there is an opportunity between the lines of the conversation to engage this individual or provide resources.

As fundraisers, a common rule is to listen most of the time to the donor and speak only about 20 percent of the time. This is hard for many fundraisers, yet it is an important part of gathering information from the donor and responding appropriately. The next generation of donors wants to be seen as relevant, heard, and valued for their experiences. Consider taking a course or workshop in active listening to help learn more about how to listen—whether it is in person or online.

If you meet or know a young person currently involved in his or her family's philanthropy or is planning to be involved in the future, begin to develop the relationship early by opening up dialogue, listening to his or her concerns, and providing resources that could be useful for that individual. Be available in authentic and genuine ways, not solely for a bottom-line goal of raising money. Offer opportunities for leadership in volunteer, committee, or board roles. The concept of giving before receiving applies as a start to the relationships. Make the engagement opportunities meaningful and fun, more than just a transaction.

Cultivating these relationships can lead to everything from gifts from the foundation such as matching gifts and individual philanthropy. In the Lawrence Welk Family Foundation there are four generations engaged in the philanthropy. The members set up special site visits for the younger generations and teach them about their family's philanthropic values. The younger donors then determine where their allocated funds are distributed based on those site visits and this is often accompanied by a matching grant.

Pay close attention to young philanthropists connected to family philanthropy—they may have an investment beyond the obvious. These individuals are usually conducting personal philanthropy outside of their family's philanthropy through individual gifts, donor circles, and more. If these young donors are not being taught in their own families about philanthropy, nonprofit organizations might have an opportunity to teach them about philanthropy through their organizations and deepen the relationship, thereby increasing the possibility of lifelong donations from these individuals.

Be careful not to see young family philanthropists only as funders. Fundraisers and other staff can connect to their values and interests by providing opportunities in your organization to learn and share their knowledge. Provide meaningful experiences with active learning rather than simple administrative tasks. Offer mentoring opportunities that "help younger funders find volunteer positions, internships, or even jobs at nonprofit organizations that align with their values and interests."[34]

Invite the next generation to be part of your organization's fundraising and philanthropy. This is a great tool not only for them to learn, but it also may be one of the few places that they are invited to learn about philanthropy from this perspective. This can be an amazing stewardship tool. "There is a difference between *knowing* and being *invited*."[35] Ask these younger philanthropists with an opportunity to share their story of being involved with your organization through a newsletter or blog post and deepen their connection to your work.

Nonprofit professionals need to challenge any assumptions that young people inherently know they are welcome to participate and make an extra effort to *invite* them to participate. Ask for their opinions and listen; also provide platforms in which to participate and learn. Your organization can become a case study for philanthropy, fundraising, and learning for the next generation of family philanthropy.

In addition to experiential resources fundraisers can also help cultivate these donors by providing philanthropic resources and peer groups. For example, *Inspired Philanthropy* by Tracy Gary is an outstanding resource for young donors looking to understand their wealth and their family's wealth. It can help them develop giving plans and learn more about philanthropic practices.[36]

Develop next generation philanthropists by connecting them with or creating peer groups with other next gen donors and young funders and provide mentoring opportunities with other funders. Peer groups like Grand Street are great examples. At Grand Street their goals are:

- To build a network of young Jews in similar positions of philanthropic responsibility.
- To create a space where members can find personal development in the philanthropic realm with their peers.
- To invite participants to ask their own questions.
- To develop their Jewish analysis and capacity for strategic thinking.[37]

Sharing online resources and organizations such as Resource Generation are incredibly beneficial for these individuals, informing their philanthropy, and providing them with communities of other young funders. As a fundraiser you are establishing a long-term investment in a future grant maker that could have a great benefit. Look at these individuals not just as ATMs, but people with complex waters to navigate.

"Many view a family fund as a valuable way to help the next generation learn about generosity and giving."[38] Family funds are more than just a way to give money for many families; they are tools to teach and share values. This is a lot for nonprofit professionals to be aware of—family leadership, generational shifts in philanthropy, family members who are not yet involved in decision making, whether the foundation will sunset or remain in perpetuity. Ultimately, be sensitive to and build relationships with philanthropists in foundations, regardless of age and experience.

WHAT NONPROFITS CAN DO

The next generations of philanthropic staff are learning from one another and incorporating their knowledge in ways that can benefit nonprofit grant seekers. As one EPIP survey respondent reported, "We moved to a simpler grant process after I attended an EPIP conference, and that has improved our relationship with grantseekers." The next generations of philanthropic staff members are looking for new ways to work with grant seekers and for innovative partnership. As a fundraiser, be available for those opportunities and conversations.

Nonprofits and fundraising staff would be wise to provide opportunities for leadership roles in their organizations to next gen grant makers. As Molly Hafid Shultz, Program Officer of the Unitarian Universalist Veatch Program at Shelter Rock says:

> As a program associate, it's not like people are falling all over you to have you be on their boards of directors, or chair meetings, or be in any kind of leadership capacity because you're thought of as young and you haven't yet put in your time or earned your stripes. Being involved in EPIP provided a very concrete way for me to test out my leadership style.[39]

Awareness of organizations like EPIP can be invaluable in providing resources and connections for emerging philanthropists. Nonprofit organizations should also be encouraging their next gen staff members to participate in leadership roles outside their organization, such as on boards and committees. This is an outstanding way for young professionals to develop skills and build relationships within the community, and potential donors.

RESOURCES

Print Resources

- *Family Wealth* by James E. Hughes Jr.
- *Family: The Compact Among Generations* by James E. Hughes Jr.
- *Raising Charitable Children* by Carol Weisman
- *The Generosity Plan* by Kathy LeMay
- *Inspired Philanthropy* by Tracy Gary
- *Legacy & Innovation* by Stephanie Yang and Changemakers
- *Creating Change Through Family Philanthropy* by Alison Goldberg, Karen Pittelman, and Resource Generation
- *Wealth in Families* by Charles W. Collier
- *Preparing Heirs* by Roy Williams and Vic Preisser
- *Family Philanthropy and the Intergenerational Transfer of Wealth* by the Community Foundation R&D Incubator

Websites

- Emerging Practitioners in Philanthropy (www.epip.org)
- 21/64 (www.2164.net)
- Grand Street (www.grandstreetnetwork.net)
- National Center for Family Philanthropy (www.ncfp.org)
- Resource Generation (www.resourcegeneration.org)
- Council on Foundations (www.cof.org)
- Full Circle Advisors (www.fullcircleadvisors.net)
- New Voices of Philanthropy (www.tristaharris.org)
- Future Leaders in Philanthropy (FLIP) (www.networkflip.com)
- Thoughtful Philanthropy (www.thoughtfulphilanthropy.wordpress.com)

Notes

1. Kris Putnam-Walkerly and Rowena Robels, "EPIP Impact Assessment" (Putnam Community Investment Consulting, 2011), 12.
2. Ibid., 10.
3. Ibid., 11.
4. Ibid., 14.
5. Ibid., 8.
6. Sharna Goldseker of 21/64 interview conducted by Emily Davis on July 21, 2011.
7. Putnam-Walkerly and Robels, "EPIP Impact Assessment."
8. Ibid., 9.
9. Ibid., 7.
10. Rusty Stahl interview, conducted by Emily Davis July 7, 2011.
11. Ibid.
12. Ibid.
13. Lisa Parker interview, conducted by Emily Davis July 13, 2011.
14. Foundation Center, "Foundation Growth and Giving Estimates: Current Outlook 2009 Edition," accessed September 24, 2011, foundationcenter.org/gainknowledge/research/pdf/fgge09.pdf.
15. Community Foundation R&D Incubator, "Family Philanthropy and the Intergenerational Transfer of Wealth: Tapping into the Power of Family Philanthropy in the 21st Century" (2010), 3.
16. Ibid.
17. Alison Goldberg, Karen Pittelman, and Resource Generation. *Creating Change Through Family Philanthropy* (Canada: Soft Skull Press, 2006), 8–9.
18. Interview conducted by Emily Davis on July 21, 2011.
19. Goldberg, Pittelman, and Resource Generation, *Creating Change*, 45.
20. Ibid.
21. Sharna Goldeseker, "Beyond Duty and Obligation" (Council on Foundations Foundation News & Commentary, January/February 2006).
22. Interview conducted by Emily Davis on July 21, 2011.
23. Lisa Parker interview.
24. Ibid.
25. Ibid.
26. Lisa Parker interview.
27. Stephanie Yang and Changemakers, *Legacy and Innovation: A Guidebook for Families on Social Change Philanthropy* (Berkeley, CA: Inkworks Press, 2007), 101.
28. Goldberg, Pittelman, and Resource Generation, *Creating Change*, 16.
29. Ibid., 105.
30. Ibid., 31.
31. Ibid., 31.
32. Ibid., 17.
33. Mike Gast interview, conducted by Emily Davis on April 1, 2011.

34. Sharna Goldeseker, "Beyond Duty and Obligation" (Council on Foundations Foundation News & Commentary, January/February 2006).

35. Sharna Goldseker, "What Will Really Engage the Next Generation" (National Center on Family Philanthropy Family Giving News: August 2009).

36. Tracy Gary, *Inspired Philanthropy* (Jossey-Bass, 2007), www.inspiredphilanthropy .com.

37. Grand Street web page, accessed September 24, 2011, www.grandstreetnetwork .net/.

38. Goldberg, Pittelman, and Resource Generation, *Creating Change*, 30.

39. Putnam-Walkerly and Robels, "EPIP Impact Assessment," 15.

CHAPTER 6

Harnessing the Power of Online Communications

It is nearly impossible to talk about fundraising from the next generation of philanthropists without talking about social media. Philanthropy's Next Generation survey respondents (28.9 percent) shared that they learned about the nonprofit organizations to which they donate through some type of social media platform. Social networks are to Millennials what television was to Boomers. Nonprofits need to go where the next generation is—online! As the *Next Generation of American Giving* notes, "Major mailers have reported almost a 20 percent decline in new donor acquisition over the last 5 years."[1]

GOING WHERE THE GIVERS ARE

Millennials are the first generation to grow up with the Internet and Gen X with personal computers. Why wouldn't fundraisers go where these next gen givers are? Organizations took the same strategies with our Traditionalist and Boomer philanthropists when they were in their thirties by connecting with them in the ways that they preferred. Without integrating some level of social media into your organization's communications efforts fundraisers are ignoring an entire demographic and tools that will help us build relationships with next gen givers—no matter what the size of the gift.

Social media should be a larger part of a multichannel communications plan to engage the next generation of donors, particularly annual givers and to steward donors at every level. Social media is primarily an outlet for new audiences and for stewardship of current stakeholders. Nonprofits should not assume that if they set up a Facebook Cause that they will immediately get donations or if they set up a Twitter account that they will instantaneously have followers. Social media is a great way for people, especially young donors, to get viral recommendations and peer-to-peer solicitations, but it also takes time like any cultivation tool. Well-organized strategies will help young donors help you and connect with your mission.

Seventy percent of Gen X and Millennials are using Facebook, but the largest growing number of Facebook users, according to Facebook, in 2009 was women aged 55 to 65.[2] Here is where multigenerational engagement is useful—providing opportunities for people of all ages to engage in your organization's online community. Younger generations can use social media to recruit their parents to a cause and vice versa; Gen X and Y rely heavily on the recommendations of their online friends and family and provide their opinions to their network as well. Remain open to individuals of all ages to support and interact with your organization online.

Ask your young donors and volunteers to get involved in helping to develop your strategies for fundraising—and then *listen*. Don't tokenize. Ask individuals what they would like to do to raise money for the mission and how they would like to be recognized. Using tools like StayClassy.org, Razoo.com, and Facebook are great places to start—be sure to tell your organization's stories and make it easy for potential donors to (a) take action (donate, sign a petition), (b) spread the word to their peers, and (c) see the impact of their efforts, whether they are volunteer or financial contributions.

The next generations have been involved in civic engagement more than any generations before and tend not to give for the sake of philanthropy, but because they believe in a cause and want to change the world. Sound familiar? Boomers wanted to change the world—they wanted a place for their ideals to shape the world in which they were living. In some ways nothing really changes, there are simply new platforms for the next gen to support their causes and ideals.

Like many individuals in their twenties and thirties, there are many young people today who may not have the financial means to deliver a larger check, but who can raise larger numbers of smaller donations from their peers, friends, and family through the simple click of a button. It is likely that if young people do organize an event for your organization, they are going to use social media to market it, raise money, and gather registrations. Be open to these new communications platforms and have orientation to the strategy behind the tools, rather than only the tools themselves.

Social media is a quicker and more accessible way to reach out to young donors and their peers. Creating exciting campaigns for projects and demonstrating the results is the best way to go about this. Use video, use quotes, use stories—be transparent and share it all online. Don't forget to ask for a donation, too.

There are plenty of nonprofits out there that have mastered the social media world—leveraging all the right tools, telling their story, and raising funds through the Internet. One great example is Invisible Children. They have leveraged small donations from high school students all around the United States to make a significant impact on child soldiers in Africa. Their message has gone global and the founders meet with Oprah and win awards, constantly increasing their visibility and, therefore, their donations. There are those organizations that are chugging along looking for good reasons and ways to start to use social media more effectively. It's not all about jumping into every social media tool at once, but rather a strategy and an on-boarding process that will help the sustainability of this marketing strategy.

SOCIAL MEDIA IS A TOOL, NOT *THE* TOOL

Opinion, resources, and self-proclaimed "gurus" for social media are just about everywhere these days. The Nonprofit Technology Network (NTEN) is booming, Allison Fine and Beth Kanter's book, *The Networked Nonprofit* is wildly popular, and it seems that every other day there is a new training or platform for social media. Social networks are advancing and being created at what seems like the speed of light for fundraising professionals.

This chapter provides an overview to strategy for using any type of social media for your organization. It is not a comprehensive source on using social media, but rather a snapshot of how to incorporate social media into your fundraising efforts. No matter what the social networking platform, the same foundational concepts apply. Today, it isn't about *if* nonprofits and development professionals use social media, but *when* and *how*.

Incorporating the essentials of fundraising into your social media strategy and practices can be a fun and exciting way to diversify your communications with your current and prospective donors.

You can also refer to Appendix A, which includes a sample social media plan outline and a complete sample social media plan that are found at Idea Encore.com. Find an online source for social media definitions at Socialbrite (www.socialbrite.org). Nonprofits do not need to reinvent the wheel for their plans, policies, and procedures, but having some structure is critical to success. Use a consistent strategy for your social media and share that strategy across your organization, empowering others to help spread your message and raise more dollars for your mission.

Social media helps to reach out to stakeholders—donors, volunteers, prospective board members, and more. Nonprofits can raise funds, get their message out, and build support for a cause. However, no organization should completely rely on social media to answer all its problems. There is no magic wand here. Fundraisers did not always have fax machines and direct mail was new at some point. Remember when e-mail became the newest thing? Electronic newsletters and listservs were the first wave of online communications, called web 1.0. Now the world is deep into web 2.0 and more is coming every day.

Social media is simply another tool in the marketing and fundraising toolbox that nonprofit professionals can use. Certainly, there are more and more social networking tools every day and there are nonprofits that are using innovative platforms effectively. Many of the smaller organizations should rely on the basic social networks like Facebook and Twitter before taking on new platforms such as Foursquare, Jumo, and others. Integrate the social media activities into other fundraising efforts and be sure to use consistent messaging. A message map can be enormously helpful in using social media as one of the cultivation tools for your organization.

LISTEN TO YOUR FANS AND FOLLOWERS

The first rule of social media is to *listen* to your followers—social media provides a platform for dialogue where your organization can gain insights about what your stakeholders want and need. It takes time to leverage engagement from your stakeholders online, but be patient. The organizational website is always home base and it is important to keep the website up to date in order to have the most reliable information for potential donors.

Your electronic communications should provide a way for users to access their profiles and contact information—this allows the users and donors to opt in and update their information providing your organization with the most up to date contact information for cultivation and solicitation.[3]

Online communications are taking an increasingly important role with more donors, volunteers and others. More and more people are researching organizations' websites to learn more before investing in the nonprofit.

> Investing in technology can help make fundraising more efficient, thus making a focus on younger donors more cost-efficient. . . . . Almost 67 percent of donors under 30 and around 65 percent of donors between the ages of 30 and 39 reported that donating through an organization's website is most preferable. Only 15 percent of donors over the age of 60 agreed that donating through an organization's website if preferable or most preferable.[4]

Social media is a great place and way to share the stories your organization has. Using a blog and social media to send those stories out is an excellent way to drive traffic back to your website. In the Philanthropy's Next Generation survey, 36 percent of participants shared that they learned about the nonprofit organization(s) that they currently donate to through that organization's website demonstrating that the power of your organization's website is a powerful tool as well. All communications, whether electronic or print, should drive people back to your website.

"Donors want you to use the communications channels they use. Since the chances that you'll be on CNN.com are small, get in their Facebook feed instead."[5] Every effort made through social media should be driving prospective donors back to the organization's website. An organization's website is now one of the primary ways that the next generation will learn more about your organization before writing a check.[6]

Use your blog as a place to share stakeholder stories, written by stakeholders themselves. It can be helpful to have a blog post submission document to help manage blog content and provide pointers. Always end a blog post with a question to open up feedback from the blog readers.

Ask questions on Facebook and Twitter in addition to asking for follower and fan participation. Follow those who follow your organization (when appropriate) and watch what they are talking about to get a sense of what interests them, particularly as it relates to fundraising. Twitter, Facebook, and Foursquare, as examples, are places for your stakeholders to tell you exactly where they are and what they are interested in. Use these platforms as entry points to one-on-one conversations about how you can develop a relationship with potential and current donors. Trust truly can be created at a distance, but dialogue and responsiveness is the key to building that trust and relationship.

In fundraising, listening is one of the most important skills; social media is a great way to listen to donors on a daily basis—look for trends and ideas and respond appropriately.

SOCIAL MEDIA IS A PLANT

Social media is like watering a plant. Your organization cannot simply create a Twitter account and expect people to follow your cause. In your social media plan be specific about how many times a day and a week you will "water" your social networks so that they don't die. An inactive social network might be as detrimental as not having a social network at all. Be sure that you or your staff and volunteers have time to dedicate to social media activity rather than leaving your social media dormant.

Start by taking 20 minutes a day to populate your social media outlets. Creating a calendar for posting can be helpful as well. What is the message that you want to get out to your stakeholders and the community? Return to your message map and your social media plan to help keep your organizational message consistent. Watering the social media plan a little every day will help to create a foundation under which your organization can grow and thrive in the virtual world.

If you are uncomfortable with social media, start by taking a training class or hiring a coach to help teach you with the tools, and then begin at home. Open up your own personal Facebook Profile or Twitter account and play around. Social media can actually be a lot of fun and there are so many resources to learn from. Watch and follow similar organizations and successful organizations that use social media.

Fundraising professionals spend a great deal of time asking donors for gifts in a number of ways as well as thanking them for their contributions. Use social media in the same way—acknowledge and ask often to keep the social media plant watered. Sharing the impact of donations quickly and easily can take stewardship to new heights.

Social Media Is Stewardship

One of the great things about social media is that it is a low-cost way to communicate with your constituents. It is a great way to tell current donors and supporters how their participation impacted a goal, clients, or the mission. The closer fundraising staff brings donors into the inner circle of the organization, the more likely they are to give and to give more dollars. Using social media is a great way to open a door to prospective donors and to build closer relationships with existing donors. It is also another great way to thank donors those seven times before asking for another gift.

Share successes in short form on Facebook and Twitter. Did you reach a fundraising goal as an organization? Perhaps you have a Walk Fundraising Team who has exceeded their fundraising goal. Can you use your blog to tell the story of how donations impact the mission and your clients? Do you have pictures to share in a Facebook album or on Flickr?

Fundraisers no longer need to wait for an annual report to get published to share pictures, stories, and resources. The Colorado Chapter of the National Hemophilia Foundation shares weekly blog posts about what is happening in their organization, including stories from community members, and the posts are shared those across other social media networks. Every month with its e-newsletter, the foundation includes the previous month's blog posts in the "Blog Corner" article of the e-newsletter. In addition to writing the stories and using web 2.0 tools, foundation members incorporate their social media with their web 1.0 tools, cross-promoting everything they do as a way to reach out to different audiences. The organization has started using video acknowledgments in addition to written and electronic acknowledgments for major donors.

Diversify the ways your organization cultivates and stewards donors by adding electronic and social networking platforms. Your organization is likely to expand its reach and build buzz among the next generation of givers.

ADDING VALUE THROUGH SOCIAL MEDIA

Your organization's social media strategy should add value and not consist primarily of asking for donations or volunteer time. Be sure to share resources that will benefit your social media followers outside of your organization. Post relevant articles and share stories of impact other organizations have had. Drive traffic back to your website and increase the opportunity for face-to-face connections with donors. If you see someone who has been active on your social media and is helping to spread the word, ask to meet with them one-on-one and then build the relationship from there. Cultivate the relationship to see what other opportunities await.

Despite what many people believe, adding content to social media networks is not only about promoting your organization's events and activities. Refer to valuable resources outside your organization. In the case of the Colorado Chapter of the National Hemophilia Foundation, they mix in their organization's activities with weekly news articles about various bleeding disorders. By setting up Google Alerts for various phrases such as "hemophilia" or looking up conversations on Twitter under "#hemophilia" they easily pull up articles and topics about bleeding disorders that will benefit their community members. Using tools like Delicious (www.delicious.com) helps to let stakeholders know what you are reading online and provides resources for them as well.

A good mix of organization-specific and field-related information will demonstrate your organization's commitment to the issue, not just its dedication to self-promotion. This type of content should be covered in your organization's social media plan. Sharing resources demonstrates that your organization is connected and knowledgeable about more than just your organization that you seek resources that would be beneficial for the reader to learn. You want your organization to be seen as an expert hub for resources—the "go to" resource for any issue related to your cause.

SOCIAL MEDIA IS A TWO-WAY STREET

One of the best things about social media is that there is potential for dialogue. A direct mail appeal can't do this in the same way that a blog can. Share news and opinions, take risks, and be ready for dissent and support. Your organization is trying to enhance engagement and you should be willing to post comments that challenge your opinions. This is how strong dialogue begins. You can always respond directly to positive or challenging comments, but allowing that space means that you are open to the community. Of course, inappropriate or demeaning language is never acceptable.

Having a well-communicated social media policy will help serve as an insurance policy. When there is negative but appropriate feedback through your social media platform, be sure to respond quickly and informatively. Offer up resources or answer any questions that arise. Your organization's response will serve as a way to clarify any confusion or at least demonstrate that you are responsive to constructive feedback. Ignoring dialogue is not a useful solution to conflict online. Set up alerts and notifications so that your staff is aware of feedback that requires an immediate response.

Be prepared for positive feedback and respond to that as well. Encourage followers to share their stories and ask how your organization can do more or improve. Social media is a quick and effective way to encourage people to share their opinions. Your organization may not hear any feedback in the beginning especially, but sometimes the simple act of being asked for an opinion is what really counts.

Not Everyone "Diggs" Social Media

It's true that not everyone is going to follow your cause on Twitter, become a fan ("like") on Facebook, or join your LinkedIn Group. There will always be people, regardless of their age, that prefer direct mail, but then again direct mail isn't for everyone either. There are next generation philanthropists who will not donate to organizations that use direct mail because they see it as a waste of time and environmental resources, and there are others who want a hand-written acknowledgment sent through the mail. There are no shortages of how donors want to receive communication.

Know who your audiences are and start to prepare your organization to be in many different places. There may be an assumption that if your organization is using social media that the staff will be inundated with dialogue and interaction that may be difficult to handle. This is rarely the case, especially when starting out using social media.

Providing platforms for different types of people to get engaged in your organization is the key to casting a wide net. The more points of entry there are for engagement the greater likelihood of success. If your organization is not sure how donors want to receive information—ask them! Cross-promote social media on all your print information and ask people to spread the word knowing that your organization may not be able to ever rely solely on a print newsletter or an RSS feed.

It Ain't Free

Social media tools themselves can be free compared to websites, print publications, and other online tools, but it does cost money to implement them. Time is money and social media takes time, especially if you are asking people to manage social media who don't really understand where to get started. The learning curve for social media is steep and although it may feel like a slow start, it becomes second nature for many very quickly. Consultants and contract employees can save you some of that time, money, and energy by putting together a plan, training staff, volunteers or board members, and setting up a foundation for your online practices. There is a small environmental impact here, but many agree that it is less than using only traditional methods of outreach for fundraising such as direct mail.

Try not to let the time commitment impede your organization's willingness to use social media. Start small, perhaps with one social network, and build from there. There are new tools coming out every day like HootSuite, TweetDeck, and more that help to manage multiple social media platforms at once. On the whole, using social media can still save more time in messaging than preparing a direct mail campaign. Consider the time and cost that your organization might invest in direct mail, conference calls, travel, and more. Keep your eyes open for trends and tools that can help your organization save time in managing a wide range of social media tools.

Build a Social Media Plan

This cannot be emphasized enough and is probably one of the greatest downfalls to nonprofits taking on social media. A social media plan can be a stand-alone document or built into existing marketing and fundraising plans. Regardless of where the plan lives, it is the way to communicate the social media activities for the organization and the development function.

It does not need to be long and complex, but it should be specific and measurable.

Hiring someone with experience to write a social media plan that folds into an existing fundraising or communications plans can be helpful in the long run. You will be able to effectively keep everyone in the organization on the same page, adjust the strategy, and implement consistently. The plan should also cover how you will manage your social media—that is, will you bring on volunteers? Staff? Consultants? Most likely, your organization will need to train someone so make sure that you have someone who can train effectively on the topic. Having a strategy will help to keep the social media plant watered consistently and effectively.

Set Your Purpose

What is your overall purpose for using social media? What are your goals for individual social networks? Do you want to increase your brand awareness, explore the online world, raise funds, or share stories with stakeholders? Be clear about the reasons that you want to use social media. There may be an overall organizational purpose and/or a specific campaign purpose. Here are ideas for purposes your organization can list in your plan:

- Learn more about social media.
- Reach a different demographic.
- Connect more with a current demographic.
- Access other research or resources.
- Promote brand/event/idea/product.
- Communicate.
- Seen as an expert.
- Fundraising.
- Campaign promotion.
- Share your story.

Clarify Goals and Objectives

What are the specific social media goals you have (number of Twitter followers or dialogue on a blog) or what are the organizational goals you have for using online tools (increase annual giving numbers, etc.)? Be as specific as you can—you may start with a more general objective and make it more specific as time goes on. Plans are living documents that should always be updated. Here are some suggestions for goals and objectives:

- Increase website traffic.
- Sell more product.
- Share ideas.
- Learn about resources in your field.
- Promote an event or idea.
- Develop your brand.
- Test campaign ideas.

Identify Social Networks

Being online means more than Facebook. Web 1.0 technology like list-servs, e-newsletters, and websites are still useful for engaging people. Generation X donors give by mail and online in equal amounts while Gen Y or Millennials give more online. Both Gen X and Y participate the same amount in mobile giving, a platform that is still growing and under the watchful eye of nonprofit organizations for its return on investment.[7] "Texting campaigns can engage a large number of prospective donors who have $5 to $10 to give. These campaigns are especially useful in those cases when the need for support requires little explanation or can be conveyed in a mass setting such as a concert or sports event."[8]

Ultimately, your organization will want your interactive online presence to lead back to your website. Decide which tools are going to be the most manageable for you to begin with and work diligently to populate those tools and engage conversation. Examples of popular social networks non-profits are using include:

- Blogs
- Facebook
- Twitter
- Foursquare

- Jumo
- Delicious

IMPLEMENTING THE SOCIAL MEDIA PLAN

Who will be in charge of the information being shared? How often will you share information? What information will be shared? Are there limitations? Creating playbooks for online communications management as well as online sharing policies are great ideas for continuity and a little insurance. Be transparent with your followers and let them know when you are trying something different—ask for feedback during implementation.

PRACTICAL TIPS

Blog
- How often will you blog?
- What will you blog about?
- Who will blog?

Twitter
- How often will you tweet?
- What will you tweet about?
- How will you track?
- Who will you follow?
- Who will tweet?

Facebook
- Profile/ Group/ Page
- Who will manage?
- Facebook Ads?
- Will you link to Twitter? Hootsuite?

LinkedIn
- Group and subgroups?
- Who will you invite to join?
- Who will be admins?
- How often will you post?

In the nonprofit world, staff members are always spread thin. With the emergence of online communications it sounds like just one more thing to add to the plate. "Oh, I forgot about the blog," or "Should I tweet this?" are questions that come up frequently. Figuring out how to communicate your organization's efforts on top of the work you already have is a big task to undertake.

Do not rely solely on the perceived young "techie" on staff to take care of the social media efforts. This is the wrong approach. Just like any fundraising effort, it is best accomplished as a team with all employees contributing in ways that they are able and with a strategy behind it. There are organizations that will designate a different person each week to manage the social media and in other organizations employees are encouraged to participate in social media in any way they can, but everyone must be active (of course, you will want to have a policy in place, too). Be sure that messaging is consistent and that those people involved in the social media communications understand the difference between how the organization uses social media and how they personally use social media.

One of the struggles in nonprofits is what is appropriate to share online about the organization; a plan can help to get all your staff, board, and volunteers oriented to what the expectations are for sharing online. Many nonprofits still have social networking sites like Facebook blocked— this inhibits your staff from promoting and getting the word out about your cause, but can also make sense depending on your mission. Consider opening up the social networking sites for your staff and use your plan and policies for insurance on what can and should be shared about the organization. Let go of some control and increase your organization's transparency.

Hiring Staff

Nonprofits are starting to see the value in hiring a staff member (full or part time) who can manage all the marketing and communications for the organization. This will be increasingly necessary, but something that funders and nonprofits often do not prioritize. Having a staff member can help to provide consistent and effective messaging for your organization— building relationships that will help to improve your fundraising efforts and your cause. Having many staff members involved in social media will help to communicate differently and to provide valuable messages about fundraising events, board opportunities, program success, and staff changes to name a few.

Most people cannot hire a staff member dedicated solely to social media efforts, so they wrap in the communications responsibilities with a fundraising role. Fundraising is a big job and raising money for the budget is hard enough as it is. Often the online communications are just tacked onto that role as if it were a simple effort to complete. True, many times the services we use are free, but the time is not. Taking time from your donor visits to tweet is not a priority, nor should it be. Share the time responsibility and identify a point person for social media without asking that individual to manage the entire content that is shared through social media.

Branding your organization and opening the door to new, potential donors, especially the next generation of donors, are critical to helping your organization grow. Incorporate skilled staff to manage the social media communications in collaboration with other staff and volunteers.

Contracting for the Cause

Contracting with a consultant can be a cost-effective way to manage and sustain your organization's online communications. It can save time while helping avoid the cost of hiring a separate staff member, paying for benefits, and so on. It can also save time in the long run from trying out strategies that do not work and getting frustrated. Don't give up . . . call in an expert to help coach your staff and volunteers if you can. The downside is that your organization is not controlling 100 percent of the content or learning how to incorporate social media into the organization completely, but this can be accomplished over time.

A consultant will review the goals and purpose of an organization's online communications. A consultant should set the organization up for success by creating the online tools, building a following, and then training those individuals in the nonprofit to take over. The consultant's job is not to be in a position where she or he is at the organization long term; a consultant is involved because the nonprofit needs short-term assistance. The job is to get the organization sustainably established, and then get out of the way.

There is always the risk of not hiring the right consultant or not knowing what you need exactly. The other problem is managing the online communications after the consultant leaves. If the consultant is an expert he or she will be able to set you up with a plan first and then demonstrate ways that others can take over.

Having a playbook for each social media tool is a great way to share information about each social media outlet (blog, Facebook, Ning, Twitter, etc.) that can be shared throughout the organization, including board members and volunteers. Include why you are using a specific social media tool and how it fits into larger goals (fundraising plan, strategic plan). Include the goals for that tool; for example, the organization wants to reach 3,000 Twitter followers by January 1. Playbooks should cover best practices, step-by-step instructions, passwords, and more. It is a great way for organizations to maintain their social media efforts going after the consultant leaves. Providing goals in the playbooks and the social media plan will help keep your organization's social media efforts on target and striving to serve your mission. As organizations work with the next generation of volunteers, a key component is to include the "why" in everything you do.

Online communications can be done from anywhere. It is helpful to be in the same geographic location, but not essential. Choosing a consultant that understands fundraising and your mission is critical in building in social media to your outreach efforts.

Volunteers Leading the Effort

Hiring volunteers and interns is a great strategy for beginning a social media effort in your nonprofit. In fact, the more people you have engaged in your social media communications the better. Ideally, your board and others on staff would be involved.

Many nonprofits ask volunteers to help when they cannot find the time to manage those online communications. Volunteers are great—they can be a wonderful resource. In fact, many organizations like Young Nonprofit Professionals Network (YNPN) are volunteer-led, including their social media efforts. If you have the right people in place—recruited and oriented by a volunteer development professional—then you are more likely to have success in getting a volunteer to manage your online communications.

On the other hand, sometimes volunteers do not stick around as long as your organization needs them to, leaving you wondering what to do next with your social media efforts. Many volunteers have the best intentions and set up sophisticated or simple social media systems that are not sustainable for the nonprofit. Perhaps your organization finds someone who knows Twitter, but does not know your strategies and how social media fits into that plan. Do the volunteers understand how to write a social media plan or how to build relationships at a distance? Be sure that you have all the access to the passwords or other administrative details before a volunteer leaves to prevent lost information, duplication, and frustration. When your organization does not have access to its own administrative responsibilities, it only leads to frustration and confusion.

Volunteers can be a perfect option for many nonprofits, but beware of the questions to ask ahead of time and make sure that your organization is setting itself up for long-term sustainability and success. Nonprofits are powered so much by volunteers—make sure that your goals and expectations are clear before you throw all the social media efforts on top of a volunteer. Conduct an interview with your volunteer(s) supporting the organization's social media efforts.

It is a good investment to bring in a social media trainer for staff and volunteers. An overview training class that teaches why social media is important and how it builds into your stewardship and cultivation of donors and stakeholders is critical. In a perfect world there would be a social media plan that you could share at that time, but most times the planning is an afterthought. An hour to an hour-and-a-half of training that explains how all the social media and fundraising pieces fit together is a great idea. This will help folks understand how they are connected to a larger project and to one another. At the Nonprofit Cultivation Center in Colorado, a six-month training program is offered on how to build strategies for social media and how to use basic social media tools; the end result is a social media plan created by participants for their organization.

Every volunteer, no matter what she or he is doing for your organization, should have a job description. Include in the job description your organization's mission, tasks for the role, qualifications for the role, and benefits to the person's involvement in a volunteer capacity. Set a realistic time commitment (i.e., two hours per week for six months) for the volunteer role and additional growth opportunities. Always explain why the role is critical to organizational success. Consider having a letter of commitment for the volunteer to sign. She or he may take the responsibility more seriously if this is a requirement. Of course, if you can do background checks that is the best as it provides you with some insurance on who is communicating on your organization's behalf.

Offer regular evaluation and conversations with volunteers about their progress. There is no doubt that they will have learning opportunities to share that will keep your staff learning, too. Share resources that you know might help them to expand their ability to serve your organization (i.e., free webinars on social media, blogs to follow). Volunteers deserve a reasonable amount of attention and the return on investment can be fantastic. This will also allow you to provide successful updates to your board and the rest of the staff about your volunteer program. Remember, often volunteers are looking to build their skills to apply to different professional capacities. Be the organization that they remember for giving them that opportunity and caring about their work!

When you work with volunteers—whether it is board members, interns, or others—recognition is a key component to maintaining relationships. Linking volunteer efforts to organizational successes is so important. The next generations of givers view the donation of time equally as important as donation of money. You just never know who your next major donor might be. He or she may be a volunteer. Offer up opportunities for the social media team to meet the board and other staff. Play and have fun. Moving to End Sexual Assault's (MESA's) recognition event is an annual kickball game with other volunteers and staff. Current and past volunteers come together to enjoy one another; this effort increases volunteer investment in the organization and can lead to financial contributions.

Designing a volunteer development program, fundraising program, or marketing program at a nonprofit is no easy task. Finding and funding staff to make your programs and outreach operate requires a team approach. If your organization cannot hire staff or a consultant consider using these ideas to build a team that can support you. Build leadership and offer learning experiences for volunteers. In other words, invest in them so that they will invest in you.

No matter what direction you go in pursuing online communications, be clear about your plan, goals, and management. Set your organization up for an effort that can be continued, modified, and effective. Remember that many of us are new to the online communications world, so being strategic and thoughtful will save you lots of time in the long run.

EVALUATING SOCIAL MEDIA STRATEGIES

Evaluate your social media strategies and implementation on a regular, periodic basis depending on what works for your organization. Use tracking and measurement tools (there are free ones available; see for instance www.tinyurl.com and www.twaitter.com) to help you with the management and evaluation. Be flexible and willing to adjust your messaging and strategies based on the metrics. Put metrics in place from the start of your social media efforts so you can track what is a good use of your time and has the best return on your investment.

There are entire publications dedicated to the number of ways to demonstrate your social media metrics. For nonprofits, using simple tracking tools to get started (like Feedburner, Feeblitz, or hash tags) is a good foundation. As your organization gets more comfortable using social media, find more sophisticated ways to measure your efforts. Without a baseline, your organization cannot determine where you have been and where you are going.

Evaluation is more than numbers; it's qualitative and quantitative. Read feedback from your stakeholders on social media to gain a sense of how the organization is doing. Ask staff members to participate in evaluations of your social media efforts by asking for feedback on how your organization can improve for the future. Encourage honest and transparent feedback as a way to strengthen the social media interaction offered at your organization.

SOCIAL MEDIA POLICIES

Your organization's social media policies are an important insurance tool that allows your organization to set the boundaries and parameters of online sharing. If you use web 1.0 tools such as listservs and e-newsletters it might be a good idea to have a single policy called an *online sharing policy* or *online sharing guidelines*. Make sure that anyone who is active online has access and is made aware of these policies to the best of your abilities. There are at least two ways to think of using social media policies: (1) policies for the use of social media by your staff and (2) policies for the use of social media by your stakeholders whether they are members, donors, volunteers, or other organizational participants.

Infrequently there are social media posts, comments, and so on that are inappropriate for the platform, but your organization should be prepared.

Outline the purpose of your social media tools, how to use the tools, what is acceptable, and what will not be tolerated, including spam. Always reserve the right to ask someone not to participate or block them from posting; it is not appropriate to post information that is related to real estate on a nonprofit-focused network. Have action steps clearly outlined in your policy when someone has violated that policy.

Placing the policy on your website as well as online communications is important. For groups like LinkedIn, it is possible to place social media policies directly in the welcome message. For membership organizations, send the online sharing policies along with the new member welcome e-mail. Whenever organizations highlight a new online networking member benefit through their blog they are sure to include a link or reference to the online sharing policy. Reminding your members on a regular basis (annually, quarterly, monthly) that there is a social media or online sharing policy is critical. Whenever there is a violation of a policy, remind the user that you have a policy by sharing it with them.

Elements of your policy should include:

- Organization mission.
- Purpose of each social media tool for the organization.
- Who has access to which tools and why.
- Examples of information that are appropriate to share and examples that are not appropriate for sharing online.
- User guidelines.
- Consequences for violations.
- Reinforce your organization's commitment to its mission and the use of social media as part of that effort.

In no way should your social media policies hinder dissenting opinions or experiences that might be difficult to hear. Social media is a great platform for two-way communication, dialogue, and provides opportunities for your organization to communicate, educate, and solicit feedback. If your organization receives negative commentary related to your organization on one of your social networks, for example your Facebook Page, respond in a timely fashion. Respond appropriately and professionally and try not to take the feedback personally. This is an opportunity to demonstrate that your organization is open to feedback and will respond appropriately and quickly. It can also be an opportunity to educate your followers about your organization or clear up a misunderstanding. Don't shy away from these opportunities—engage in them.

Social media policies create clear boundaries and protect your organization from verbally violent or unacceptable online behavior. In every online platform, always include that the organization reserves the right to ask a participant to leave and then back up that statement with the policy.

If the negative feedback is unrelated to your organization, violates your social media policies, or is offensive, respond to that appropriately according to your policy and remind the person of your policy. Start with a warning where appropriate and, if necessary, eventually remove the person from the network.

If you are looking to create a social media policy look for resources that already exist. Here are social media policy resources for your organization:

- IdeaEncore: IdeaEncore Social Media Policy Resources at https://www.ideaencore.com/search/node/social+media+policy.

- NTEN: Tips for Writing Your First Social Media Policy at www.nten.org/blog/2010/02/17/tips-writing-your-first-social-media-policy.

- Social Media Examiner: How to Create Social Media Business Guidelines at www.socialmediaexaminer.com/how-to-create-social-media-business-guidelines/.

- Social Media Governance: Social Media Governance Policies at socialmediagovernance.com/policies.php.

- Nonprofit Law Blog: Social Media Policy Resources for Nonprofits at www.nonprofitlawblog.com/home/2010/09/social-media-policy-resources-for-nonprofits.html?utm_source=twitterfeed&utm_medium=twitter.

- Mashable: 10 Must-Haves for Your Social Media Policy at http://mashable.com/2009/06/02/social-media-policy-musts/.

- Wild Apricot: Creating a Social Media Policy for Your Nonprofit at www.wildapricot.com/blogs/newsblog/archive/2009/01/08/creating-a-social-media-policy-for-your-nonprofit.aspx.

Conclusion

Social media is an outstanding way to diversify your communication efforts and to meet the next generation of donors where they are. Create sustainable online activities through planning, training, and insurance policies. Know that your organization will make mistakes, but that is part of the transparency of social media. Social media is evolving almost more quickly than we can measure it, but social media engagement should be a serious consideration for every organization that wants to focus on engaging the next gen givers.

Also remember to see Appendix A for some practical materials to assist you in getting started with some of the ideas presented in this chapter.

RESOURCES

Print Resources

- *The Networked Nonprofit* by Allison Fine and Beth Kanter
- *I'm on Facebook, Now What?* by Jason Alba and Jesse Stay
- *I'm on LinkedIn, Now What?* by Jason Alba
- *Mobilizing Youth 2.0* by Ben Rigby
- *The Complete Facebook Guide for Small Nonprofits* by John Haydon
- *Twitter Jump Start: The Complete Guide for Small Nonprofits* by John Haydon

Websites

- Nonprofit Technology Network (NTEN) (www.nten.org)
- Beth's Blog (www.bethkanter.org)
- Mashable (www.mashable.com)
- Idealware (www.idealware.org)
- Netsquared (www.netsquared.org)
- Nonprofit Tech 2.0: A Social Media Guide for Nonprofits (www.nonprofitorgs.wordpress.com)

- Socialbrite (www.socialbrite.org)
- Mgive (www.mgive.com)
- Social Media Examiner (www.socialmediaexaminer.com)
- Socialnomics (www.socialnomics.net)

Notes

1. Vinay Bhagat, Pam Loeb, and Mark Rovner, "Next Generation of American Giving: A study on contrasting charitable habits of Generation Y, Generation X, Baby Boomers, and Matures" (Convio, March, 2010), 2.
2. Socialnomics 2011 video, accessed on September 24, 2011, www.youtube.com/watch?v=3SuNx0UrnEo.
3. Sarah Fischler and Alyssa Kopf, "Engaging Tomorrow's Donors Today: A Toolkit for Success" (Community Shares of Colorado, 2007), 16, www.cshares.org/publications.
4. Fischler and Kopf, "Engaging Tomorrow's Donors Today," 4, 7.
5. Trista Harris, "How to Engage the Next Generation of Donors Now" (*Nonprofit World*, 2011), 6.
6. Bhagat, Loeb, and Rovner, "Next Generation of American Giving," 11.
7. Ibid., 5.
8. Center on Philanthropy at Indiana University, "Charitable Giving and the Millennial Generation" (Giving USA Foundation Spotlight, 2010), 9.

CHAPTER 7

Conclusion

Despite everything that has been covered in this book, it is critical to continue the conversation about the generations by including your organization's staff, board, volunteers, and donors. Use the opinions and insights from your stakeholders to allow space for dialogue about working with multiple generations, whether it is with your staff or your donors. Read research, books, and publications from other authors about the multigenerational workplace and marketing; attend trainings; and be open to new ideas. Cultivating relationships across every generation will have a significant impact on every aspect of your organization because it will develop insights and investment into everything your organization does. The act of opening up dialogue with and about younger donors demonstrates a commitment and investment to diversifying your organization's funding base.

WHERE TO GO FROM HERE

Where you take those conversations is entirely up to you. It is easy—and understandable—for nonprofit leaders to allow the day-to-day work distract from addressing underlying, cultural challenges in their organizations that can help open up funding opportunities with next gen givers. The strongest and healthiest leaders are the ones who embrace change and ask questions on ways to best serve their community—whoever those individuals might be. Demonstrating quality leadership means facing challenges head on and learning what is possible to help the organization grow and thrive. Empower your staff and board in the process because they are your most important resources; invest in them and they will invest in you.

New research and trends will emerge every day. Although many folks in the nonprofit sector are already overworked and stretched too thin, they may not have the time to read a whole book on this or other topics. Training and blogs are a great way to learn about research and trends and engage in dialogue at a distance about next generation philanthropists.

Embrace social media. Be open to creating connections and to innovative ideas, not only in reaching out to the next generation of donors, but also in learning about them.

RESOURCES

Blogs and Blog Resources Worth Noting

- Alltop Nonprofit
- A Small Change—Fundraising Blog
- AFP Blog—Recent News of Note
- AFP Blog—Youth in Philanthropy
- Allison Jones
- Amy Sample Ward's Version of NPTech
- Beth's Blog
- Chrisbrogan.com
- EDA Consulting
  - Nonprofit Consulting Café
  - Fundraising and the Next Generation
- Engaging Volunteers
- Event Fundraising Blog
- Fistful of Talent
- Frogloop
- Fundraiser Ideas
- Fundraising IP
- Future Leaders in Philanthropy
- Getting Attention Blog
- Giving in a Digital World
- Nonprofit Leadership 601
- Idealist Blog
- Inside Facebook

- Inspiring Generosity
- Kivi's Nonprofit Communications Blog
- Mashable!
- Momentum San Diego
- Netsquared
- New Voices of Philanthropy
- NonProfit2.0
- Nonprofit Cultivation Center
- Nonprofit Law Blog
- NTEN
- OnlyUp
- Rosetta Thurman
- Social Media Examiner
- Social media marketing hacks for nonprofits
- Social Media Today
- Step by Step Fundraising
- The Non-Profit Press
- Thoughtful Philanthropy

BECOMING A LEARNING ORGANIZATION

To become a learning organization means that you lead an organization or department that is willing to adapt and embrace new ideas. There is always something new around the corner and this book merely scratches the surface of possibilities. Fundraising professionals may never feel like they are completely caught up or ahead of the curve, but that is the beautiful challenge in the development world; it keeps the work innovative and exciting. There is never a dull moment.

With anything new—or old—your organization should evaluate in both qualitative and quantitative ways what works and what does not work. If a venture fails, fail forward and learn all that you can about how to get better in the future. Just because the first attempt at a new strategy doesn't work, it does not mean that your organization should not try again. Take a good look at why the effort wasn't successful, adapt and try again. Chances are there is going to be some value in the effort and debriefing and evaluating the experience can reveal valuable information. Ask anyone—your staff, donors, and volunteers—what are their opinions? Their answers may just change the course of the work for the better. Always be willing to experiment. The mantra here is to never stop evaluating; there is so much to be learned.

Be careful not to take negative feedback personally. It is important to remember that your work is for the mission of the organization above all else. Constructive feedback is often not about you personally, but it is about the mission and the people you serve. Try looking at any difficult situation from the outside in as a way to be more objective and ask for support when needed. Attribute successes across the organization, publicly acknowledging that any accomplishments are a result of team contributions. Great leaders share accomplishments as much as they share the challenges. There are certain to be roadblocks and bumps along the road, but there will be successes and surprises to be celebrated. And remember to celebrate.

Take calculated risks that could turn out to be more beneficial than you ever thought was possible, and have unintended, positive outcomes. When trying something new start slow and steady, then grow from there. Take on one step at a time or a new, small project that can be successful and build your team's confidence. Let your team (staff, board, volunteers, donors) know that this is a new endeavor and that there will be mistakes to learn from. Set yourself up for success by underpromising and overdelivering.

Ultimately treating everyone with respect and opening up to new approaches will benefit the long-term sustainability of your organizational mission. These concepts are not only applicable for fundraising from the next generation of philanthropists, but for working with any donors and building the strength of all your fundraising efforts.

Worksheets, Plans, and Templates

This appendix includes the following materials:

- Fundraising and the Next Generation Worksheet
- Organizational Readiness Assessment
- Stewardship Plan Worksheet
- Sample Memorandum of Understanding (MOU)
- Sample Board Recruitment Plan
- Social Media Plan Worksheet
- Social Media Plan Outline
- Blog Post Template

FUNDRAISING AND THE NEXT GENERATION WORKSHEET

This activity is great to use with your board and staff to help start the conversation before moving into the assessment or as an alternative to the assessment.

Which generations do you think are represented in your organization (staff, volunteers, and board)? Mark all that apply.

❒ Traditionalists/Greatest Generation

❒ Baby Boomers

❒ Generation X

❒ Generation Y/Millennials

Do you know if you have any next gen donors?

❒ Yes

❒ No

❒ Not sure

Do you currently have any strategy or strategies to engage the next generation of donors?

❒ Yes

❒ No

❒ Not sure

Write down three steps you and your organization can take in the next week to engage next gen donors.

1. _____

2. _____

3. _____

How can you implement each of these steps?

1. _____

2. _____

3. _____

Who needs to be involved in these efforts in your organization?

_____

_____

_____

How will you get others in your organization (staff, board, and volunteers) involved in these efforts?

_____

_____

_____

What changes would you make to the plan or what other ideas do you have?

_____

_____

_____

ORGANIZATIONAL READINESS ASSESSMENT

The following assessment questionnaire will help you and your organization develop a program or programs for attracting, engaging, cultivating, and stewarding younger donors. There are a number of ways you can assess your organization's readiness for engaging young philanthropists and the following questionnaire is based on Sarah Fischler's and Alyssa Kopf's toolkit published by Community Shares, "Engaging Tomorrow's Donors Today: A Toolkit for Success."

I recommend asking as many board members, staff, volunteers, and donors as you can to participate in completing this assessment in either print or in online form. The more input you receive on your organization's readiness to engage next gen givers, the better you can determine where to focus your efforts.

This questionnaire also addresses your organization's planning preparedness. That is, do you have a fundraising plan, communications plan, social media plan, and/or stewardship plan? In order to effectively execute and measure your efforts related to fundraising and the next generation you'll need plans and activities that are documented and shared across the organization and its stakeholders. Plans and policies will also help with continuity as you have staff and volunteer changes. Be sure of your orientation process to make sure that anyone involved in your organization is knowledgeable about these types of plans.

This assessment might be used in conjunction with training as well as worksheets listed in the appendices. The worksheets in the appendices encourage more open-ended responses than the responses listed in this section, which are useful for fundraising strategy meetings, staff meetings, and board and committee meetings. Use the questionnaire for an assessment of where to begin and follow with the worksheets on concrete actions that volunteers and staff can use.

Working with Younger Donors

Generally, how appealing is your mission to younger donors?

a. Our message is specifically targeted to an older audience because they make up the majority of our donors.

b. Our message is universal and our language is not targeted to any specific age groups.

c. Our message has specific elements that may appeal to younger donors.

d. Our messaging is varied and specific to different donors by age.

Does your organization engage younger donors?

a. We do not have existing, young donors.

b. We do not track donors by age, but we likely have young donors.

c. We have young donors that fit into our traditional fundraising program.

d. We have young donors engaged in a variety of ways in our organization.

Does your organization have the resources and capacity necessary to develop fundraising efforts focused on younger donors?

a. We do not have the funding or resources (staff, volunteers, etc.) to reach out beyond our core donors at this time.

b. We plan to invest resources that will expand our donor program and outreach to younger donors.

c. We have the capacity to expand our overall donor program, but would need a solid financial return.

d. Pursuing young donors is a necessary step to realize our mission and we have the capacity and resources to create measurement successes other than financial.

Does your organization have the ability to track a donor's giving and involvement over time?

a. We do not have a formal database for tracking donors or volunteers.

b. We track donor gifts or volunteer contributions, but not both.

c. Our database tracks all contacts with our volunteers and donors in a single database.

d. Our database tracks all contacts with our volunteers and donors in a single database and can sort by various categories.

Does your organization have a culture that is accepting of younger donors and welcomes their active involvement?

a. We have not discussed or considered the culture of our organization as it relates to younger donors.

b. Our culture is not specific to any age group; younger donors would feel as comfortable as everyone else.

c. Our organization is exploring how our culture can be more welcoming to younger donors.

d. We have a culture that intentionally invites younger donors to become actively involved at every level of our organization.

Does your organization have meaningful ways for younger donors to become involved in your organization?

a. Young donors would be welcome to participate in our existing programs, but they are not specifically designed for a younger audience.

b. Young donors would enjoy our existing programs because they are built to appeal to all ages.

c. We have planned one to three programs or events targeted to young donors.

d. We have events, volunteer programs, and engagement strategies specifically targeted to appeal to young donors.

Does your organization engage young professionals in leadership roles?

a. We do not have anyone under 40 on our leadership staff, our boards, or committees at this time.

b. We do not have anyone under 40 on our boards or committees, but do have staff under 40 in leadership roles.

c. We have a small group of young professionals as leadership staff or in board and/or committee roles.

d. We specifically recruit young professionals for leadership roles. We have a good mix of all generations represented on all our committees, on the board, and in staff leadership roles.

Do you feel that your organization is ready to engage younger donors?

a.   No, not at this time.

b.   The staff is prepared, but needs greater investment from board and committees.

c.   We are in the beginning stages of planning and implementing efforts to recruit younger donors.

d.   We have programs, events, leadership roles, volunteer opportunities, and communications that are appealing to young donors.

Do you have at least one person in your organization championing the effort to fundraise from younger donors?

a.   We do not have any champion identified at this time.

b.   We have at least one key staff person who dedicates time to engaging young donors.

c.   We have at least one staff person and one board member who serve as champions for engaging next gen philanthropists.

d.   We have a commitment from the majority of our board and staff leadership that engaging young donors is a key component to our fundraising efforts.

Planning

Does your organization have a comprehensive fundraising plan?

a.   We do not have a fundraising plan, nor track our fundraising at this time.

b.   We have a way to track our fundraising efforts, but do not have a fundraising plan.

c.   We are building a fundraising plan with staff, board, and committee participation.

d.   We have a comprehensive fundraising plan including timelines, goals, and activities.

Does your organization have a stewardship plan?

a. We do not have any stewardship plan at this time.

b. We have stewardship activities, but they are not part of formal plan.

c. We are building a stewardship plan.

d. We have a comprehensive stewardship plan as part of our fundraising plan.

Does your organization have fundraising policies and procedures?

a. We do not have any fundraising policies and procedures at this time.

b. We have fundraising procedures and policies, but they are not documented in a formal way.

c. We are developing documented fundraising policies and procedures.

d. We have formal fundraising policies and procedures approved by our board.

Does your organization have a communications/marketing/outreach plan?

a. We do not have any kind of communications plan at this time.

b. We have communications strategies, but they are not recorded in a formal plan.

c. We are in the process of creating a documented communications plan.

d. We have a comprehensive communications plan including timelines, goals, and activities.

Online Communications

How would you describe your organization's online communication tools?

a. We do not use any online communications.

b. We have a website only.

c. We have a website and regular e-newsletter.

d. We have a website, regular e-newsletter, and other social media (i.e., blog, Facebook, Twitter).

How would you describe your organization's website?

a.   We do not have a website.

b.   We have a website, but it is not updated regularly.

c.   We have a website that is updated regularly and allows us to measure website traffic.

d.   We have an interactive website that is updated regularly, allows us to measure traffic, and includes our social media tools.

Does your organization use social media as a communication strategy with donors?

a.   We do not use social media.

b.   We are using at least one social media tool (i.e., Facebook, blog, Twitter) to reach out to our donors.

c.   One or more staff members participate in our social media communications, which include multiple social media tools.

d.   We have a social media plan and policies that the staff manages and evaluates.

Evaluate Your Score

The following section outlines recommendations based on your scores for the assessment tool. Most likely, your organization had a mix of responses and should consider implementing various recommendations as outlined in this section. Ask multiple staff, volunteers, and leaders in your organization to participate in this assessment as a way to gain additional insights into the perceptions of your fundraising efforts with younger donors. Engaging internal stakeholder participation will help your development efforts beyond the scope of your development department.

Mostly "a" = Your organization is most likely not ready at this time to launch any campaign or specific efforts to reach out to younger donors. You will want to remain aware of younger donors and leaders in your organization as you continue to develop fundraising strategies, but isolated efforts may be perceived as incomplete efforts to engage younger donors. At this time, your organization's resources may be best used in another area of fund development. As your organization's resources or capacity increases or organizational barriers are diminished, consider taking additional steps outlined in the next section.

Mostly "b" = Your organization is most likely ready to begin to fold in strategies for engaging young donors. Although you are likely not ready to engage in a full-fledged campaign to attract young donors, your organization can start incorporating small shifts into creating an increasingly welcoming culture for young professionals and donors. Begin to talk with staff, board, committees, and volunteers informally about how they might see your organization reach out more to young donors.

Mostly "c" = It's time to get going. Adding in or expanding on current efforts will help to continue the growth of engaging young donors in your fundraising efforts. Other considerations, like support from board or other organizational priorities, will factor into your decision to move forward with developing additional young donor engagement. It may be worth your organization's time to conduct a more detailed assessment and feasibility study for a campaign to attract, engage, and retain younger donors. Your organization could start with a small pilot project in an area that makes sense to see if it is worth devoting more resources and time to the project.

Mostly "d" = Excellent work! You are already well into the planning and implementation of strategies for working with and engaging younger donors. Continue your efforts in a more targeted way that will really capitalize on the knowledge and tools you have developed. Through the support of a consultant, committee, and/or staff, develop a measurable plan for your young donor engagement efforts. Conduct independent evaluations of your young donor fundraising efforts at least annually. Continue to maintain and support leaders who champion your efforts and look at ways to strengthen your existing activities.

STEWARDSHIP PLAN WORKSHEET

Throughout *Fundraising and the Next Generation* there has been discussion of stewardship and touchpoints. Below you will find a worksheet on how your organization can create a stewardship plan for working with donors of every generation. It may make sense to use the worksheet for various generations and/or donor levels.[1]

What is stewardship? The AFP Fundraising Dictionary defines stewardship as "a process whereby an organization seeks to be worthy of continued philanthropic support, including acknowledgment of gifts, donor recognition, the honoring of donor intent, prudent investment of gifts, and the effective and efficient use of funds to further the mission of the organization."[2]

What is a touchpoint? "The term *touchpoint*, which originates with marketing, is defined as 'all of the communication, human and physical interactions customers [donors] experience during their relationship lifecycle with the organization.'"[3]

Organizational History

1. List all the tools that you have used for touchpoints in your donor stewardship efforts for the last one to three years. Examples include: direct mailings, one-on-one meetings, events and programs, website, e-newsletters, social media, mobile communications.

2. How often do you use each of these touchpoints and who are your target audience(s) for each? This may be a helpful place to create a table or spreadsheet. Explain why you use each tool. What is the purpose of the touchpoint?

3. What is the success rate you have with each of the touchpoints? Your organization should have systems in place that will help you track the success of an annual campaign, track hits to your website, provide statistics on e-newsletter opens, and more. Be honest about the success rate—this information can only help your organization become clearer about what tools work with whom.

4. Who is involved with managing your touchpoints and oversees the stewardship process? This may include staff and volunteers such as

board members or interns. Your organization's executive director should always be involved with stewardship in some way.

5. What is the donation size of your small-, mid-, and high-level donors?

6. How many donors do you have in each of these categories?

7. What are the age ranges of your donors and how many donors do you have in each generation or group?

8. What are the five strongest touchpoints for donors based on their type (i.e., individuals, corporations, foundations) and donor size?

9. What are the five weakest touchpoints for donors based on their type (i.e., individuals, corporations, foundations) and donor size?

10. Have you conducted an evaluation or survey of your donors in the last one to three years to determine their satisfaction with the organizational touchpoints?

11. Are there are other critical pieces of information necessary in creating your stewardship plan (e.g., seasonal mailing addresses)?

Assumptions for Implementation

There are assumptions that will be essential for your stewardship plan regardless of the details in your plan. Read below for sample assumptions that can be used in your stewardship plan.

- For increased success with a stewardship plan it will be critical to identify success factors in the past to repeat and improve on for the future.

- Staff and board will invest in the evaluation process and commit to the agreed-on stewardship plan.

- Each recommended touchpoint will be customized based on donor needs and interests.

- Fundraising team members will solicit donor feedback, either formally or informally, on a regular basis and respond proactively to that feedback, adjusting stewardship accordingly.

- Program and fundraising staff will work closely to provide necessary, high-quality information to donors.

- Executive director and board members will be available for touch-points with donors as directed by the stewardship plan.

- The organization will develop the capacity within the organization to implement and update the stewardship plan.

Stewardship Activities

Create touchpoints with a calendar of deadlines, target audiences, and intended and actual outcomes for touchpoints. See Table A.1 as a sample.

Touchpoint	Donor Level and Age	Donor Type	Primary Contact	Deadline/Schedule	Notes
One-on-one meetings	High-level donors; all ages	All—individuals, corporate, foundation	Executive director	Within one month of donation	
Site visits and volunteer opportunities	Mid- to high-level donors; all ages	All—individuals, corporate, foundation	Development and program staff	Quarterly	
Electronic newsletters	Small- to high-level donors; all ages	Individuals, corporate	Development/marketing staff	Monthly	
Text invites	Small- to mid-level donors; Gen X and Y	Individuals	Development director	As needed, one week before event	
Annual report (print form)	Small- to high-level donors; Gen X—Traditionalist	All—individuals, corporate, foundation	Executive director, development director, program staff	Fall, annually	
Hand-written acknowledgment letters	Mid- to high-level donors, volunteers; Gen X, Traditionalist	All—individuals, corporate, foundation	Board members	Within one month of donation	Conduct at board meetings
Acknowledgment phone calls	Small- to mid-level donors; Boomers and Traditionalists	All—individuals, corporate, foundation	Board members, staff, executive director	Semi-annually	

Other stewardship activities might include those like the ones in Table A.2.

TABLE A.2	STEWARDSHIP COMMUNICATIONS EXAMPLES		
Print	**Online**	**Social Media**	**Phone**
Event invitations	Website	Facebook (Page, Cause)	Phone calls
Program invitations	Electronic newsletters	Twitter	Text invitations
Donor appeals	E-mail	Foursquare	Mobile giving
Newsletters		Flickr, Picasa	
Annual report			
Site visit invitations			
Acknowledgment letters			

Sample Memorandum of Understanding (MOU)

Organization #1/Organization #2 Partnership

Memorandum of Understanding

[YEAR]

Nonprofit #1 to provide Organization #2:

- Ability to promote [abc program] through Nonprofit #1's monthly e-newsletter and blog postings. Organization #2 will provide content by the first of every month (approximate number of subscribers: 123).

- Ability to send messages, with support from Organization #1's staff and volunteers, through the Nonprofit #1's listserv (approximate number of listserv members: 123).

- Weekly, recurring Twitter posts and retweets from Organization #2.

- Web page dedicated to Organization #2 for 12 months (renewed annually based on changes). Content provided by Organization #2.

- Display and distribution of Organization #2's flyers or other collateral, when and where appropriate such as on Nonprofit #1's community table at programs.

- Members of Organization #2 can receive membership benefits or discounted member rate from Nonprofit #1.

- Endorsement of Organization #2's programs. For example, "This program is endorsed by Nonprofit #1."

Organization #2 to provide Nonprofit #1:

- Invitation to have Nonprofit #1 board member serve on the advisory board or committee for Organization #2; to be a legacy position that would pass onto a Nonprofit #1 board member each year.

- Invitation to have Nonprofit #1 board member attend programs and events at a discounted rate and represent Nonprofit #1.

- Invitation for Nonprofit #1 board member to guest speak at appropriate Organization #2 program(s) about Nonprofit #1.

- Promotion of upcoming Nonprofit #1 programs in quarterly e-mail blasts (approximate number of subscribers: 123). Inclusion of Non-profit #1 logo where applicable and appropriate.
- Recommendations of and connections to possible volunteers for Nonprofit #1.
- Donation of space to Nonprofit #1 at Organization #2 for meetings (based on availability).

Term

Term for this MOU will be 12 months beginning on the day both parties have signed this document.

Read and agreed by:

Nonprofit #1: _____ Date: _____

Organization #2: _____ Date: _____

SAMPLE BOARD RECRUITMENT PLAN

The Board of Directors recruits new members to begin service in [month] of each year. Board terms are for [number] years with the option to renew for [number] terms according to the organization bylaws (a total of [number] years). The Organization Board of Directors has no less than [minimum number] board members at any time with up to [maximum number]. Below is the step-by-step process for recruiting board members for organizational board service. If you have any questions, please contact the Board Development Committee Chair(s).

Preplanning

- The current organization board members complete a board matrix and determine areas of need for the current Board.
- After determining areas of need for the Board, the current Board considers any candidates based on those needs. Frequently, committee members are excellent candidates for the Board because they have some orientation and experience to the organization and have demonstrated a commitment to the mission as well as hard work.
- Draft recruitment language to be distributed by the Board Development Committee where appropriate. Include benefits to joining the board, expectations, and board recruitment process.
- Identify individual from the Board Development Committee who will accept and respond to board applications as they come in. This person will need to:
  - Thank individuals for their board applications and resumes promptly after receipt.
  - Explain the next steps and timelines for the recruitment process.
  - Keep applications well organized (this may be done through the DropBox).
- Distribute the board application announcement through individual board networks. Be sure to announce the board recruitment process and timelines at any and all upcoming events.

Application Process

- Applications can be downloaded through the organizational website. Applications and resumes are sent to the organizational e-mail that is managed by the [board member]. Applications are due on [date] each year, three months before the board term begins (*Note: This allows time to review the apps, interview, and invite people to one board meeting*).

- Organize a call to action event to describe opportunities to get involved with the chapter, including board service.

- Board Development Committee member responds to prospective candidates thanking them for their application and notifying them of the process and timelines for the application process including:

  - How many spaces are open and available on the board.
  - Date of the board meeting for candidates to attend, including time and location.
  - Dues expectations and board commitment letter.
  - Timelines for when they will be notified about their acceptance onto the board.
  - Other ways that they can get involved in the organization if they are not a good fit for the board at that time (e.g., committees, volunteer opportunities).

- The Board Development Committee member collecting applications gathers and distributes the applications to the entire Board for its review.

- All candidates will be invited to the [month] board meeting as an opportunity to see the organization's activities in person and ask questions of the board. At this board meeting, after the potential candidates have been excused, the board will discuss applications and who to accept onto the board.

- Board buddies should also be identified at this board meeting and their efforts to reach out to the new prospective candidates are reviewed.

Welcoming New Board Members

- Within one week of the [month] board meeting, prospective board candidates should receive an e-mail/phone call from the chair(s) of the Board Development Committee notifying them of their acceptance onto or refusal onto the Board.

- Prospective candidates *not invited* onto the board—this e-mail should be very gracious and appreciative; encourage continued participation on the organization's committees; and explain any reasons why the individual was not accepted onto the board, but highlight the positive qualities that individual holds.
- Prospective candidate(s) *invited* onto the board—this e-mail should provide a general welcome onto the board and include any logistical information including their new board buddy to help orient them to the board. Include the following details:
  - Dates of board meetings.
  - Orientation dates and process [month].
  - Board buddy contact (be sure to copy the board buddy on this e-mail).
  - Committee participation—any current committee needs or leadership roles that may be available to the new board member.

Orientation [Month]

- Prospective board members will need to participate in an orientation process in [month] each year preferably before the [month] board meeting.
- If the prospective candidate cannot attend the orientation date, he or she will need to schedule a separate time to meet with someone from the Board Development Committee or the Board President.
- Orientation takes approximately [time] (see complete orientation process) to conduct in person, but can also be coordinated through a conference call. Each new board member should receive an orientation packet including the following information:
  - Organizational collateral materials—brochure, packet.
  - Organizational case statement.
  - Plans—strategic, fundraising, social media.
  - Chapter bylaws and related documents.
  - Letter of Commitment.
  - Board job description(s).
  - Committee descriptions.
  - Annual self-evaluation process.

Social Media Plan Worksheet

Step 1. Identify Three Purpose(s)

1. _____
2. _____
3. _____

Step 2. Goals and Objectives—Be Specific!

1. _____
2. _____
3. _____

Step 3. Tools and Strategies

Blog

1. _____
2. _____
3. _____

Facebook Page/Cause

1. _____
2. _____
3. _____

Twitter

1. _____
2. _____
3. _____

Other Social Media

1. _____
2. _____
3. _____

Step 4. Implementation—What, When, Where, and How

- How will your social media plan fit into existing plans?
- How will you get board, staff, and volunteer investment?
- Who in your organization will participate in the implementation process?
- When will you use each social media tool?
- Other considerations?

Step 5. Evaluation and Measurement

- How will you measure your overall efforts?
- How often will you measure and/or evaluate your efforts?
- What will you use to measure your impact using social media, overall and for each tool?
- Who will track measurement?
- Are you prepared to change your course of action if evaluation indicates that is appropriate?

Social Media Plan Outline

Social Media Plan [Year]

Purpose   Identify your purposes related to social media. Why are you using social media at all? An organization does not participate in social media just for social media's sake. Are you trying to market an event? Services? Brand your organization in general? Perhaps your organization is looking to establish itself as an expert in a certain field. List those items here.

Be sure to list goals that are clear and measurable, which will help increase accountability and ownership for your social media plan. It will also allow you to review and adjust your communications within social media as needed.

Examples:

- Steward and cultivate current supporters.
- Attract new supporters.
- Tomorrow's donors today.
- Position your org as an expert.
- Promote brand, programs, events.
- Share your story.

Goals and Objectives   Your goals and objectives should be concrete and quantitative as well as qualitative. What do you want to see happening for your organization in the first three months? Six months? Year and so on? Examples include: increasing donations, recruiting x number of volunteers, increasing recognition in the community.

Examples:

- Raise money! How much?
- Bring in new prospects. How many?
- Share ideas from your org. Which ones?
- Get feedback.
- Promote programs and events.
- Build relationships.

Target Audience(s)   Your organization can have multiple target audiences with your social media. If you are using social media for different campaigns, indicate that here and differentiate timelines for various target audiences where necessary. Your organization may even want to break out independent social media plans for different campaigns.

Examples include:

- Current donors.
- Prospective donors.
- Prospective board members.
- Prospective committee members.
- Volunteers.
- Clients.

Social Media Outlets and Strategies   Evaluate previous strategies and implement new strategies in targeted social media tools to leverage awareness as well as reach goals and objectives. Below, describe how you will use each of these social media tools and who will be responsible for "owning" the messaging and management of each tool.

Blog

- Create a calendar of weekly blog posts and schedule time to create those posts.
- Identify topics for blogs.
- How will you track blog posts (analytics) and promote across web 1.0 and 2.0 tools?

Twitter

- Identify point people who will tweet for your organization.
- Identify tracking strategies (hashtags, etc.).
- Build value into tweets beyond organizational promotion and outreach.
- How will you schedule your tweets?
- What will be the minimum number of tweets daily?
- Will you have bloggers (twitter and blog) for your events? How will that be managed?

Facebook: Fan Page, Group, Cause

- Will you use a Page, Group, and/or Cause?
- Why?
- How will you promote your fan Page/Group/Cause?
- What type of content will you populate the Page/Group/Cause with?
- How will you leverage networks to increase your following?

LinkedIn

- What types of resources will you post to your LinkedIn group?
- How will you generate conversation?
- Will you post jobs and if so, what types?
- Does it make sense to host subgroups?
- How will you promote your LinkedIn Group?
- How will you use other LinkedIn Groups?

Implementation   It is important in any planning to look at specifics of who will lead the efforts and make sure that the strategy is being implemented. Ideally, everyone in the organization will, in some way, be involved with your social media efforts, but there should be at least one individual overseeing the strategy and how it is implemented. Here are some questions to consider when thinking about implementation of your social media plan.

Blog

- How often will you blog?
- What will you blog about?
- Who will blog?

Twitter

- How often will you tweet?
- What will you tweet about?
- How will you track?
- Who will you follow?
- Who will tweet?

Facebook

- Profile/Group/Page/Cause.
- Who will manage?
- Facebook Ads?
- Will you link to Twitter? Ping?

Other Social Media

- What?
- Why?
- How?
- When?

Metrics and Evaluation   Evaluate your social media strategies and implementation on a regular, periodic basis depending on what works for your organization. Use tracking and measurement tools (there are free ones available) to help you with the management and evaluation. Be flexible and willing to adjust your messaging and strategies based on the metrics.

Remember, social media evaluation is both qualitative and quantitative. Without any kind of a baseline, you won't be able to determine where you have been and where you are going. Hashtags and link-shortening/tracking tools can be a great help.

- What tracking tools will you use?
- What will you track?
- What are your baselines for measurement?
- How often will you measure your tracking?
- Who will be responsible for setting up the tracking, maintaining, and reporting?

Blog Post Template

Use the blog post template as a way to gather content for guest posts. The template can be used in a document format that is submitted to the blog master for editing without posting directly to the blog. This provides the blog master with greater control and final editing rights to a blog while providing the writer with guidelines, formats, and tips. This template can also be downloaded at https://www.ideaencore.com/item/nonprofit-blog-post-template.

[Name of Organization's Blog]: Creating an organizational blog post

Thank you for your interest in contributing a blog post for the [organization's name] blog. Your story and perspective can help strengthen our community, create a more dynamic network, and gain a valuable following of community members and donors. Our blog is a way to tell our organization your story. We appreciate your joining in this effort.

Below you will find formatting suggestions as well as hints and tips for your post. We will be in touch with you about when your post will go up; we may need to save your post for a later date depending on other events and announcements happening through the blog. We also reserve final editing rights although if there are any major changes we will consult with you first. The deadline for submitting a draft of your post is: [day, date, year].

In addition to submitting your post below, please send us a picture of you, your family, or a relevant image to accompany the post. If you have any questions about writing the post or the image you would like to submit, please do not hesitate to contact us at [e-mail address] or [phone number].

Hints and Tips:

Your blog post can be as short as two to three paragraphs, but can also be much longer. For samples of other blog posts, please visit our organization's blog at [www.sampleblog.com].

In writing your blog, there is no need to add in hyperlinks, we will take care of that in the formatting process, but you are welcome to include hyperlinks if you wish.

To engage more dialogue, please include a question at the end of your post. For example, "What has been your experience with this?" "Do you agree or disagree and why?"

Use the first person voice. The benefit of a blog is to share opinions and experiences so please make your blog posting personal.

Once the blog posting goes up we will promote the blog through our online networks including Facebook and Twitter.

Your Post:

Please include the following (you can write the information directly into this document and submit to us):

Title:

Please write your title directly into this document. Feel free to design a catchy or creative title. Shorter titles are best and we can help you with this part if you need it.

Post Content:

Write your content here. We will edit as necessary, then copy and paste your content into our blog. From there we will add links and images.

Closing Question(s):

Be sure to include at least one question at the end of the blog post to encourage comments and feedback. We are happy to help with this if you have questions.

Contact:

For any additional questions or comments, please contact [Name], [Title] at [e-mail address] or [phone number]. Thank you again for sharing your story and/or opinion with our network—it means so much!

■ ■ ■

Notes

1. Adapted from the Blue Root Consulting stewardship plan template.
2. AFP Fundraising Dictionary, online at www.afpnet.org, Barbara R. Levy, editor, R. L. Cherry, lexicography editor. Copyright 1996–2003. Association of Fundraising Professionals (AFP) formerly NSFRE, all rights reserved.
3. Hank Brigman, "Defining Customer Touchpoints," www.imediaconnection .com. Published November 2, 2004.

Selected Interviews

This appendix includes interview material with the following leaders in this field:

- Mike Gast, Resource Generation
- Jason Franklin, Bolder Giving
- Sharna Goldseker, 21/64
- Lisa Parker, Family Circle Advisors
- Mary Galeti, The Tecovas Foundation
- Alan Frosh, The Gordian Fund
- Jennie Arbogash, Social Venture Partners of Boulder County

NEXT GEN PHILANTHROPIST: MIKE GAST, RESOURCE GENERATION[1]

Michael Gast is co-director of Resource Generation (RG). Mike has been involved with Resource Generation since 2002, when he attended his first RG program, the Making Money Make Change Retreat. Over his many years with RG, Mike has become an experienced social change philanthropist, donor organizer, and fundraiser. He co-coordinated the Movement Generation Support Committee, a donor circle supporting young progressive leaders in the Bay Area, and has led multiple young donor delegations to events such as the U.S. Social Forum and multiple Council on Foundations conferences. Last spring, Mike organized the Creating Change Through Family Philanthropy Retreat, where 40 young people involved in their families' philanthropy came together to learn, build skills, and develop their leadership. He is a talented facilitator and educator with years of experience leading programs, workshops, and trainings on topics from environmental justice to creating a giving plan. Mike lives in Seattle, plays rugby with the Seattle Quake, and is a graduate of Vassar College.

Q: What is the story of how you became involved in the philanthropic world?

A: I was never really aware of any philanthropy in my family when I was growing up. We talked about politics and my parents were involved in the community in different ways (I remember door knocking for Jesse Jackson with my mom), but there wasn't a sense that they were philanthropists.

I started giving after college when I had money left over from my trust fund (which my grandmother established) that paid for my undergraduate education. At the time, I was working at an organization that focused on youth organizing around environmental justice.

During college I learned about oppression, injustice, and social justice movements and was trying to figure out my role. Around that time I learned about Resource Generation's (RG's) Make Money Make Change (MMMC) conference. I wanted to figure out how to take ownership over the money in my life and how to organize in the wealthy communities I grew up in San Francisco.

My first MMMC conference was in 2002 and it was both a challenge to identify as a young person with wealth and so unique to have space to talk about money, giving, class, and wealth in the context of my values. I became involved with RG's Bay Area chapter and the first thing I did was to work with other local RG members to create my first financial and giving plan. For my first two to three years of organized giving I was donating between $2,500 and $5,000 per year. I tried out different ways to give like donating to community foundations, monthly giving, and donating to small projects.

A few years later, the rest of my trust for college went towards my brother's education. Then, several years ago, I ended up inheriting 50k from my grandma when she died.

Q: How do you engage in philanthropy?

A: I have made a commitment to donate at least half of my inheritance. Right now, around 10 percent of my giving budget comes from my personal income and the other 90 percent comes from inheritance. In the last couple of years, I've given over $23,000, just $2,000 shy of my initial goal. I have used the money to support not only social change organizations I believe in, but also friends who need some financial help.

Half of my donations go to organizations that I am familiar with and half go to organizations selected by foundations with decision-making processes that are activist-led. One hundred percent of my giving for nonprofits is to social change organizations. I like that leaders in the communities are being funded or on the issues being addressed make the decisions about where my money goes. I also like that the foundations know about a range of organizations that I would never hear about.

I also like to join other donors in giving, including through matching gifts and donor circles. These kinds of donor-organizing projects help to leverage the resources of other donors and moves money collaboratively to benefit an organization. It means my donations are inspiring others to give and my dollars are going further.

Somewhere around 25 percent of my giving is processed through recurring donations on a monthly or quarterly basis. Recurring donations through a nonprofit website help me to reach my giving goals without even having to think about it and provides my charities with constant and dependable income. I haven't used Facebook Causes much but am not against doing so in the future.

If I am going to make a larger donation, I am going to write a check so that the organization doesn't have a processing fee taken out of the donation.

I gave $5,000 to a friend who needed money for school and I have talked to other RG members who have given to individuals who need money. My friend was asking for support to pay for college from her community and I was happy to be in the position to help out. In another case I was able to give a friend a loan, again for school expenses.

Giving money to friends can bring some tricky dynamics to the relationship. It's important to remind myself what my friends want from me and that is my friendship and not my money. The priority is always my friendship—my time and energy are way more important than any dollars. If I am giving to an individual, it can't come from a place of guilt or it will ruin the relationship.

Q: How do you learn about charities that you support?

A: I learn about organizations through my personal activism, social change work, conferences, and workshops. I meet organizers who are involved in causes and make a personal connection. I also read e-mails and Facebook links that are recommended by my friends. For me, it is really about personal relationships and my analysis of how change happens.

I give to organizations that are being led by the communities they serve. I value organizing and advocacy as a strategy; I give to groups that are building power in marginalized communities and groups that are organizing folks with privilege to be in solidarity with those struggles.

Q: How long have you supported your top charity/charities?

A: I started giving to organizations I care about when I was 21. There are probably five to seven that I started donating to eight years ago. If you explain to people in their twenties the reason and need for giving early and consistently, they get that concept and are more likely to help.

Q: What, if anything, limits your amount and frequency of giving?

A: I would say my limited time is a big factor. Since I am often helping people learn how to give through my paid work, it can be hard to set aside time for my own personal giving.

I like having accountability for my giving. For example, having a community to report back to about my giving, such as RG, helps me to make commitments and reach my goals. This support has helped me to move my philanthropy forward more than it would have otherwise.

Q: How do you prefer that these charities communicate with you?

A: I like personalized messages from someone involved in the organization. Whether it's through a letter with a personal note, a phone call, or a personal e-mail, knowing someone took the time to thank me individually makes a big difference. I do like a multichannel approach to remind me to give. I'm not really inspired to give by Facebook. Recently, I've liked thank-you phone calls where there is no pitch or outreach, just a simple thank you. We did this at an RG board meeting and it was a great experience.

The coolest example of engaging donors I have seen lately is a personalized video message from the executive director thanking the donor. I saw this done quite effectively by Tim Shriver from the Special Olympics.

Q: How many nonprofit boards have you served on?

A: None actually. I have been asked, but I feel like board work is too similar to my day job right now. I do this work professionally so I don't want to spend my personal time serving on boards. I want my free time to do something more social and fun.

Q: What would you recommend nonprofit boards think about when recruiting young professionals to board leadership roles?

A: Have a clear answer to "why" you are recruiting the person to your board or committee. There has to be a clear and compelling purpose to having young people on the board that matches up with their interests. If you don't have any programs that serve young people at your organization it could be hard to recruit young people at the board level.

I think the best board members are those who come up through the organization's work. This isn't easy advice and it can be really challenging for the organization if they are trying to bring in folks from outside their community. Organizations really need to have ways for everyone to get engaged in the work and the mission.

Q: What have been your best experiences sitting on committees and why?

A: I have always really liked having time to have social interaction with other committee members after the meetings. It's all about the personal relationships and I have made lifelong friends in those experiences.

Q: What have been your worst experiences and how could the organizations have improved?

A: The worst committee meeting I went to was primarily my fault. I flew on a red-eye to a meeting in New York and went straight to the meeting and changed into my work clothes in the bathroom. I was sick during and after the meeting, with a big pile of Kleenex next to my chair. I soon realized never to take red-eye flights and to make sure I am giving myself the proper space and time before meetings to prepare.

Q: Any final thoughts?

A: One thing I am proud of is that because of my own giving, my dad was inspired to give money to me and my siblings to start giving together. This is the first time we have ever done any family giving. In our first year, we decided to give $10,000 to a woman who helped raise us when we were kids and who we have stayed close to. She is an immigrant from El Salvador, and a domestic worker, and has done so much for us—it felt real good to give back to her.

NEXT GEN GRANT MAKER: JASON FRANKLIN, BOLDER GIVING²

Jason Franklin serves as executive director of Bolder Giving, which encourages donors to "Give More, Risk More, Inspire More." He brings to this work more than 15 years of experience in philanthropy education, nonprofit strategy, and urban policy and education advocacy. He is also an award-winning lecturer and doctoral candidate at New York University, where he teaches and conducts research on philanthropy and policy making. He serves on the boards of Resource Generation, North Star Fund, Proteus Fund, 21st Century School Fund, Social Justice Philanthropy Collaborative, Wealth for the Common Good (advisory), and the Chartered Advisors in Philanthropy program (advisory).

Q: What is the story of how you became involved in the philanthropic world?

A: I became involved in social change work in high school. Oregon was proposing major funding cuts to the public school system and I organized a group of students to advocate for stopping the cuts. Our group—Oregon Students Supporting Education—grew from 4 student members to 10,000 in six months and working with teachers, parents, and others from across the state we were able to reduce the budget cuts from 25 percent to 2.5 percent. I served as executive director of OSSE and graduated high school convinced that one person truly can make an impact.

From there I became involved in a number of human rights and equity issues that I was passionate about, worked as volunteer in the White House AIDS Policy Office during the Clinton administration, and completed a graduate program for nonprofit management in New York City.

I was passionate about social change and the nonprofit sector, but hadn't formally been involved in philanthropy. In 2002, when I was 22 years old I received a phone call from my grandfather's secretary letting me know that my grandfather wanted the younger generations to get involved in the family foundation. I had no idea up until that phone call that a family foundation even existed.

As I learned more and more about philanthropy as well as the nonprofit sector, I started speaking on the topic of generational philanthropy issues and organizing other people around their giving. Last June, I became executive director of Bolder Giving, which works to inspire donors to "Give More, Risk More, Inspire More"—especially since then I've been working hard to walk our talk of giving big in my own life.

Q: How do you engage in philanthropy? Family foundation? Personal checks?

A: There are a number of ways that I engage in philanthropy. Annually, each member of our family is able to make small, discretionary grants through our family foundation, directed to a wide range of issues based on each of our passions and interests. Additionally, today I give at least 25 percent of my annual income to a range of causes.

Every year I create a giving plan to guide from my personal giving. I divide my giving plan into six areas including issues I am passionate about such as education equity and local community organizing and what I call "impulse giving." The impulse giving pot is for one-time gifts when I want to support a friend's efforts or a single project that catches my attention and heart. This impulse giving is both the hardest and most fun part of my giving—it allows me some flexibility in my giving but also leaves me open to being irrational and "unstrategic." But after a couple years of budgeting every gift I realized I had to leave room for the unexpected.

I would say that about 50 percent of my current giving is directed through ongoing, monthly gifts, often with a multiyear commitment of $500 to $1,500 a year. I'm also in the process of setting up a local NYC next gen giving circle and serve as a board member for two public foundations—the North Star Fund and the Proteus Fund.

My gifts mostly range from $25 to $2,500, with my bigger gifts going mostly to groups where I am actively involved in their work. I also tend to support smaller organizations where my gift may be among the larger gifts they receive thus making a big impact on their missions. While large social change groups are critically important, in general I believe in investing in the smaller and more marginalized organizations and communities to help get their voices heard.

Q: How long have you supported your top charity/charities?

A: The first gift I remember making was when I was 12 years old. I ran a lemonade stand for a summer with three friends—but it wasn't your average stand selling "Dixie cups for a quarter." Five to six days a week we offered to our neighbors and golfers between the ninth and tenth holes not only lemonade, but extensive morning and afternoon menus—coffee, sodas, baked goods, candy, fruit, and more. We thought we were "budding businessmen" . . . I didn't realize until years later that our parents spent more on our supplies than we made selling them!

My mom sat me down at the end of summer and encouraged me to give some of my earnings to those who needed them more. After much discussion, when I returned to school in the fall I told Principal Marder I wanted to donate half of what I had made from my lemonade stand to help buy books for our "sister school" in Latin America. He was shocked when I handed him an envelope with $1,200 in it—half of my share from the almost $10,000 my friends and I made that summer.

Q: What, if anything, limits your amount and frequency of giving?

A: It is 100 percent budget restrictions. It's an ongoing balancing act. I love to give and it gives me a great deal of personal satisfaction, but I struggle between what I want/need/should spend on myself and wanting to do more philanthropically.

Q: How do you prefer that these charities communicate with you?

A: I'm really open to all kinds of communications. Because giving is such a big part of my life, I do read annual reports. I think about my philanthropy as part of my self-development and I know I spend much more time thinking about giving than most people my age.

I do appreciate when organizations ask me how I would like them to communicate with me. I don't like when I contribute an "impulse gift" to a walk, run, or bike ride and then get overwhelmed with e-mail and print mailers. I feel I get inundated with information from these organizations after I contribute a very small gift to help or support a friend. Recently I set up a new e-mail account for my donations just to help hold off the spam.

Q: How satisfied are you with how often your top charities communicate with you and the way they communicate with you? Do you have any suggestions on what to maintain or improve?

A: About 50 percent of my annual gifts go to organizations that I am personally involved with as a leader and so often I already know what's happening in the organization. I appreciate the acknowledgment letter or being added to an e-mail list. But I also know that it's about scale. For the few larger institutions I support, I get that with my small gift I'm simply a name on a long list rather than someone they hope to build a relationship with.

One approach I particularly like is used by a local New York City organizing group I support. They set up a meeting with every person who gives over $250 between the donor, a staff member, and at least one of their constituents. It becomes a learning experience on all sides. The organization learns about me more as an ally and a pipeline to other resources, the constituent(s) get comfortable talking with donors—often people with wealth they've rarely or never had the chance to connect with before, and I get a deeper understanding of the organization and how it is impacting the community it's organizing.

While it is nice to be recognized, I am also an executive director who struggles to find enough time to effectively recognize every donor to our organization. I understand the competing priorities and the juggling act. I am a philanthropist, but I also share the perspective of those running the organizations and cut a lot of slack to groups about acknowledgment—ultimately I'm supporting them because I believe in their work, not because I'm seeking a thank you.

Q: How many nonprofit boards have you served on?

A: I am currently serving on five boards and two advisory boards; I have served on three others in the past. I have a different experience than many people my age in the nonprofit world because I started working part-time for a nonprofit when I was 17 and then was working almost full-time by the time I was 20. I've spent the last eight years in philanthropy—teaching philanthropy at NYU, working on my PhD dissertation looking at philanthropy and policy making, and serving as a major donor.

At the North Star Fund, one of the foundation boards I sit on, they've set as one priority a goal of building a younger donor base and engage younger people throughout their work. My position on the board among other actions communicated the message that our community is important to North Star, which has helped increase their next gen participation on boards and committees. I think the difference here is that they are clear about their expectations and follow through with their goals of engaging the next generation. I also loved the experience of serving on the Resource Generation board, which is a youth-led board and gave me a chance to learn with a group of my peers.

I've probably turned down seven or eight board invitations in the last six months because groups are so actively looking to find next gen members for their boards. My goal now is to serve as a bridge to other next gen leaders . . . and also to help nonprofit leaders realize that young leaders can do more than just "party and tweet." Boards need to open up other opportunities based on the individual's skill set, not make such big assumptions based on age.

MULTIGEN FAMILY PHILANTHROPY: SHARNA GOLDSEKER, 21/64[3]

Sharna Goldseker has 14 years of experience in the nonprofit sector including 11 years in the philanthropic field as a grant maker and as a consultant to families, foundations, and advisors on next generation and multigenerational philanthropy.

Sharna is currently vice president of the Andrea and Charles Bronfman Philanthropies (ACBP) where she directs 21/64, a nonprofit consulting division specializing in next generation and multigenerational strategic philanthropy. In that capacity, Sharna facilitates Grand Street, a network of 90 18- to 28-year olds who are or will be involved in their family's philanthropy; speaks and consults on generational transitions using 21/64's uniquely developed tools such as the "Grandparent Legacy Project" and "Picture Your Legacy"; and trains other grant makers and advisors on 21/64's approach to multigenerational philanthropy.

Previous to ACBP, Sharna was a program officer at Philanthropy Advisors, a multifamily foundation office in New York, where she managed grant making in the areas of legal rights, reproductive health, social justice, and the environment. Sharna was also a project coordinator for Enterprise Homes, a subsidiary of the Enterprise Foundation, where she developed affordable rental and for-sale housing in Maryland.

Sharna graduated with a bachelor of arts from the University of Pennsylvania with majors in urban studies and religious studies. She has a master's in public administration in nonprofit management from New York University's Robert F. Wagner Graduate School of Public Service where she was the inaugural Charles H. Tenney Fellow. She also has training in organizational development and group dynamics.

Sharna currently serves on the board of directors of the Council on Foundations and the Goldseker Foundation, as well as the advisory board of Strategic Philanthropy Ltd. The following is a summary of an interview conducted with Sharna Goldseker.

With four generations of families over the age of 21, it is difficult to engage everyone. The life span was much younger with previous generations; there was always one generation in a leadership role and the next generation in training to serve in leadership. Today, the passing of the baton doesn't happen in the same way; now every generation is trying to share the baton.

Traditionalists are retiring into their philanthropy and volunteerism. Boomers are staying in the field longer. Gen X and Millennials are struggling to be included and be part of it all. The capacity to give for younger generations is going to look different than their parents or grandparents; the next generation sees giving as an investment.

For nonprofits it can be difficult to know where to put our resources with the generations, but if we don't invest in younger generations now they won't be around in 10 to 20 years. Our investment in the next generation is a human capital investment for both the shorter term, such as volunteering and annual giving, and long-term investments including planned gifts.

21/64 intentionally conveys the message that family philanthropies and advisors working with them should not assume that the next generation is going to participate because they have been invited to participate in an existing system or infrastructure. By inviting younger family philanthropists doesn't mean that there will be young funders at the existing family philanthropy table; rather, the next generation have their own skills and experiences to integrate into the existing generations' skills and experiences which changes the philanthropy.

What 21/64 often sees is that younger funders may expand the range of the board or decision makers, but the leadership doesn't take into account the different values and expectations around operating the philanthropy. What 21/64 is seeing is that next gen funders don't join boards unless they are fully committed to service on those boards.

With so much transition happening in their personal lives, such as school, family, and homes, they are looking for more than name recognition. They want to serve on a board that will give them transparent access to information and how decisions are made. Next gen funders expect orientation and training that will help them serve in the best way they can. Mentorship, coaching, or board buddies are all great ways to support next gen funders in board roles.

Q: What dynamics in family philanthropies do fundraisers need to be aware of?

A: Most nonprofits have a relationship with a single member of a family and that person brings a generational lens to his or her passion for that nonprofit. Traditionalist family members might have a 40-year commitment to an organization that is local and mirrors their personal interest in creating opportunities for a particular program. The philanthropy they engage in may reflect that donor's journey or understanding of their experience of living through generational experiences, such as the Great Depression.

It is important to remember that every generation is shaped by his or her experiences during a specific time in history. Succeeding generations will have a different experience and generational lens. Nonprofits might be surprised to find that the family is not "homogeneous." As nonprofit professionals, we need to spend time learning about unique family members and their various approaches to philanthropy.

Q: What trends or changes are you seeing in the next generation of donors?

A: There was a Gen Y/Millennial funder who was the third generation involved in his family's philanthropy. His grandparents had given significantly to a particular organization and that organization approached him about his grandparents' legacy. The organization asked to meet with him in person to let him know about their organization and his family's history with that organization.

The following day, the same Gen Y funder met with a different nonprofit who had conducted research on the funder himself and learned that he had an MBA. In their meeting, the nonprofit presented him with a PowerPoint and connected to his business approach related to organizational performance (this analytical lens is not uncommon for younger donors). What was unique about this is that the nonprofit did not assume that there would be a relationship between them and the Gen Y funder because of previous family connections; they treated him as a unique individual and appealed to his motivations.

It is critical that nonprofits not take for granted that because there is a relationship with one family member there will be continued relationships with other family members. Nonprofits need to see each family member as unique. Gifts made from the family may not be inherited values through the generation.

Q: Do you see the communication styles and needs being different across generations? If so, how?

A: It is important to remember that there are actually two distinct generations in the next generation. Gen X and Gen Y/Millennials did have different experiences with technology growing up. For Gen X, the greatest technology invention might have been the home video game, Atari. Many Gen X folks didn't get an e-mail account until late in college or well after. For Millennials, they are really the first generation to grow up with cell phones, e-mails, and personal computers.

Many nonprofits might focus on technology as ends itself rather than a means to an end. Social media is not going to be effective unless you have built some kind of community. Technology is a great advantage because it gives us better access to individuals living in vast geographies, which is the case with many Millennials who are living all over the world.

Certainly, social networking and technology is no substitute for building relationships, but it allows nonprofits to make appointments quicker and confirm use tools like text messages. We need to be very focused on continuing those in-person opportunities to build relationships with younger funders in conjunction with online cultivation and stewardship.

In an example of one community foundation, the foundation was having a hard time attracting younger members to participate in the foundation. Their assumption was that if they created online invitations for younger donors, then those next gen givers would show up for the organization at events and programs. The problem was that these invitations were still coming from strangers in the minds of the younger donors.

The foundation hired someone from the targeted peer group that conducted 200 personal interviews as well as organized a retreat to gather next gen donors. From these interviews, the foundation was able to build a community of 50 young donors. The foundation hosted open sessions, which resulted in five specific activities they could engage in to take their efforts to the next level.

Q: What are some creative/unique/effective ways that you have see nonprofit organizations engage family philanthropists of all ages? Do you have any stories about nonprofits engaging multiple generations in family philanthropy?

A: In one family's philanthropy, they had three generations involved in their giving; "G3" were the parents and "G4" included their children from Gen X and Y. At age 18, the children were invited into the foundation where they collaboratively participated in the giving process.

The family was intentional about their commitment to multigenerational philanthropy and hired an outside philanthropic advisor to help guide them through building trust across all generations. They recognized that their children needed to feel trusted and vice versa for effective and rewarding philanthropy to occur.

One of the G4 family members was invited on a donor trip to Africa with an international organization as a representative of his family foundation. As a result of the amazing experience this family member had, the family provided a collective grant to the organization. This is just one example of the kinds of entry points nonprofits can use to engage donors of all ages.

Q: What are some tools that 21/64 uses in the multigenerational conversation, both in philanthropy and nonprofits?

A: 21/64 uses "Motivational Values" cards and "Picture Your Legacy" cards to help individuals identify their specific values and visions in their lives and in the specific philanthropy in which they want to engage. There are foundations that have used these cards within grant-making committees to ensure alignment with the grant-making vision. Foundations are certainly not the only ones who can use these tools; nonprofit boards, fundraisers and advisors to families have used the cards and exercises to help bridge generational gaps as well.

21/64 has been invited by nonprofits to facilitate the organizational legacy using the Values and/or Vision Cards. One nonprofit has even used the cards to use with their donors. When they are pitching to new donors, they use the cards to help the family learn about their own values before determining if their nonprofit is a good fit for the family's giving. This is a great way to give to a donor before the donor gives to the organization.

Volunteers running fundraising campaigns have also taken the cards to use them during one-on-one cultivation opportunities to help the prospective donors articulate their vision rather than simply asking the individual for a gift. These cards can be an excellent way to arm your volunteers with the tools they need to help you fundraise for your mission.

FAMILY PHILANTHROPY CONSULTANT:
LISA PARKER, FAMILY CIRCLE ADVISORS[4]

Lisa Parker works with families looking to engage in philanthropy in meaningful ways through greater understanding and intimacy. Lisa collaborates with wealth advisors and other philanthropy professionals.

In family foundations, Lisa notes that older family members should be designated to involve younger generations in the family philanthropy. In her experience, simply inviting them to a meeting isn't going to cut it. These retreats deliver hands-on activities that demonstrate the ideas and concepts behind philanthropy. Family foundations can offer creative ways for family members to inspire one another's giving and engagement.

Lisa focuses primarily on youth philanthropy (giving from those under the age of 18), but she shared that philanthropists in their twenties want to get their hands dirty and it isn't philanthropy as usual. Next gen donors want their philanthropy to be an experience, an act of service, rather than solely transactional.

Volunteer management and development is challenging for nonprofit organizations, but it is a critical component to engaging young philanthropists and increasing their access to them. Hands-on experiences allow people to see the real-life super heroes in the nonprofit sector who are giving up leisure and material wants to do incredibly important and vital work for the community and the greater good. In Lisa's words: "The impulse to give isn't fully borne until there is a personal experience from giving."

Lisa facilitates retreats for families involved in multigenerational philanthropy. These retreats always involve nonprofit organizations in some way. The family pays nonprofit staff for the time to help share their stories and provide the family with an understanding of the work the organization does. This partnership between the family and the nonprofit organization creates a powerful conversation and provides the next generation with strong insight into nonprofit work and philanthropy.

Lisa shared the story of one father who achieved significant financial success when his company was bought out. The father hadn't known the kind of wealth as a child that he was experiencing as an adult; he and his wife did not want their children to grow up entitled and behave like "rich kids."

Lisa designed a retreat for the family where the parents and children had to come together to physically build something. Lisa developed a transformational experience by sharing a surprise once the final project was complete—the final project was created in service to someone else. In this way, the children could actually experience philanthropy and how their participation can change the world. Although the children were initially resistant to participating in the activity, the family now works together to partner with nonprofits and make grants to organizations with whom they visit.

In another story, a third-generation mother in the family had her daughter, Amy, collect money in a giving jar annually throughout the year for the funds to be distributed on Valentine's Day every year. Her mother asked Amy to find something she loved and share the money. Amy brought her money to the local zoo where she wanted to give her money to an old deer, Archie from the petting zoo.

Amy brought her giving jar up to the check-in counter and she was welcomed to visit with Archie where she shared her whole story about saving her money and shared the jar with the deer. It was not a large donation by any means, but three weeks later Amy received a photo with all the zookeepers and Archie also signed by the zookeepers. It was a powerful experience for not only Amy, but also for the entire family. The family foundation ended up making an additional donation to the zoo. The greatest connection that exists is the human connection.

When the element of creative fun is present, people come out from all over. One organization asked its group of younger advisors to organize a fundraising event and the advisors orchestrated an underground, free show. The text invite went out two days before the event and was a great success for the nonprofit. This shift from e-mail to text is an important communication strategy for nonprofits to be aware of when they are working with and fundraising from next gen donors.

The San Francisco Bay area has the Carrot Mob that puts out announcements via social media and text to support socially responsible businesses. A group of people then gathers at the business for the day in support of the business to draw attention and support their work. It's another creative way to communicate and provide financial support to people doing good work in the community. Philanthropy is going outside the norm including in grant making; even organizations like the Case Foundation are opening up their grant-making decisions to the community.

Although all generations involved in philanthropy may desire the same outcomes, the next generation of family philanthropists is looking to overcome and compensate for power differentials they are experiencing within the family. Nonprofits can help create expertise with the younger generations by serving as a teacher rather than going in for a "hard sell." Invite these younger givers into your organizations and build relationships that will teach them the true impact of their giving on your mission for many years to come.

FAMILY FOUNDATION: MARY GALETI, THE TECOVAS FOUNDATION[5]

Mary's family foundation started in 1998 and her family has a long-standing tradition of philanthropy. Her grandmother in particular has been highly involved in philanthropy; her last large project was in Amarillo building a performing arts center.

When Mary was 16 the family engaged the cousins and other stakeholders in the conversation about how to launch their strategic, family philanthropy. By 18, Mary had joined the board when the majority of the foundation's assets were designated for the Amarillo performing arts, but the foundation started accepting grant proposals of small amounts. In 2004, the foundation's assets went from $500,000 to $14 million in the wake of Mary's mother and aunt passing away and the foundation inheriting their personal investments.

Because of her professional experience in political campaigns and non-profit service, Mary has become a leader in her family's philanthropy and has a strong commitment to social justice. Since 2008, Mary has played a pivotal role in her family foundation as well as other institutional philanthropic organizations beginning with Council on Foundations.

Mary's own philanthropy comes primarily through the family foundation, but she does engage in individual giving, primarily through online gifts, no more than a few hundred dollars at a time. When Mary does give financial gifts of larger sizes she will write a check because she has a close understanding of how online donations are processed and feels somewhat skeptical.

Mary describes her donation of volunteer time as "Puck-ish mischief." She serves in leadership roles, rather than "working in the trenches" as a way to stir things up at the board level.

Mary shared a friend's story that inspired her about a man who spent time raising funds to buy socks for homeless people. She was so inspired by the story that she made a large anonymous donation online at a great time of need. Mary continues to be connected to the organization and follows their work through Twitter. For Mary, she describes this as a less strategic and more "knee jerk" reaction to a solicitation, rather than dealing with root cause issues that she normally funds. This was a purely emotional donation and she continues to track their status as an organization.

The foundation does not have a website so few nonprofits know about it. The foundation typically receives grant requests through word of mouth from friends and family and it enjoys supporting organizations that are young in their organizational life cycles; the foundation focuses on capacity building, but outside that it can be difficult to communicate what it focuses on specifically. In short, the foundation focuses on organizations that are high risk, high impact, and high reward.

The foundation is still developing its infrastructure, which makes it hard to do simple things like site visits. The foundation is looking to do more with metrics and evaluation, but for now the process if fairly haphazard. The grant-making process is still being defined as well.

All of these processes are affected by family dynamics and funding negotiations. Finding projects that the entire family can agree on is a huge time commitment especially because so much of the grant-making process is based on relationships. Time and family dynamics are probably what affect their grant making the most.

Although Mary likes staying connected through social media, she realizes that it has its own limitations. An e-newsletter is far better in her mind than a print newsletter, which she sees as a waste of time and resources. For her, meeting in person is ideal whenever possible. She has more projects nationally than in her home state, so those in-person meetings can be challenging. A hand-written thank-you note still makes a huge difference.

Mary is currently serving on four boards outside her family foundation and participates on committees for the Council on Foundations. Often she sees young people joining boards because the organization is young, there is a special program with young people as a target audience, and/or there is some level of tokenism at play. In the 1960s the average age of a board member was 35 and now it is 70. The same people are sitting in board positions; the nonprofit and philanthropic communities need to have self-awareness about how they function and what they need to diversify perspective. It can be a great advantage for nonprofits to invest in individuals who will be powerhouses in the next decade.

Being young and having an opinion can often ruffle feathers and Mary has been criticized for her strong opinions. This can make her a target in some ways, but people do stand up and support her. Young people need to have their voices heard and know that there are people who will support them. If you have the right name and family history it can be insulating so that you, as a young person, can have experiences that will develop you as a professional.

Although there are more and more programs investing in the training and development of young leadership, one of the gaps that exist is teaching young people what leadership actually is and how to create self-reflective space. This is something that few businesses and foundations do. Often, people feel that they are ready for leadership when actually they are ready for management roles.

Mary shared that she would like to see more organizations she can support that are invested in succession planning: Can your current director leave and your organization continue? She felt that this is something that is missing from the conversation; we need to make it clear that this conversation is needed. As a sector, we need to acknowledge the gaps in leadership and know what information we need to fill those gaps.

Mary's opinion is that we don't need another organization, but we do need more conversations about what is great leadership and management.

GIVING CIRCLES: ALAN FROSH, THE GORDIAN FUND[6]

A sixth-generation Denver native, Alan H. Frosh has spent a decade serving countless Colorado nonprofits as a staff member, board member, consultant, volunteer, and advocate. His career began during high school at the Young Americans Center for Financial Education and after graduating from the University of Denver, he joined the El Pomar Foundation Fellowship, a premier postgraduate program in leadership development and nonprofit management. After three years at El Pomar, Alan entered the Sturm College of Law at the University of Denver in 2008, where he studied corporate and nonprofit law while working with the College's Community Economic Development Clinic. Alan graduated from law school in May 2011 and is pursuing jobs in the foundation or philanthropic sector. Outside of school, Alan serves as the founding chair of the Gordian Fund, as the chair of the Daniels Legacy Circle and the Pioneer Leadership Program Alumni Advisory Board, and as a member of the Kent Denver School Alumni Association Board and the El Pomar Fellowship Alumni Advisory Board.

Q: What is the story of how you became involved in the philanthropic world?

A: My philanthropic involvement began as a child, as my parents taught me the Jewish values of tzedakah (charity or giving back) and tikkun olam (repairing the world). I gave a quarter every Friday night, along with my parents and siblings, and at the end of each year, we decided together where to give that money. My parents, to ensure we learned the lesson of service, paired our financial gift with a day of service at the recipient, so we learned the experience of volunteering and making a direct, personal impact. These lessons have stayed with me as my involvement has deepened.

My first job involving philanthropy started when I worked at the Young Americans Bank in high school, as I was asked to sit on the Youth Advisory Board. This bank was unique, as the only bank in the world just for children, and this advisory board offered direct feedback in helping the bank better serve its young customers. Through this process, Young Americans recognized that alumni of the advisory board and its programs were the best examples of Young Americans Bank's value and wanted to make sure that those stories of impact were communicated to larger audiences.

Later, during college at the University of Denver (DU), I moved into Young Americans' development office and was charged with building connections for Youth Advisory Board alumni. Our advisory board alumni ranged in age from 15 to 40 and the organization wanted a way to keep them involved as donors, ambassadors, and volunteers, since no process existed at the time. In 2003, I co-founded the Daniels Young Leaders Circle (now the Daniels Legacy Circle) to connect alumni with Bill Daniels' charitable legacy serve as the primary opportunity for the Young Americans' alumni to get involved. This group contributes nearly $5,000 annually to Young Americans' summer programs and serves to groom the next generation of leaders for this organization.

After college, I was selected for the El Pomar Foundation Fellowship, a premier postgraduate program in leadership development and non-profit management at El Pomar Foundation in Colorado Springs. In working with El Pomar's community stewardship programs, many of which focus on building resources and philanthropic education, I recognized the need for programs that teach young professionals how to be philanthropic and how to contribute more than money to the state's nonprofits. This recognition led to the beginning of the Gordian Fund in early 2006, as a giving circle to encourage and educate the next generation of philanthropists. I invited members from different social circles—Young Americans colleagues, high school classmates from Kent Denver, DU classmates and fraternity brothers, and other Fellows—to join the original board, to build a solid concept from my original idea.

At this point, I became aware of the Eagle Fund, a giving circle founded by alumni from Denver's Graland Country Day School. These alumni have worked together for many years, with the same group of donors since inception, and tremendous support from the Denver Foundation. Brian Abrams, a successful entrepreneur and one of the Eagle Fund's founders, served as a wonderful mentor to me as the Gordian Fund grew, as he had so much experience with donor-advised funds and giving circles for young professionals.

The Gordian Fund is based on the concept of collective giving—to get young professionals engaged in and learning about philanthropy, while leveraging smaller donations together for maximum impact. So many young professionals simply had no opportunity to enter the philanthropic world, for many reasons—lack of education, lack of interest, and lack of connection to nonprofits. Therefore, I looked at examples of alumni groups and associations, which had connected with this demographic, for inspiration and structure in forming the Gordian Fund. My collaborators and I were very conscious about the process itself and wanted to appeal to a broad demographic, while focusing on grant making as our primary activity.

The Gordian Fund does not have any specific area of focus, like education or human services, but the model targets encouraging philanthropic participation and activity from the next generation of philanthropists (ages 18 to 40 approximately). Our membership currently includes young professionals between the ages of 22 and 40; while we accept members of any age, our bylaws dictate that the board will always be comprised of young professionals to ensure that the organization's focus remains on this demographic. On our roster, we have a great mix of personal and professional backgrounds, with members who are experienced philanthropists and members who are entering into philanthropy for the first time.

Q: Do you have a giving plan?

A: Yes, I have an annual giving plan that primarily supports organizations in which I am personally involved. For example, as an alumnus, I give to my high school and college, and I give to several organizations where I have worked as a staff member. Eighty percent of my giving is processed through recurring online donations, but I leave some money for one-time donations, like races, events, or relief efforts. My recurring donations are mostly processed through Giving First's monthly online donations and my annual gifts are usually given at year-end or during a specific fundraising campaign.

Q: How long have you supported your top charity/charities?

A: Outside of my family philanthropy, I have been involved in my own philanthropy since working with the Crohn's and Colitis Foundation of America in 1992. I was affected personally by these diseases and received such meaningful support from this organization during my treatment that I got involved personally after recovery. For the other organizations I support, I have been donating for 5 to 10 years.

Q: What, if anything, limits your amount and frequency of giving?

A: I use both a budget and a strategic approach in my giving. When I give, I give because I trust in the organization's activities and leadership, so I want to make a meaningful gift. Therefore, I use the overwhelming majority of my budget to give larger gifts to fewer organizations, while leaving a smaller portion to distribute smaller gifts to many organizations.

Q: How do you prefer that charities communicate with you?

A: I do appreciate when organizations use tools like e-mail, their website, and Facebook and I encourage the organizations I support to use these tools. These methods are cost-effective, direct, and easily personalized, while direct mail and phone calls seem antiquated to me—when organizations use the latter strategies, I feel like they are looking to attract a demographic different from my generation. I strongly prefer direct messages from an executive director or board member through Facebook or recruiting to an event, instead of generic year-end appeals through mail or by phone.

Q: How many nonprofit boards have you served on?

A: I currently serve as the chair of three boards—the Gordian Fund, the Pioneer Leadership Program Alumni Advisory Board, and the Daniels Legacy Circle. I also serve as a board member for the Kent Denver School Alumni Association and the El Pomar Fellowship Alumni Advisory Board, and I recently completed my term as the DU Law liaison to the Colorado Bar Association—Young Lawyers Division. I also have served on the planning committee for TEDxMileHigh, a recent event to showcase local leaders, innovators, and motivators. In the past, I've served on many more boards, but I am working to limit my involvement, in order to provide a valuable contribution to every board on which I serve. To do anything different would be irresponsible, in my opinion.

The Gordian Fund has a secondary goal of educating young professionals to be really effective board members and in order to achieve that purpose, we have been providing training on positive and sustainable board practices. Through my experience, I have found that there are not enough interested or qualified members of our generation to fill all the board needs in our community, so those who are involved are overwhelmed, overburdened, exhausted, and unfocused. Organizations need to do a better job of training young people to be effective board members, because if the organizations fail to involve those young professionals who are interested, the organization loses that generation of volunteers for good. If organizations are not investing in professional trainings for their staff and volunteers, these people will not be fully capable to serve the organization.

Q: What would you recommend nonprofit boards think about when recruiting young professionals to board leadership roles?

A: Don't be satisfied to ask an older board member's daughter or son to sit on the board. Make intentional asks to young professionals who embody the organization's mission, represent a target demographic, or have specific skills that the board needs. The organization needs to focus on functions and responsibilities by defining certain positions and seeking out personalities that will complement the current board. Look to a diversity of professional backgrounds and experiences to capture a variety of perspectives.

I think there is some hesitation on the part of nonprofits to ask young professionals to serve as board members because there is the assumption that young professionals are transient and unreliable. While young professionals are often changing jobs, finishing graduate school, or starting families, we still have a tremendous amount of enthusiasm, passion, and dedication to commit to important causes. An effective organization will already have term limits in place for board members, so it is important to allow young professionals to serve the organization profoundly for a few years, just like their older peers, without burning them out or burdening them with inappropriate responsibility.

Ask us to get involved—I think it is better to have more investment for a shorter period of time rather than very little investment over a longer period of time. Young professionals are often handled with "kid gloves," which makes us feel less effective and valuable.

The recruitment process is really important for a young professional, as it needs to include a job description for board members and a distinct set of responsibilities. The board needs to be intentional about how and who they recruit to the board. It's about the tide raising all ships to one level; if you ask for nothing, then you'll get nothing. Set high standards.

Ask your board for their expertise, especially when it comes to financial management. I would rather be overasked than underasked for support as a board member.

Q: Any final thoughts?

A: We are still writing the stories about our generation's impact on these organizations; we are still on the cusp of an enormous transition of leadership and with it, we'll see the beginning of these stories.

Young professionals are making the choice to start their career in the nonprofit sector rather than starting in the corporate sector and moving into a nonprofit organization later. This is a new situation, so we have not seen the long-term effect yet and how it might change the non-profit paradigm. Young professionals are generating momentum and see how much there is to be done. Our generation takes a very new, high-impact approach to philanthropy and bridging the gap between our generation and current nonprofit leadership will be a pressing challenge for this sector.

I think this research and the publication of *Fundraising and the Next Generation* will bring awareness to this important topic, as it is a critical conversation for the nonprofit sector's future.

GIVING TIERS: JENNIE ARBOGASH, SOCIAL VENTURE PARTNERS OF BOULDER COUNTY[7]

Jennie Arbogash is the executive director for Social Venture Partners (SVP) of Boulder County. In 2011 it launched a tiered partnership program to help recruit interest and partnership from a diversity of generations.

Q: SVP Boulder started a tiered partnership program this year. Can you share what the tiered partnership opportunities are and why SVP Boulder wanted to do this?

A: SVP Boulder has been talking about it for several years because of our desire to have more diversity of perspective and involvement in the organization. We are committed to expanding what we are doing in the community and better serving our community. We felt that diversity of experiences will better serve the investees. We wanted to leverage new opportunities to engage; the fellowship was especially created with this goal in mind.

As an organization, the partners had an issue with being seen as an exclusive group or club, but they did not see themselves that way. It was certainly a perception we wanted to change by opening up more to new partners.

We also recognized the importance of diversifying our resources financially and creating a pipeline to future partners. This isn't unique to SVP Boulder; certainly organizations everywhere are asking the question about funding for long-term sustainability and that means diversifying funding and opening up to new strategies.

It is an important value for us that no one is treated differently based on their financial participation so we are careful not to publicly differentiate between different partnership levels; the partnership level participation is more of an internal record. As an organization we want to be aware of the nuances in generational conversations and engage in a learning culture. We all need to be learning from each other—we all have something to share.

Q: Can you describe the partnership tiers?

A: There are really three tiers of partnership that were developed out of researching other chapters of SVP; I know that 10 other chapters have similar partnership tiers. I spoke with about 9 or 10 other chapters that have associate partnership levels to find out what was working and what was not. I wanted to learn lessons from other affiliates and from those conversations we developed the following partnership options:

Full Partner

- Commitment to give $5,000-plus annually for three years; after the initial three years, a partner can remain involved on a year-to-year basis.
- The financial contribution can be paid for by the individual or another entity.
- There is volunteer requirement, but it is highly encouraged.
- There are no limits on how many people can become full partners.
- Full partners can be a family, couple, company, or foundation.
- Full partners have all rights and benefits as defined by the policies.
- We currently have 38 full partners at SVP Boulder.

Associate

- Commitment of $2,500-plus annually for three years plus a minimum of 36 hours of volunteering annually.
- This is only available to individuals or couples at this time.
- The financial contribution can be paid for by the individual or another entity.
- Eligible candidates are under 40 years of age or work in the nonprofit sector.
- Have all other rights as a full partner, but can only comprise up to 25 percent of the executive committee and total partnership.
- We launched this partnership level in February 2011 and have three associate partners.

Fellowship

- Fellowship partners do not have a set amount that they are required to contribute financially, but must make a donation that is significant for them and one of the top donations they make to any organization.

- Fellowship partners are expected to volunteer a minimum of 90 hours annually.

- Fellowship partners are single individuals that must be 21 or older and are chosen through a competitive process.

- They cannot serve on the executive committee or vote on policy issues that relate to the cost of an annual financial contribution.

- Fellowship partners may comprise up to 15 percent of the partnership.

- We launched this partnership level in 2004 and we have five fellowship partners.

When we were determining the criteria for these partnership tiers we knew it would be a tricky conversation because it was important for there to be some kind of value associated with the associate and fellowship partners that would be comparable to the full financial value of the full partner.

We wanted to engage as many people as we could while accounting for the financial needs of the organization. We felt that this mix would allow for SVP Boulder to engage a diversity of individuals as volunteers and donors in ways that were meaningful, but not overwhelming.

Q: What has been your success with the tiered partnership program to date?

A: It has brought a diversity of thought to SVP in terms of projects, pro bono consulting, capacity building, how the organization is run, how they engage other people in the community. The various partnership opportunities have helped us to maintain a culture of respect while improving our community image. We are seen less as being "top-down" experts.

We have also been able to get about twice as much accomplished with the additional people on board; 45 to 50 percent of our volunteer time for the organization and our investees is coming from our Associate and Fellowship Partners.

We are really appreciative of all these individuals who are doing so much—we really couldn't do what we are doing without these programs and partners.

Q: What are the challenges with this program?

A: There aren't a ton of challenges. Having the different levels does require more staff and management time. We had to make the choice to implement these programs knowing that human resources would be affected, which is why there are some participation limits that we have built into the partnership tiers.

I would say that the other challenge might be that some full partners may know that others are paying less while receiving the same partnership benefits. This comes up infrequently, but we need to be conscientious of how we are being fair to all the partners.

Q: How have you recruited individuals to this program?

A: There have been varied strategies based on the partnership level. For the Fellowship Partners, we have a large listserv of nonprofit professionals that will announce the opportunity to their networks. We also promote to corporations that may be help to us where we have gaps and needs related to specific skills. We are constantly revisiting our need for diversity so look to organizations and companies that can help us find diverse individuals related to ethnicity and age. Of course, we always use existing networks wherever we can.

For the Associate Partners we access lists of personal contacts from prior years, in-person connections, and simply talking with younger professionals that I know in the community. We also try to be strategic in how we leverage certain programs. For example, this fall we are hosting the Board Match program with engaging next gen philanthropists as a main focus. This helps the larger community, but also our organization.

Q: What would you recommend to other organizations looking to engage next gen philanthropists?

A: I would say there are three things I would recommend:

1. Engage young people within your organization to help determine the strategies for bringing in younger generations to your organization.
2. Evaluate what work you are doing internally for your organization to encourage a culture that is welcoming to new people of all kinds.

Think about how your organization can have an inclusive culture. Identify specific things your organization can do to welcome others. For SVP Boulder, we had an educational opportunity for our partners about welcoming Associate Partners.

3. Be very clear about your goals and purposes—don't just launch strategies because you think you should do it. The organization really needs to be invested in the value without tokenizing.

■ ■ ■

NOTES

1. Interview conducted by Emily Davis on April 1, 2011.
2. Interview conducted by Emily Davis on March 7, 2011.
3. Interview conducted by Emily Davis on July 21, 2011.
4. Interview conducted by Emily Davis on July 13, 2011.
5. Interview conducted by Emily Davis on April 20, 2011.
6. Interview conducted by Emily Davis on March 21, 2011.
7. Interview conducted by Emily Davis on June 13, 2011.

APPENDIX **C**

Survey Summaries

This appendix includes summaries of the following surveys' results:

- Multigenerational Development Office Survey
- Philanthropy's Next Generation Survey

Multigenerational Development Office Survey Results

The results of the Multigenerational Development Office Survey are presented in this section. The survey was distributed nationally between June 15, 2011, and July 18, 2011, and 174 individuals participated in the survey. This survey was an effective start to researching generational impact in the development function, but more research is needed including differentiating between organizational size and field (i.e., arts, education, environment).

The results for this survey were, in some areas, consistent with other research about the multigenerational nonprofit workplace. In other areas survey respondents shared experiences outside the norm for nonprofit organizations including providing professional development opportunities for fundraising staff. This is a positive trend that should be continued along with resources such as mentorship or coaching and volunteer development.

It is recommended that a longitudinal study be conducted and follow-up interviews help to create a more comprehensive sketch of the impact of the multigenerational develop function on nonprofit effectiveness and donor impact.

The survey and responses are printed here as they appeared in the original. The boldface responses indicate that these are the most popular responses from survey participants.

Section 1: Overview: The Fundraising Office

Thank you for participating in this survey for the upcoming book, *Fundraising and the Next Generation*. Your participation will help fundraising professionals better learn strategies for engaging and cultivating the next generation of philanthropists; work in a multigenerational development office; and plan for the future of their missions. All information will remain anonymous unless indicated at the end of the survey.

You should complete this form if you are an executive director or working in fundraising in any capacity. In this section, I will be gathering general information about your experience as an executive director or fundraising professional in fundraising and the nonprofit sector.

Question 1: When were you born?

- Born between 1900–1945 (Traditionalist) 2.9%
- **Born between 1946–1964 (Baby Boomer) 36.8%**
- Born between 1965–1979 (Generation X) 32.8%
- Born after 1980 (Millennial) 27.6%

Question 2: How long have you worked in fundraising?

- Never 3.4%
- Less than 1 year 5.7%
- 1–3 years 14.4%
- 3–5 years 17.8%
- **5–10 years 21.3%**
- 10–15 years 13.8%
- 15–20 years 9.2%
- 20–25 years 4.6%
- 25–30 years 5.2%
- More than 30 years 4.6%

Question 3: Which title best describes your role?

- Executive Director 24.1%
- Development Director 25.9%
- Development Associate 14.9%
- Development Assistant 3.4%
- Development Intern 2.9%
- **Other (please specify) 28.7%**

Question 4: How many generations do you think work in your development department?

- One 9.8%
- Two 36.8%
- **Three 43.1%**
- Four 6.9%

- Not sure 3.4%
- Other (please specify)
  - Sole practitioner doing philanthropic advising to families.
  - We have no development department.

Question 5: How many generations do you think work at your nonprofit?

- One 4.6%
- Two 12.1%
- Three 38.5%
- **Four 42.0%**
- Not sure 2.9%
- Other (please specify)
  - None less than 1 year-old.
  - Our nonprofit has well over 300 employees. My generation is however, is the minority.
  - Answering as board chair for YWCA.

Question 6: How many generations do you believe you have represented on your organization's board (advisory or governing)?

- One 5.7%
- **Two 44.3%**
- Three 30.5%
- Four 15.5%
- Not sure 4.0%
- Other (please specify): less than a year

Question 7: Please rate the following questions.

How important do you feel academic training is for fundraising professionals? (i.e., Master's programs, certificate program, CFRE)

- Very important 25.9%
- **Somewhat important 46.6%**
- Somewhat unimportant 9.2%
- Neutral 14.9%

- Very unimportant 3.4%
- Not sure 0.0%

How important do you feel experiential or "hands-on" training is for fundraising professionals?

- **Very important 85.0%**
- Somewhat important 11.6%
- Neutral 2.3%
- Somewhat unimportant 0.0%
- Very unimportant 1.2%
- Not sure 0.0%
- Comments:
  - A background in the liberal arts is helpful. Eventually, you need a broad core knowledge to appreciate and interact with the diverse people and ideas you need to incorporate into philanthropy.
  - Academic training is important because of the way philanthropists and donors in general perceive a PhD VS a College graduate or dropout.
  - I particularly do not like undergrad certificate programs—I've encountered too many certificate holders with no clue about daily fundraising operations or relationship building but a sense of entitlement about deserving management jobs right out of college. I fear that makes me sound like a fuddy-duddy, but I see these people make huge mistakes that jeopardize other people's work.
  - Skill set—listening skills, attention to detail, ability to relate with wide range of people.
  - Note: CFRE is *not* exclusively academic because it requires real experience for certification.
  - There's a difference between "academic" training and the sort of practical, professional training available through conferences and associations. Training is important, but not necessarily with an academic orientation.
  - Having a mentor has proven to be the most important of all my support systems.
  - Training for fundraising professionals should be integrated within training of organizational management.

- I have that masters degree and have found that the OTJ training is more valuable. Fundraising is a world of relationships which is hard to teach in a structured way.

Question 8: Does your organization currently provide and pay for external professional development training for fundraising staff? (i.e., in-services, webinars, nonprofit association trainings, AFP workshops)

- **Yes 67.8%**
- No 28.7%
- Not sure 3.4%
- Other (please specify)
  - We have in the past but just stopped this year.
  - Some in-house training through AFP is covered, but not membership.
  - To a limited extent, yes. Colorado Nonprofit Association, Meals on Wheels.
  - Association of America, etc.
  - Pays for attending annual meeting of corporation.
  - We do provide funding but it is *very* limited and only amounts to about $1,000 total (for everyone) per year.

Question 9: Do you feel you have opportunities for career advancement within your organization?

- **Yes 43.1%**
- No 42.0%
- Not sure 14.9%
- Other (please specify)
  - As a consultant, advancement is my responsibility.
  - I am about as high as you get in this organization. The ED is next highest.
  - It's possible but probably not likely unless my boss decides to leave.
  - Currently the Executive Director.
  - As ED, I personally do not need career advancement.
  - As the ED, I am the only staff member.
  - Once our campaign is complete, my position will no longer be in existence. If another position does not open up, I will have to move to a different organization.

- 4 filled from outside, 2 promoted from inside, 0 from my dept[.] I already at the highest staff level. However, I have opportunities for career development through training.
- NA—I'm the Exec.
- I'm a one woman development department.
- With two staff members the only advancement is into ED position.

Question 10: What are the TWO (2) most important characteristics your organizational leadership looks for in hiring fundraising staff members?

- Has at least 1–3 years of experience 19.0%

- Has at least 3–5 years of experience 18.4%

- Has at least 5–10 years of experience 6.9%

- Has 10 or more years of experience 2.3%

- Has nonprofit experience 32.2%

- Strong leadership and management skills 39.1%

- Academic experience 10.3%

- Connection to potential donors 24.7%

- AFP member 0.6%

- **Has met ambitious fundraising goals 28.3%**

- Other (please specify) 19.0%
  - Ideally a candidate has years of experience and a track record of success, but great rapport building skills and a willingness to learn and receive constructive input from experienced staff members goes a long way.
  - Has passion for the mission.
  - Organizational fit.
  - One who is passionate about our out-reach and understands the importance of such programs. One must know the areas of concern and the avenues to bring relief.
  - Is tenacious about meeting goals.
  - Leadership has no FR experience and does not actually know what to look for.
  - Can describe clearly the exact steps taken to reach those goals, and can also describe mistakes along the way. I've interviewed too many people whose Resumes show meeting ambitious goals but

who cannot describe how they did so - if they don't know, how can they repeat that success (or learn from any failure if they can't describe some)?

- Effective donor account management.
- In general, the org seems willing to hire on drive, talent, potential more than proven accomplishments.
- Sales & Marketing experience.
- Rather than "years of experience," we look towards an understanding of what development is and what it means. We look for individuals who have and can successfully steward donors, who will take development to heart.
- Years of experience depends on the position.
- International exposure/experience/global worldview (we are an international school).
- In theory—we aren't hiring . . .
- Good fit with the team.
- Since I'm both Executive Director and the person responsible for fundraising, I can only reflect on what I brought: over 30 years of professional experience, but not specifically fundraising expertise.
- Not in a hiring role, so I cannot comment.
- Character.
- Only hire from within the government and non-profit sectors.
    1. Is from the community we are fundraising in (has the network).
    2. Is an alum of our NPO.
- Strong belief in philanthropy.
- Has traits and characteristics that have are common among successful Fundraisers.
- They will be volunteers.
- Personal 'connection' or feeling about staff member re experience and fitting in with department.
- Ability to relate to persons of influence and wealth.
- Would want ministry experience.
- "Friend" of the CEO or of another c-level executive, literally (both are family members).
- Charm and brains.
- Embodies abundance-mentality and orients to possibility.
- Thinks outside of the box.

- Willing to work for cheap (i.e., usually younger, less experienced people).
- Passion for the mission.
- Is a person they would like to have lunch with.

Question 11: What ONE (1) recommendation would you provide for your development office or organization to improve their access to leadership opportunities for younger staff and/or development professionals?

- Availability of training and professional development opportunities.
- Encourage participation in AFP and CASE (if appropriate).
- Open a dialogue, rather than a monologue.
- Let us into their circle—attend the meetings that they attend and meet the folks on their advisory and other boards.
- Ongoing dialog between managers and staff on career development.
- Networking.
- Get more involved with the younger staff. They may have ideas that we don't.
- Volunteer with AFP.
- There needs to be a better organizational respect for the younger generations.
- Take risks on young professionals with less than 5 years of experience.
- Believe this is God given opportunity to serve fellow human[s] and inspire each other to stay on course passionately.
- Encourage attendance at professional seminars.
- Maintain data that supports your programs.
- A larger budget for memberships in fundraising organizations that seek volunteer leadership. In my department of eight, I attempt to give younger staff leadership responsibility for creating and running programs, including giving clubs, young professional organizations, etc.
- Unknown—this org is very small.
- Education and training.
- Enroll in a Fundamentals of Fundraising class to better understand the science behind fundraising.

- Study issues of what the individual whom you are looking to hire believes and expects in employment (generalized studies often reflect their perspectives).
- Involve program staff in fundraising—invaluable skill for all non-profit leaders to have.
- Put your eyes on those who have experience doing it. . . . Learn.
- First have leadership with fundraising experience who believe strongly in professional development of all staff.
- Not sure!
- Help them plot out a career that may take them out of your office/ organization. If your org. values longevity in staff, your younger/ newer staff will need to go elsewhere if they can't grow in your office—no one can be development assistant forever, but it is a valuable job to start from—so talk frankly with them about helping them learn all they can & then helping them network with other great orgs. They'll get training elsewhere & may come back when they are ready to lead and the baby boomers are FINALLY ready to retire.
- Provide clear pathways of promotion and encourage uptake from Apprentice scheme (vocational training) to allow diversification of workforce.
- More actively seek out and present training opportunities to us; we mostly have to find them ourselves now.
- Include more internships and volunteer opportunities with the development department.
- To allocate budget for professional development opportunities.
- Get to know and use social networking.
- Career planning within the organization.
- Create more opportunities for movement up the ladder.
- Provide access to leadership opportunities for younger staff and promote younger staff.
- Find a mentor, someone who doesn't always agree with you, but whom you can learn from.
- Make available to young staff discounted conferences on nonprofit. As a youth, I am interested in learning more about how to manage a

nonprofit but am finding organizations understaffed and overworked to be able to show me how to perform the duties of a development job.

- Spend more time out of the office.
- Inclusion in meetings between leadership and potential donors.
- Networking is the key.
- Recognize and cultivate existing staff's skills rather than looking for a mythical "magic fix."
- Offer internship opportunities to identify strong potential employment candidates.
- Expand recruitment to a wider and more diverse network of people.
- Follow first, then lead.
- Walking with the Lord guiding.
- VP of development needs to be a champion mentoring and encouraging involvement in fundraising professionals organizations such as AFP, CASE, PGRT, etc.
- Open up more opportunities to network with other leaders.
- Network as often as possible.
- Setting a solid budget aside for professional, on site training/conferences.
- I would rather my employer pay tuition for one whole education course than offer to pay half my tuition for multiple courses. I just don't have a lot of money right now!
- Mentoring.
- Capacitation.
- Join professional and/or business groups for networking.
- Learn patience; visit prospects regularly; listen to donors and prospects while helping them reach their aspirations.
- Approve funding for it.
- Have programming that reaches young people who could be future development staff.
- If our organization grows to the point of having a possible career path for an employee, serving as a younger development officer might be a step toward larger duties.

- Ask us what we want to learn in relation to development and take the time to serve as a professional mentor.
- Stop following a hierarchical model and start rewarding the people who have genuine results.
- Participate in AFP activities, webinars, workshops, meetings.
- Increase salary to attract experienced professionals.
- Communicate your interests to senior management and supervisor.
- Establish a more comprehensive budget, not for just a select few.
- Finding a way—not sure how—to market what being a development professional means (i.e., that it's about furthering a mission, not simply getting checks in the door). A career of just asking for money doesn't sound very appealing, but building relationships, enjoying people, and helping further a mission seem to be very alluring to those interested in the nonprofit sector.
- Provide time to pursue such opportunities.
- Improve visibility by getting out there to the people with branding!
- I think we're very open to new and different ways of training and providing leadership to our younger staff members. It is our culture.
- Be sure to have the conversation with staff about their goals and objectives then work to provide meaningful ways to help them accomplish their goals. Doing so will allow you to retain top talent longer.
- Understand what learning process connects with the demographic you are trying to communicate with.
- Professional org memberships.
- Gain experience, even if it is volunteer experience.
- Be more of a mentor.
- More training from seasoned fundraisers—in the same field, if possible.
- Allow younger staff to make more decisions and try new techniques.
- Be open to change.
- Emphasis the good the organization is accomplishing and the opportunity to help spread the impact.

- Develop real relationships and stop treating people like a check.
- Adopt nepotism policy and open up to other prospective leaders from rest of staff.
- Training and encouragement.
- None—our E.D. is strongly connected to Midwest Ctr for Nonprofit Leadership, GKC Comm. Fdn., Kauffman Fdn, national YWCA training . . .
- Be willing to relocate.
- Go external from the host organisation and seek self development that suits you!
- Solicit ideas and feedback on training opportunities in the community.
- Allow them to take on a project (with background guidance) so that they can learn to lead and have ownership in that project. Then promote their successes.
- More strategic approach and plan with commitments from both the org. and the staff members with measurable results.
- Reward success.
- Provide higher-level leaders exciting new opportunities to lead so they have positive motivation to cultivate a successor and leave a positive legacy in their transition.
- Mentorships.
- Be creative in your approach.
- Allow them to make suggestions. Give honest feedback and use what works.
- Don't judge effectiveness and experience based solely upon age.
- Develop a mentor program.
- We already have young professionals in our development staff, who ideally would be trained to take over when other staff retires.
- You must be open to change to keep up in this business.
- Encourage younger staff to join AFP and other fundraising membership organizations in the area.
- Have more opportunities to collaborate with other local organizations.
- Have them begin taking responsibility for annual renewals and events.

- Sign up with a support organization such as Young Non Profit Professionals (YNPN).
- Senior Staff Mentoring programs for younger staff.
- Just giving them information on what all is out there so they can pick the opportunities they need to participate in.
- Establish mentoring/educational programming as a priority.
- Allowing staff time for regularly scheduled professional development opportunities—both traditional learning events and pure networking events.
- Mentoring.
- Outreach opportunities.
- Provide a hierarchical structure that provides clear incentives for younger individuals who are obtaining and surpassing goals.
- Give them small fundraising projects to lead so they can get their arms around them.
- Budget for staff development courses, not taking supply dollars and paying for a conference/seminar/class sporadically.
- More educational opportunities and small projects (that can fail without taking everything with it).
- More staff to allow for personal development.
- Provide more mentoring opportunities.
- Not sure.
- More information about the priorities of the larger organization. (I recently got promoted thanks to several managers who welcomed my participation in projects outside of my job description.)
- Provide mentoring within the organization.
- Continue to provide the opportunity for professional development but, in addition, allow a space for staff to share that learning, report back to the team and agency about what they've learned. Making this more of a formal/ongoing process to help bring the education and value back to the org. not just the individual.
- Encourage attendance at networking events for nonprofit (and other) professionals.

- Access/funding for outside training and professional development seminars.
- External training, seek leadership in employees.
- Hmmm . . . Not sure. My org is pretty good at providing these opportunities for training even if the actual opportunity to move up isn't there.
- Professional development opportunities and/or student loan reimbursement program. Many of us with the Master's degrees in nonprofit management can't pay off our student loans on our nonprofit salaries.

Question 12: How many people from Gen X and Y (Millennials) do you believe you have serving on your organization's board?

- Zero 32.2%
- **One–Two 37.4%**
- Three–Five 14.4%
- Six–Ten 7.5%
- More than ten 4.6%
- Not sure 4.0%

Question 13: What, if anything, is your organization doing to recruit and retain next gen board and committee leadership (mark all that apply)?

- We have a next gen/young professionals group or committee 13.2%
- We have next gen/young professionals events 14.4%
- We are using social media to find next gen leadership (i.e., LinkedIn, Facebook, Twitter) 20.7%
- **We don't have a specific plan 51.1%**
- The organization does not see recruiting next gen board and committee members as a priority 29.9%
- Not sure 14.4%
- Other (please specify) 7.5%
  - I see lots of organizations doing the young leader thing, but too [many] may see it as short-term fundraising work instead of long-range relationship-building and leadership cultivation. Fundraisers

end up being the groups' organizational liaisons—wish the whole org. would focus on the value of these groups.

- We try to maintain an inclusive board that represents the demographic of the community. Age is part of this demographic but we don't specify generations.
- Providing stepping stone leadership volunteer opportunities for next gens. but not board service yet.
- We are specifically focused on building the leadership of the next gen.
- Our organization is very good about recruiting and retaining a diverse group of next gen board members by using traditional print media to find leads for potential board members.
- We're establishing a development board to recruit younger professionals in our work.
- Our dept is starting to outreach and network with next gen/young pros. We have one person in the dept in that category and she is leading the project. We are working on getting our Board to understand the importance of connecting with this new group.
- Currently in survival mode to rescue organization from past board and CEO failures. Board is a transition board for 18–24 months. We WILL have a board skills matrix approach to board development including diverse ages, ethnicities, geog., skills, experience . . . but not right now.
- Recruitment of next gen leadership is passive and what we naturally attract; our organization has actually discussed the idea of cultivating a Wise Woman's Circle as we hope to attract women in their 50's, 60's, 70's and beyond and funnel to board leadership.
- Networking with next gen individuals.
- I work for an incredibly conservative medical college, in a conservative Midwestern city, which does not place a value on next generational leadership. Our institutional leaders are all Baby-boomer or older—it is a silver haired mafia mentality.
- Honestly, we have not had a problem recruiting "next-gen" donors or volunteers—I think because our mission appeals to a younger base. We need more "greatest generation" folks!
- We have an event geared toward Gen Xers—that was created, spearheaded and run by Xers. These ladies have joined our board

(the leaders) and have significantly helped with our fundraising efforts (well outside of the event).

Question 14: What recommendations do you have for your development office or organization to improve their recruitment and retention of next gen committee and board leadership (mark all that apply)?

- We have a next gen/young professionals group or committee 21.3%
- We have next gen/young professionals' events 20.1%
- We are using social media to find next gen leadership (i.e., LinkedIn, Facebook, Twitter) 23.6%
- **We don't have a specific plan 29.9%**
- The organization does not see recruiting next gen board and committee members as a priority 20.1%
- Not sure 16.1%
- Other (please specify) 16.1%
  - We are all gen. X and do not have it as a priority to recruit Next Gen board members. We hope that through our work with youth—that there will be a natural progression in leadership to them.
  - We are more concerned with having a diverse board reflecting different cultural backgrounds and ethnicities. We have one 'Gen X' member.
  - Let your light so shine that people may see you good works and glorify the Father who is in heaven.
  - The organization needs to raise its visibility in the community. So far, it's been an uphill battle getting a commitment to spend some dollars on advancement/marketing.
  - If you only focus on younger people who currently have substantial fundraising value, you will alienate too many potentially valuable supporters. There is great value in having 10 20-somethings who can only give $25/year be deeply engaged in your mission—that passion will yield great fruit in monetary and non-monetary ways. Trust in the long-term plan.
  - Keep doing what we are doing.
  - We are trying to start a Young Philanthropists group to identify and recruit potential leaders.

- Hiring a specific staff person to work with students and young alumni.
- Enlist to other volunteer leadership opportunities to prove commitment and ability.
- We're doing pretty good on this. Maybe more college organizing.
- Find volunteer opportunities that next gens are interested into keep them engaged and active with the organization outside of meetings and events. This will better connect them to the mission and help ensure they become future cash donors.
- Develop a plan; continue to participate in seminars provided by the Center for Nonprofit Management such as Training the Next Generation of Leaders.
- We seek and target talent, we do not seek to fill positions with a specific age group.
- Provide more leadership opportunities for next gen individuals.
- The options for this question don't seem to fit[.] If you are asking what we should do then we should have a group/committee, have events, and have a plan to move volunteers into leadership roles.
- Create a cultivation strategy targeting selected individuals.
- I would add that it's not just age, but diversity that will reflect all future nonprofit governance - based on demographics, not just values.
- Continue empowering staff members who themselves are all next gen to assist in recruitment of peers to assist in volunteer fundraising positions and committees that serve as pipelines for hire.
- Outreach to local high schools and colleges.
- Listen to their advice and let them lead projects that inspire them.
- Develop at Next gen/YP group/committee, host YP events, utilize social network connections to recruit.
- Again, it hasn't been an issue for us.
- I am not sure if this needs to be a priority right now—and honestly we have to raise a lot of money for our new hospital. If this happens organically—fantastic! But we need high capacity donors who don't have any lingering commitments (like children, sending kids to college, weddings, etc.).
- Recruitment is not an issue—retention is. That is where mentoring is key.

- We have those that are interested but many of the "older" board members will not give up control and help mentor these emerging leaders. I think utilizing a mentoring program would be a HUGE help to our (and any) organization struggling with this problem. This way the current "older" board members would feel they had a hand in training the new leaders, which may help them give up some control (in addition to stroking their egos).
- I think a young professionals group with events is a great idea.

Question 15: Please answer the following questions about communications (see Table C.1).

TABLE C.1   QUESTIONS/RESULTS ABOUT COMMUNICATIONS

	What communication strategy do you most prefer with your colleagues in your organization?	What communication strategy do you use primarily WITHIN your organization (i.e. with staff or volunteers)?	In general, What communication strategy do you most prefer with your donors?	What communication strategy do you use primarily with your current donors?
In Person	39.9%	17.2%	58.5%	19.1%
Phone	2.3%	4.0%	11.7%	16.2%
Email	54.9%	74.7%	19.3%	27.2%
Instant Messaging (IM)	1.2%	1.1%	0%	0%
Text (SMS)	1.2%	0.6%	0.6%	0.6%
Facebook	0%	0%	1.2%	1.2%
LinkedIn	0%	0%	0.6%	0%
Twitter	0%	0%	0%	0%
Blogging	0%	0%	0%	0%
Snail Mail	0%	0%	3.5%	20.2%
Electronic Newsletter	0.6%	2.3%	4.7%	15.6%

- Other (please specify):
  - Skype & phone.
  - A "one size fits all" approach to donors will never work. Major gift donors require TLC, older donors who aren't tech savvy still like

print newsletters and annual reports. Strategies need to be adapted for the individual donor.

- Whatever works for them—I try to be present in all media to see where they engage me.
- We send donor acknowledgements via snail mail but we communicate more frequently via electronic newsletter.
- I do annual giving so I don't really have one primary method. We use phone, email, snail mail, social media.
- Communication strategy with donors varies between email, in person, and phone depending on the objective of the message and the preference of the donor.
- Email used to schedule appointments, etc.
- Donor communication strategy will vary based upon the contribution level. The larger the contribution the more likely a person to person strategy is deployed.

Question 16: Do you vary your communication style with donors relative to the donor's age?

- **Yes 68.4%**
- No 24.1%
- Not Sure 7.5%
- Other (please specify)
  - Vary communications by donor preference.
  - Varies per the donors preference.
  - We vary our style based on what we know about them and/or their request.
  - When possible based on contact information.
  - I tailor the communication style to the donor and how they like to communicate regardless of age.
  - We try!
  - The older ones want a phone call. The younger ones want email.
  - And relative to donor's preferences.
  - But not strategically—our gift officers adjust to what is most effective. Our annual fund is strong and for now is based in direct mail & telemarketing. We are exploring strategies now—have tried them in the past but they weren't effective.

Question 17: Would your organization like to increase their outreach to younger philanthropists (under age 40)?

- **Yes 87.9%**
- No 1.7%
- Not sure 10.3%
- Other (please specify)
  - We would like to increase our outreach to philanthropists of all ages. In general I feel we have a very balanced plan.
  - Don't have the resources to do everything we WANT to do.
  - My organization does not have a strong history of reaching out to young philanthropists, but personally I would love to engage younger high capacity donors.
  - Of course—always interested in connecting with potential donors of any age!
  - We would like to increase outreach to ANY philanthropists.

Question 18: Does your organization have specific strategies for fundraising from younger philanthropists (under age 40)?

- Yes 35.1%
- **No 58.0%**
- Not sure 6.9%
- Other (please specify)
  - Recommending that clients create this strategy.
  - We would love to connect with those under 40. Almost all of us are under 40 and we have been focusing our effort on trying to get funding from older philanthropists/had not considered the under 40 crowd as a viable means of funding for our organization.
  - But we use some of the following strategies (not just for younger people).
  - Social media.
  - We are in the process of developing a plan.
  - Bringing in the donors through lead volunteer fundraising events (that these donors themselves pitch, create and initiate with our support).

Question 19: If so, what strategies is your organization using? (Check all that apply.)

- Next gen/young professionals' events 36.8%
- **Social media 70.5%**
- Email/E-newsletters 58.9%
- Committee recruitment 33.7%
- Board recruitment 20.0%
- Partnering with other young professionals' groups 22.1%
- Connecting with older family members 17.9%
- Networking events 43.2%
- Personal outreach 49.5%
- Other (please specify) 3.2%
    - Getting them aware of the need and get them involved in the project, so that it becomes their project and they are happily involved in lifting others to significance.
    - Anything that works.
    - Charging for membership.

Question 20: What recommendations would you have for your development office or organization to IMPROVE THEIR COMMUNICATION with current young (under age 40) donors? (Check all that apply.)

- Next gen/young professionals' events 47.7%
- **Social media 75.3%**
- Email/E-newsletters 42.5%
- Committee recruitment 40.8%
- Board recruitment 38.5%
- Partnering with other young professionals' groups 52.9%
- Connecting with older family members 9.8%
- Networking events 48.9%
- Personal outreach 57.5%
- Other (please specify) 5.2%

Question 21: What recommendations, if any, would you have for your development office or organization to improve their RECRUITMENT AND RETENTION of next gen philanthropists? (Check all that apply.)

- Next gen/young professionals' events 53.4%
- **Social media 66.1%**
- Email/E-newsletters 40.8%
- Committee recruitment 49.4%
- Board recruitment 40.8%
- Partnering with other young professionals' groups 47.1%
- Connecting with older family members 17.8%
- Networking events 51.7%
- Personal outreach 62.1%
- Other (please specify) 5.7%
  - Engage them fully—include active next gen donors in decision-making.
  - Do more of everything we are doing.
  - All of the above AND finding out what is important to them through the process of communication they most favor.
  - The rest we already do.
  - Make the networking events novel and fresh. No wine and cheese cubes!
  - Improve cross training and advancement opportunities with specific goals.
  - Giving circles, which allow young professional[s] to pool donations and thus have a larger impact. Many Giving Circles create social events and fund raising activities thus providing a social outlet for their members.
  - Talk to them [to] devise programs to meet personal and organization needs.
  - Hosting educational events, such as panels or workshops, about next gen philanthropy by invite and open to public.
  - Don't know.

Philanthropy's Next Generation Survey Results

Section 1: Financial Contributions to Charitable Organizations

Question 1: Please identify your generation.

- Traditionalist (Born between 1900 and 1945) (0.4%)
- Boomer (Born between 1946 and 1964) (6.2%)
- **Gen X (Born between 1965 and 1980) (58.9%)**
- Gen Y (Born between 1981 and 2000) (34.4%)

Question 2: Do you make financial contributions to nonprofit organizations either personally, through workplace giving, or a family foundation?

- **Yes (97.1%)**
- No (2.1%)
- Other (please explain): (0.8%)
  - I have, but do not do so on a regular basis and almost never to the same organization.
  - Only to the non-profit I work for.

Question 3: Approximately how much money cumulatively do you donate annually personally?

- $0/NA (0.4%)
- $1–$500 (41.8%)
- $500–$1,000 (16.5%)
- **$1,000–$5,000 (27.0%)**
- $5,000–$10,000 (7.2%)
- $10,000–$50,000 (5.1%)
- $50,000–$100,000 (0.8%)
- $100,000–$500,000 (0.4%)
- $500,000–$1,000,000 (0.0%)
- $1,000,000–$5,000,000 (0.4%)
- More than $5,000,000 (0.4%)

- Other (please specify):
  - I give personally. My workplace matches it. I also direct discretionary funds through my family foundation.

Question 4: Approximately how much money cumulatively do you donate annually through your family foundation?

- **$0/NA (85.4%)**
- $1–$500 (1.4%)
- $500–$1,000 (0.9%)
- $1,000–$5,000 (0.9%)
- $5,000–$10,000 (1.4%)
- $10,000–$50,000 (3.2%)
- $50,000–$100,000 (0.9%)
- $100,000–$500,000 (2.7%)
- $500,000–$1,000,000 (0.9%)
- $1,000,000–$5,000,000 (1.8%)
- More than $5,000,000 (0.5%)
- Other (please specify): The foundation allocates approximately $4–5m.

Question 5: At what age did you begin making financial contributions to charitable organizations either personally or through another giving vehicle (workplace giving, family foundations, etc.)?

- 0–5 years old (7.2%)
- 6–10 years old (8.9%)
- 11–15 years old (14.0%)
- 16–20 years old (30.1%)
- **20–30 years old (35.6%)**
- 30–40 years old (4.2%)
- Other (please specify):
  - Sunday school we had to save—but that was not always a self-motivated donation—"encouraged" by the Sunday school teachers!
  - I donated to telethons and my Dad "matched" me.

Question 6: What is the single largest financial contribution you made to a nonprofit organization?

- $0/NA (0%)
- $1–$100 (22.9%)
- **$100–$500 (34.3%)**
- $500–$1,000 (11.0%)
- $1,000–$2,500 (11.9%)
- $2,500–$5,000 (5.5%)
- $5,000–$10,000 (6.8%)
- $10,000–$25,000 (4.2%)
- $25,000–$50,000 (1.3%)
- $50,000–$75,000 (0.4%)
- $75,000–$100,000 (0.0%)
- $100,000–$500,000 (1.3%)
- $500,000–$1,000,000 (0.4%)
- $1,000,000–$5,000,000 (0%)
- More than $5,000,000 (0%)
- Other (please specify):
  - That's me personally, not my family's foundation. I have no say in my family's foundation so I find it difficult to include those numbers when the question clearly asks "you."
  - I give $25/month to Amnesty International which adds up to $300/year.
  - (I have a monthly gift to one org that is around $600/yr.). Gave $500 at once, maybe once.
  - This was a personal gift. The foundation makes much larger gifts.

Question 7: How often do you think you financially contribute to nonprofit organizations?

- **1–5 times per year (43.6%)**
- 6–10 times per year (17.9%)
- 11–15 times per year (15.4%)
- 15–20 times per year (11.1%)

- 21–30 times per year (5.6%)
- 31–40 times per year (0.9%)
- More than 40 times per year (5.6%)
- Other (please specify):
  - Not sure what you mean by how many times—most of my big giving happens only twice a year (June & Dec) but little gifts as the asks come, probably at least twice a month.
  - As often as I can. It varies each year. Typically between 1 and 10.
  - Tax time, Christmas time and times of disasters.
  - At least 24 times, if not more.
  - I work in non-profit and feel my low salary is part of what I'd consider a donation.

Question 8: How many nonprofit organizations do you think you financially donate to annually?

- **0–5 (59.1%)**
- 6–10 (28.7%)
- 11–15 (6.8%)
- 16–20 (3.4%)
- 21–25 (0.8%)
- 26–30 (0.8%)
- More than 30 (0.4%)
- Other (please specify):
  - Right now I'm making donations ranging from $500–10,000 to about 20 organizations, but I also regularly respond to requests from friends for $20 for this group or $25 for that group . . .
  - A bulk of my giving is to United Way, while they are "one" organization who knows where my specific donation is going to because they support 50 nonprofits in my community.
  - I have 3–4 personal orgs that get my most thoughtful gifts, but as an active athlete I will generally sponsor any fellow athletes in their charity events.
  - I think my number may be skewed a little low here. My work had a "donations for casual days" program where we support a different

nonprofit for a month. Because I was traveling for 1/2 a year, I participated less in the workplace giving.

Question 9: What vehicle(s) do you use for making financial contributions to nonprofit organizations? Mark all that apply.

- **Check or cash (82.2%)**
- Family fund or foundation (10.8%)
- Personal fund or foundation (6.2%)
- Donating online through organizational website (73.0%)
- Donating online through social media (Facebook, Twitter, etc.) (15.4%)
- Mobile giving (text) (10.8%)
- Special event attendance (56.0%)
- In-kind contributions (36.5%)
- Donation at a special event (in addition to registration) (40.2%)
- Direct mail prompt (25.7%)
- Online, recurring donations (25.7%)
- Gifts of stock or real estate (2.9%)
- Planned giving (6.2%)
- Workplace giving (28.2%)
- Other (please specify):
  - Through eBay/PayPal (charity donation option at checkout).
  - Sometimes fundraising by selling something I have, like tickets, and donating the proceeds to a charity of my choice.
  - Direct debit (monthly automatic transfer). And I work at one for 2/3 of what I used to earn. Buying products of which a part will go to a charity.
  - PayPal, or through DonorsChoose or Kickstart.
  - I didn't check family foundation because although my family has a foundation, I have no say in it.
  - Personal solicitation.
  - By credit card over the phone when an organization calls me[.] I make recurring donations to Amnesty International through direct debit (from my bank account)[.] I sponsor friends and

colleagues for walks/runs/yogathons etc. I usually do this online.

- Credit card recurring donations.
- Began donating through check/mailers, until I began working at JustGive[;] now I set up my monthly recurring for multiple charities on their site.
- Donations at register (Have seen this at Ralphs, Vons, Petco, etc.)
- Regarding donating online: I don't have a credit card, so I can only donate to websites that accept PayPal, which limits to which organizations I can give.
- I don't have a credit card, so I can only make donations if the website accepts PayPal.
- Monthly giving online.
- Through my organization providing matching gifts.

Question 10: Who was involved in your learning about philanthropy? Mark all that apply.

- **Family (74.5%)**
- Friend or colleague (47.3%)
- School (36.0%)
- Financial institution (0.8%)
- Foundation (13.4%)
- Nonprofit organization (59.4%)
- Other (please specify) (16.7%)
  - Church.
  - My education in social work.
  - Church.
  - A foundation consultant group.
  - Workplace.
  - My faith in Christ-Bible.
  - Church.
  - Donor networks like Resource Generation, serving on foundation and nonprofit boards.
  - Myself only!
  - Myself—I was volunteering at nonprofits at a young age and realize it's important to help the causes you feel strongly about.

- Reading more about it.
- Grand Street—a peer network of philanthropists.
- Presentations at school, reading the newspapers. The one I work for, I once read an article about how they were the last NGO to evacuate Bosnia.
- Social Justice allies.
- Consultants.
- The Philanthropy Workshop, Global Philanthropists Circle.
- Resource Generation.
- Independent research.
- Union.
- Church Attendance.
- When I was teaching at a private school I realized how fortunate the children were and we established a school shop and the money we raised we donated to a number of charities. I started donating personally from then on.
- Work.
- No one in particular.
- I worked at an agency for 12 years that worked exclusively with not-for-profit organizations.
- Growing up poor and working for non-profits.
- It was not until I started working in the sector that I realized how easy it was to give.
- My own interest.
- Religious Institution.
- Church.
- Religion/Church Community—values from being raised Catholic and Catholic education.
- I work in nonprofit.
- Church.
- I believe I learned through the media (e.g., commercials showing starving children).
- Work in philanthropy (development manager for a nonprofit).
- My Christian church, my family, my alma maters.
- Work place giving. I have always worked for non-profit organizations.
- Philanthropic and member-based groups like COF, Jewish Funders Network, Resource Generation, via their conferences.

- U.S. Navy.
- Youth service organization (4-H).
- Myself. I took a personal interest in it.

Question 11: Do you have an annual giving plan? (An annual giving plan includes a budget for pre-selected charitable organizations that will receive your financial contributions.)

- Yes (29.1%)
- **No (67.4%)**
- Not sure (3.5%)
- Other (please specify):
  - I have a plan for significant donations but I tend to not have a plan for smaller gifts.
  - But occasionally think about developing one for some charities yes, some are unplanned gifts.
  - Sort of. I have a budget for some pre-selected organizations, but often make some additional, unplanned contributions.
  - Working on it right now.
  - Theoretically.
  - Not really—we give based on monthly income—which can vary based on what bills we have (i.e., insurance, medical, car work, etc.). I am a student so there is some fluctuation in my annual income, and that plays a factor as well.
  - I am working on putting one together as I need to become more targeted/planned in my giving efforts as there are so many worthy causes.

Question 12: How did you learn about the organization(s) to whom you donate?

- **Word of mouth (friend, family, colleagues) (80.9%)**
- Fundraising or networking event (43.2%)
- Training (4.1%)
- Website (36.9%)
- Social media (Facebook, Twitter, blog, etc.) (29.0%)
- Organizational staff or board member (36.1%)

- Traditional media (print publication) (22.8%)
- Other (please specify) (20.3%)
  - Conferences, networking events & house parties.
  - My own involvement.
  - Radio and Church.
  - Research into causes that interest me.
  - Personal experiences.
  - Organizations I work with.
  - Volunteer for them.
  - Being an alumnus of my university.
  - I'm a type 1 diabetic, so by virtue of having the disease, I'm tied to the nonprofits that help my community.
  - In-person volunteering.
  - Personal engagement—attendance at cultural events, educational. institutions, etc. NPR.
  - TV, the news.
  - Through my work in the community.
  - Church.
  - They all have personal significance to me. (Schools I attended, my local Jewish federation, a non-profit organization I used to work for.)
  - Alumni.
  - Local causes I just knew existed and that I believe are important in our community (Food Bank, Hospice, Library).
  - From working directly with the nonprofit.
  - Founded, partnered with, worked for.
  - College internship.
  - Independent research.
  - Areas of interest.
  - Television.
  - Educational institutions or churches we are associated with.
  - Work.
  - Volunteer at the organizations.
  - Work.
  - Direct mail.
  - They are all organizations that I closely work with.
  - An organization I participate in regularly.

- Personal connection.
- First donated to ASPCA in college, after watching commercials. Learned about other charities through friends/colleagues.
- Not really sure, I generally donate to groups I've known about for most of my life.
- My own experiences—attendance at Arts events, etc.
- Family.
- Church—organizations in addition to giving to the church as well as pledging annually.
- Already affiliated/alumnus.
- Main donation is to my summer camp "alma mater."
- I either have a personal affiliation or I did research to identify an organization that addressed a cause I'm interested in.
- Alumni, workplace giving or recipient of services (NPR), etc.
- Church.
- Volunteer.
- Radio, and organizations I am personally connected to like my son's school, or through membership to Institute for International Education and Returned Peace.
- Corps, Alumni groups.
- Alma maters.
- University student giving program.
- They are always my employer.
- I am associated with the non-profit either directly, or a friend asks, or I give in honor of a friend.
- I use the organization's service (i.e., NPR).
- Organizations I am part of/volunteer for.

Question 13: Who most influences where you make financial contributions? Please select one option.

- Friends (25.3%)
- Family (26.1%)
- Colleagues (7.5%)
- Traditional media (5.8%)
- Social media (Facebook, Twitter, Ning, LinkedIn, etc.) (3.7%)

- **Other (please specify) (31.5%)**
  - Strategy & impact.
  - Charity Navigator (fiscal responsibility).
  - My personal involvement and feeling toward the org.
  - I'm influenced by the work of the org. There are people who introduce me to the org.
  - Personal values.
  - I'd say I'm uninfluenced and make these decisions completely on my own accord.
  - Programs or organizations that are taking a unique approach and are making a meaningful impact.
  - Friends introduce me to organizations that I become passionate about.
  - Organization itself—their community impact.
  - Faith in Christ.
  - My personal beliefs.
  - None—where I decide to donate is a very personal thing to me.
  - Current events, political/economic climate.
  - Organizations themselves.
  - I'm an independent thinker and am not easily influenced by anyone/anything other than my own values.
  - This answer changes from moment to moment.
  - The organization (do they meet needs).
  - The values of the organization.
  - I choose where to contribute based on my interests.
  - My values and the communication from organizations who I support.
  - I really give to those organizations my family and I are most involved in or have a connection.
  - Self.
  - Spouse.
  - Personal connection.
  - I do based on my research.
  - Life experience.
  - Hearing the CEO of the organizations speak.
  - My personal goals and values.
  - I believe it is a spiritual practice.

- Just causes I want to support.
- Myself mostly and what my beliefs and values are centered around.
- The organizations themselves influence my contributions if they are effective in making an impact in the areas I'm interested in.
- Personal preference, values.
- I mostly influence myself. If it is a mission I believe in and it is a good organization, I donate.
- Reputation of agencies and their outcomes . . . asking the agency questions.
- Personal decision.
- Personal morals/belief tied to giving back.
- Myself.
- Organizations that offer me something.
- Those I work for and organizations whose mission aligns with my personal values.
- My own research.
- For me it's the organization itself. I carefully research organizations before I donate. I also take in to account how often I am solicited/ how I'm treated as a donor, if I think the organization is fiscally responsible, and if they are mission focused.
- Who I volunteer with.
- I give because I want to give.
- Variety of influences.
- Organizations that I also volunteer my time to.
- Husband—which I realize is technically family, but I think there is a difference in "family" as in parents, siblings, extended family, and my immediate "family," as in my husband.
- Myself.

Question 14: Do you ask friends, family members, and colleagues to financially support causes that you care about?

- **Yes (75.5%)**
- No (19.9%)
- Other (please specify) (4.6%)
  - Depends on the commitment level and resonance of the org, and if it is an event with auction items vs. check writing (more likely to

send around auction item list to family than ask for a check over $50).

- I have only started to do so and I would say I am not very good at it. Many of my friends live on a tight budget so I am not particularly aggressive.
- Rarely.
- But not as much as I might. It's tricky to do. The times I most do that is in place of birthday or x-MAS presents.
- Sometimes.
- Only by sending social messages through my networks (Twitter, Facebook, Hyves, LinkedIn).
- Occasionally, if the appeal is clever and easy to "sell" to friends without much disposable income.
- I ask people to attend events that may interest them, which may be sponsored by non-profits.
- Only in rare situations.
- No but if friends ask me who I would recommend donating to then I will make recommendations. I get asked as I have worked in the not for profit sector.
- Not personal friends unless there is a direct relationship with the organization.

Question 15: If you ask others to support your cause(s), how do you ask them to contribute? Mark all that apply.

- **Cash or check (66.8%)**
- Sponsorship (33.2%)
- In kind donation(s) (skills, expertise, rental space, etc.) (44.0%)
- Event attendance (61.0%)
- Volunteer time (board, committees, projects, etc.) (54.4%)
- Social media (Facebook Causes, Twitter, etc.) (38.2%)
- Gifts of stock or real estate (1.7%)
- I do not ask others for support (0.7%)
- Other (please specify) (15.8%)
  - Beer garden or other fun purchasing events like silent auctions or benefit concerts.

- Event fundraising/collecting pledges.
- Grants from their foundations.
- Emails for making online donations online through website.
- Depends on the situation, but most support I get involved with involves monetary donations.
- I feel people can make up their own minds on which nonprofit they want to support.
- Credit card Online.
- Online (the individual non-profit's website).
- Contributions on my behalf.
- If I were to speak to them about giving it would be to say to them "find something you are passionate about and support it in any way you can."
- I include them in annual appeal on occasion (I'm on a board).
- Online.
- Buy merchandise.
- Online donation.

Question 16: What inspires you to give?

- Those who have something more have a responsibility to give back. Along with cute animal faces and maintaining my rights.
- The fact that even our little contributions might make a difference to someone else's life.
- Personal connection to organization and its mission.
- Helping others, making a difference.
- Their mission.
- The mission of the organization.
- I have the ability to give and I like helping others.
- I love to help those less fortunate than I in any way I can.
- Feeling of being lucky to be in a position to give when others are needy.
- Giving feels good! I appreciate so much of the good work folks are doing in this world and giving is a way to be involved and show solidarity and love.
- Personal interest in the cause, alignment with my beliefs and values, organizational reputation, personal connection to employee or constituent, demonstrated urgency.

- Believing in the mission, having a passion for the organization's future.
- I want to give back to the community or organizations that either I get enjoyment out of (NPR) or that benefit the community. I also give through my church—the teachings inspire me to be a part of the whole.
- My ability to actively participate in the cause, supported by my financial contribution.
- It's just part of my "make-up."
- A sense of community.
- I feel like it's my responsibility to give back because of the opportunities I've had (access to education, family foundation). At the same time, it feels good to be altruistic, whether it's giving money, time or just helping people out whenever I can.
- Passion for the cause.
- Making the world a better place.
- The cause and vision of the organization & the impact it makes in the community.
- Passion.
- I have been blessed by God. He has provided for me and my family in many ways. I want to give back to Him.
- My personal belief in giving back.
- A cause I believe in; sometimes with a personal connection.
- I'll give to causes that I care about, but don't have time to volunteer for.
- Wow, what a question! I give because I have more resources than I need and believe that it is our collective responsibility to work in all ways possible for a world we desire. I also give today, because I consider it an opportunity to learn and prepare for the future. I have been told that within the next few decades (probably in two waves, the first within the next ten years) I will likely inherit significant wealth and I plan to give away much of this inheritance. Therefore, as I have grown my giving over—particularly over the past ten years—I have used my giving as a chance to reflect and learn about my priorities, what I want to support, and what form I want that support to take so that I will be prepared to responsibly give at larger levels in the future.

- A strong mission and solid foundation of good work. Also, family legacy—it's something we've always done and feel good about.
- Wanting to help communities become stronger and healthier.
- A sense of responsibility to give back as well as coming from a family with a philanthropic tradition.
- Causes that inspire me with their work. Those that are financial sound and well managed.
- This is what we should do to be good citizens and humans. Get jazzed by systems change, programs addressing root causes of societal issues, personal passions.
- A mission that I care about, confidence in their leadership and ability to make an impact, and a sense that they will use my donation well.
- Personal experience, recognition, ability to network.
- I'm motivated to donate by the organization's cause, and its ability to carry out its mission.
- The people who work in nonprofits.
- Organizations that provide skills and support to help people be self-sufficient.
- Supporting work I believe in.
- Shared values between me & the organization.
- I think it's right to if I can afford to.
- The hope of a better future.
- The idea that I am making a difference. And the belief that I'm contributing to solving the root cause of a problem, versus its symptoms.
- A friend or family connected to the cause.
- Intrinsic/internal inspiration; relationship with the organization; hearing people's stories; ability to see how my investment is used to support someone.
- It is healthy, it is right and it is what I like to do.
- Making change!!!
- Org. that demonstrates their hard work & passion, transparency and easy way to connect my contribution to impact of their work, causes that I have personal attachment to.
- The belief and knowledge that my individual contribution makes a difference.

- People in the struggle that I have met over the years and their strength, generosity and love for others and the world.
- Driven by our [my husband and my] values of community, creativity and compassion, we engage in philanthropy in order to create a more thoughtful, welcoming and just world.
- I believe in helping your fellow human. Every day I realize I could have been born on the other side of the earth and be in less fortunate circumstances. My parents were asylum seekers before they invented that term, we were stateless and I was born stateless. I feel it is my duty to help others.
- Evidence of tangible change towards liberation for people of all ethnic and economic backgrounds. And the planet.
- The missions of the organizations I donate to.
- Knowing how much it matters.
- Christ. I've been blessed and everything I have belongs to the Lord. I need to be better about sharing it.
- Either being an employee of the nonprofit itself, being asked to give to an entity by a friend and being inspired by the organization's mission.
- A 13 year old boy who lives in Kenya and could not go to school if I did not sponsor him
- I can't afford to give much, so appeals for small amounts usually win me over. I ignored the Wikipedia appeal banners for months until they posted one that said, "if everyone gave $5 this campaign would be over today." That inspired me to give!!! But in all seriousness, it means a lot to me when an organization makes my small contribution feel valuable.
- Social justice, groups that are working on a local level, usually where I have some kind of connection, through a friend who works or volunteers for the organization.
- I've been blessed in life and want to pass those blessings on in the support of causes I believe make a difference.
- Causes I believe in. Seeing a difference made.
- I give because I know it has an impact on service delivery in my community, and also generates more money for the community.
- Close personal association with cause.

- The idea of giving back to the community and making the world a better place.
- Because they need the money.
- 1) The knowledge that I personally have been blessed. 2) Working directly with a nonprofit and seeing the need. 3) Causes that are tied to my own personal interests/hobbies. 4) A desire to set an example for friends and others.
- Better emotional returns than other activities.
- It's not enough to be the change you want to see in the world . . . you have to enable others to change as well.
- Just the simple act of giving—good karma!
- Working to make God's world a better place, supporting organizations that fight for social justice.
- It's a responsibility that comes with privilege.
- Personal connections.
- Obligation, how I was raised, sense of being thankful for what I was given.
- The cause and my personal relationship to the cause.
- Personally knowing someone who has been affected by a cause.
- Personal connections to causes and or extraordinary creativity and vision.
- I believe in the causes I donate to.
- The causes themselves . . . and the work the charities do to support the people and causes I believe in!
- Faith.
- The desire to help bring about real positive change in the world.
- I'm inspired by groups working on issues in their communities with a multi-issue perspective and groups that have in leadership positions people from the groups most impacted by that issue.
- Self-awareness of privilege, recognition of need to redistribute wealth to those structurally disadvantaged.
- News events (disasters, etc.).
- I believe in their causes.
- Simply my common humanity.
- The need, the story.
- Wanting the organization to do well.

- Helping the organizations to continue the valuable work they do—usually it is a cause personally close to my heart but sometimes it's just because of the work they do for the community as a whole.
- Volunteers who make a difference inspire me to give.
- 'Tis better to give than to receive. Simple as that.
- A personal passion for or tie to the mission of an organization.
- A belief that it's incumbent upon anyone who can make a difference to do so.
- Results in causes that I care about.
- Honoring family members with breast cancer. Want to find a cure.
- Need.
- I give for selfish reasons—it makes me feel good to help others.
- A powerful story with someone I connect with.
- Strong belief in the work of the nonprofits and the value of the work they do.
- Knowing that my donation will directly improve someone's life.
- Worthy cause.
- It is something that I have done from a young age. It is simply part of my life. And, my parents instilled in me the sense that I need to give back.
- Need Desires to make a difference.
- Not what, who. Jesus. God.
- Children, birth, families.
- Personal experience.
- I think I am "called" to give—called both as a Christian and a community member. I love trying to give back *lots,* because I know I've received *lots.*
- The nature of the work that the organization does.
- Need, and positive outcome.
- Personal experiences.
- I'm inspired by the cause, the organization's ability to fulfill its mission and its sustainability.
- Seeing that my money, regardless of the amount, makes a difference. Having the organization make an effort to stay connected to me.
- I have learned so much from nonprofits that I have to give back.
- Causes that I'm passionate about—like human rights. I like to support friends and family in the causes they are passionate about as well.

- The cause. A well run agency.
- Personal connection to the cause.
- Friends/family supporting a cause by running a marathon, etc will inspire me to donate to support their fundraising goals. I also volunteer at an animal shelter and donate to that organization because I see the great work that they do.
- Seeing the people involved genuinely committed to their cause and actually accomplishing something.
- Biblical commandment, the desire to help.
- Knowing that a small donation to Africa can provide clean drinking water to a village.
- People. The human race never ceases to inspire me.
- What inspires me to give is my life experience—things that I see, been exposed to good, bad & ugly. I am so thankful for the life and have not gotten where I am alone. I believe and wish that everyone just had someone/something to assist them and I try to be that help. It can be money, time and/or other resources to just make a difference.
- My Christian faith.
- Environmental concerns, personal connection or involvement, local issues that impact my community.
- It is up to our generation to make the changes we want happen. We need to put our money where our mouth is.
- A personal connection—my school, my passions, organizations that have helped my friends and family in times of need.
- Personal connection.
- Knowing I can improve another life, when I have been so blessed in my own. I think we all have an obligation to give in whatever way we can—time if not money.
- We have so much wealth, and there are so many others that don't.
- The cause and the desire to help in things I believe in.
- The way it makes me feel and the tax deduction I get.
- Supporting the causes I care about, which in turn helps to leave the world a better place.
- Lifelong affiliation with Jewish community philanthropy (Jewish Federation).
- Increasing urgency about environmental issues.
- Personal membership on Board of Directors.

- Personal ethics and faith.
- A cause that directly impacts my life or the life of someone I care about.
- People's passion for making this world a better place, socially, environmentally, financially, culturally through organizations, AND wanting to do my best to leave this place better than I found it.
- Mission.
- Sound mission[.] Established realistic goals[.] Family history with an organization.
- I am lucky to be able to give; I don't believe that we should be selfish and I DO believe that we need to do all we can to make sure that every human being has the essentials.
- Giving to things that I believe in and knowing I can make a difference.
- Strong belief that b/c I have the ability to help others, I have a responsibility to do so. Desire to change systems to end the root of problems. Seeing the positive impact that organizations are able to make.
- Helping others.
- I'm not sure.
- The inequalities that we see in our world today.
- It is what people should do if they can. I have been very lucky. Re: my camp, I want other kids to have the life-changing experiences that I had.
- Anecdotal evidence.
- We need to make changes in this world. You can't wait for someone else to do it.
- Just knowing I am helping something that is important to someone I care about. For example a friend has a daughter with CF so donate to that same with Juvenile Diabetes, no one in my family has it, but a friend's daughter does and it is very important to her.
- Knowing that I am able to make a difference in someone's life. I have the ability to give back and want to be a good role model for my children.
- Knowing that my generation needs to be more empathetic and understanding than past generations in order for countries to get along better.

- Positive impact of the organization on me, my family, my friends.
- The joy of giving. You cannot out give God and in turn you cannot out give your community.
- I am a nonprofit fundraiser and understand firsthand what it means to build a sustainable donor base. I also know from this experience that every gift counts, whether it is $5 or $500,000. I understand the critical role that nonprofit organizations play in our society and believe that we all must do our part in assuring their sustainability.
- I know that every little bit helps. Even if I can only make a small contribution I know that combined with the support of others I am making a difference. I look for organizations that are effective in making an impact and I believe that in supporting them I am helping to make a better world. The causes/organizations I choose to support are those that have been important to me in my own life.
- The cause.
- Positive impact on my community/the world.
- I am rarely inspired to give; it has to be something that moves me personally, and at a time when I can afford to give.
- Connection to the mission and being asked directly.
- Good governance (knowing my money is going where I'm told) causes that I connect to personally, a strong "ask" without being pushy.
- To help others.
- Outcomes.
- Brought up to give, ingrained to give at a very young age. Have chosen to continue the tradition.
- My belief system . . . Christian belief system and I was taught an early age to give back.
- Passion about the mission; the desire to be contribute to my community (civic engagement).
- I believe in the mission of the organization.
- Being able to have the opportunity to really make a difference in the lives of those who are less fortunate than you.
- I love being involved in my community and "seeing" the effects of my donations.
- Being invited to spend time with the organization/people I give to.
- To support friends.

- Justice/equity. Compassion for those in need.
- Knowing that my funds will make a difference.
- Faith in Jesus Christ, opportunity to serve him by giving to others.
- It's my responsibility to give back when I can.
- Responsibility to share resources and talents with NPOs and individuals in needs.
- Seeing change in the world.
- Outside of my support to my colleges, I give to organizations that I believe are actively helping individuals while working to reshape our country.
- I give my time, and give my money only when required.
- A good cause, with a well-run fundraising organization. Clear communication of organizations goals and process is key. I distrust large org's like United Way, etc.
- My religious beliefs and my experiences as an undergraduate student.
- My duty.
- Quality of work for dollars received.
- A good cause.
- Knowing my $ may be small as a % of my annual income can make a huge impact on recipient organization.
- I believe in the mission.
- Being able to identify with the mission of the organization and the effectiveness of the organizations' programs.
- To help important issues and it feels good.
- The stories of what has been accomplished by the nonprofit and the obstacles the population is overcoming.
- Client stories.
- My mother's example.
- Something that I am passionate about, or that someone I care about is passionate about . . . and I do respond well to clever written communication.
- An organization's mission and the staff.
- Helping Others.
- Kids, good programs.
- Belief in the cause, organization's management structure, urgency of the issue I know what it takes to do the work of nonprofits and I want to be of assistance where I can.

- The fact that I am in a position to be able to when so many others are in need.
- Organizations that I know could greatly impact my community or orgs that I received service through as I was growing up. If the org supports a cause that I am deeply committed to and am equally passionate about, I give as well.
- Causes that have impacted me personally.

Question 17: What types of causes are you most passionate about (i.e. health care, human rights, environmental, etc.)?

- Reproductive rights & justice, environment, media reform & policy and election integrity.
- Health care, children education.
- Health care, human rights, environmental.
- Health care, specifically gastrointestinal diseases and cancer young professional philanthropy.
- Animal welfare, environment, wildlife/conservation, children, human health social service my religion.
- Children, health care.
- Human development (education) and economic development (small business development).
- Education.
- Jewish Identity, needy kids (backpack drives, secret Santa drives, etc.), Cancer research.
- Human rights. Youth development/empowerment through the arts. Woman's empowerment (internationally). Local food (locally). Non-corporate news outlets.
- Human rights, gender equity, animal rescue, HIV/AIDS, human services. Health organizations, animal causes.
- Homelessness, hunger.
- Environmental, education, children, health/food.
- Animal welfare, education.
- Animal rights.

- Innovative approaches to education/teaching life and job skills and empowering under served or at risk youth.
- Children's causes.
- Agnostic. It's more about which non-profits are making the most impact in their particular sector and which ones have amazing missions, but need help.
- Human rights & helping people.
- Food justice.
- Spreading the Gospel. Supporting the family. Human rights.
- Animals and health.
- Animal welfare.
- Environmental; child health/safety.
- I divide my giving in six categories—1) community organizing 2) social justice philanthropy and donor organizing 3) progressive electoral and non 501(c)(3) work 4) queer rights 5) educational equity and access 6) local arts & cultural activities.
- Holistic approaches to helping people solve their own problems.
- Social justice, health, environmental, leadership development.
- My giving runs the gamut in terms of organization and focus and changes from year to year . . .
- Women's empowerment.
- Youth civic engagement education.
- Conservation.
- Education, health care, human rights.
- I am most passionate about programs that improve the lives of children, especially education.
- Education, health care, safety net services.
- Jewish issues, Israel, women.
- Health organizations, humane societies/animal rescues, military/veterans.
- Support, environmental, disaster relief, church groups, political causes, youth.

- Groups, sports (Olympic team/Special Olympics), memorial funds.
- Art, College Access, Equitable access to opportunities for youth in the US. Child protection, health & human services (AIDS related), pet organizations, arts.
- Environmental.
- Environmental.
- Personally, human rights. But donate a lot to health-related organizations. Health care, housing, hunger, children, education
- Strengths/asset based orgs, women-centered, faith-based, youth mentoring.
- Organizations that teach kids about giving and philanthropy.
- 1. Environment 2. Education 3. Peace 4. International health care (diabetes but health care on a larger scale), education, economic development, the arts, religion.
- Poverty (including hunger/homelessness), health care (esp. for causes combating cancer).
- Health care—in particular bone marrow donor registration for racial ethnic minorities.
- Immigration, education, and all issues that seek to stop the root causes of oppression both in the US and abroad.
- The arts, creating an exciting and inclusive Jewish community, social justice emergency aid (Medecins Sans Frontieres/Doctors Without Borders), human rights (Amnesty International, Human Rights Watch), development aid that is properly done, do what they promise. All three are needed for a society that is just and peaceful.
- Environment, racial justice, prison abolition, health care for all.
- Youth arts, community arts, informal education, culture, environmental justice, food safety.
- Youth, especially after-school youth arts programming.
- Environmental. Education.
- Clean water, poverty issues, sex trade.
- Literacy, animal rights, environment, public radio, at-risk populations i.e., homeless, women's rights.

- All.
- I'm actually kind of scatter-shot in the causes I support. I tend to give very small amounts to a number of causes. I might pick a few and donate more regularly once I'm making more money.
- Social justice, affordable housing rights and advocacy, youth arts, arts, urban.
- Agriculture, environment.
- Human services.
- Health care, education, Jewish and Israel.
- Environmental, religious.
- Basic needs, i.e., human service organizations that address homelessness. Also very passionate about local gov't.
- Health care (i.e., diseases, malnutrition) and Jewish causes.
- Jewish.
- Homeless and under poverty line.
- Hunger, Social Justice, Human Rights (e.g. Human Trafficking, Abortion).
- Environment and meta-nonprofits (those that help other nonprofits).
- Arts and social justice.
- Libraries[.] Preservation of wildlife and natural spaces[.] Emergency funding for families in a health care crisis[.] Hospice.
- Social justice, direct service, progressive faith groups.
- Environmental.
- Health care, environment, music.
- Rural development in Latin America, health, environment and renewable energy, the field of philanthropy.
- Education and religious.
- Health care, political.
- Environmental, educational, health, women.
- Poverty/economic equality.
- Kids Konnected (support for kids who have a parent with cancer), Equality California, MS Foundation.

- Women's rights, education, disaster relief.

- Religious/human rights.

- Social Justice, Environmental Justice, Political.

- Environmental and racial justice, gender and sexuality issues, and economic justice.

- Environmental issues, sustainability, inequality, criminal justice, human rights human rights, poverty, environment.

- Immigrant rights; access to education.

- Environmental, Animal.

- People people people.

- Education.

- FIA as a peak organization for fundraisers, research, welfare, native animals.

- Health, humanitarian, children.

- Poverty.

- I give to organizations that have given to me (i.e., girl scouts, college sorority and its foundation). At this point in my life I give much more time (3–4 hours a week) than I do money.

- Women's rights, poverty elimination and hunger.

- Community Development and Diversifying Economies.

- Human rights, environment. Also health care but somewhat less than the first two, especially as I feel that many things like health care can be bundled under human rights.

- 100 Education At Risk Youth.

- Health Care.

- Homelessness, hunger, education, health care.

- Kids and military families.

- International health care agencies.

- Animal welfare, animal rights, environmental.

- Women's rights, health care, hunger, animal rights.

- Pets, environment.

- Health care, basic human services.

- Health care, domestic violence, education, mentoring, children's health.
- Children Haiti human rights.
- Homelessness, natural disasters, children/babies.
- Health care, women's rights.
- I am most passionate about *LOCAL* causes—supporting organizations that make a contribution to my community and mostly anti-poverty, animals, choice, and criminal justice issues.
- Human rights, public service/aid.
- Human rights.
- Human rights, children and environmental.
- Health.
- Causes impacting the well being of children, especially education, usually receive my donations.
- At-risk women and children.
- Social justice.
- Human rights, MS Society of Canada, MADD (Mothers Against Drunk Driving).
- Women, peace, homeless.
- Arts and culture, environment, social justice, health and wellness, hunger.
- Animal welfare & Environmental.
- Public broadcasting, education.
- Abortion, scientific apologetics, politics.
- Human Rights, Water, Women's Rights, Hunger, Sustainability and Fair Trade.
- Human rights and environmental.
- Education & health are where my heart lives to give . . . they do touch many of the other causes—children, the environment, and civil/human rights . . .
- Poverty, especially related to children. Disaster relief, international development.

- Environmental.
- Women's rights/issues.
- Cancer research/awareness (particularly breast cancer), literacy, education (especially related to my alma mater), and the environment (recycling, trash cleanup).
- Arts environmental cancer giving opportunities to others.
- Arts, health.
- Animal rights, environment.
- Education in third world countries, socioeconomic programs that teach sustainability rather than straight handouts.
- Health.
- Health care, children's welfare.
- Environmental and animal aid.
- Arts (including public radio), eliminating world poverty.
- Community services, Environment.
- Hunger and housing, human/civil rights, environmental.
- Human Rights/Equality Visual Arts programs.
- Education, and social justice.
- Health, arts, education.
- Health and Human Rights.
- Human rights (wiping out poverty, homelessness, etc.), environmental.
- Health care (research), human rights.
- The arts (music), Aid organizations such as MSF, Oxfam, UNICEF etc. and United Way. My church.
- Basic human needs & rights issues (food, water, shelter, education, health care)—LGBT rights & equality—Animal rescue & conservation—Cures for diseases.
- Poverty and environment
- International, human rights.
- Animal welfare, microfinance and small business development in developing countries.

- Ones very personal to me, so mainly community-based things. poverty, human rights, education.
- Animal rights, human rights, and essentially the rest of the liberal agenda.
- Health, arts.
- Older adults and children's causes.
- International, human rights.
- Education, youth development.
- Christian Education, business, entrepreneurship.
- Education, historical preservation/societies, libraries/archives.
- Education[,] Environment Local community organizations.
- Education, women and girls, animals.
- Developing work opportunities or access to education.
- Animals.
- Children, saving our oceans, heath care.
- Women and youth, human rights, education for under-served populations.
- Children and health.
- Health and human services and education.
- Education.
- Christianity, global public health, historically black colleges and universities (education).
- Environmental.
- International focus, alumni and service orgs like NPR.
- Cancer.
- Veterans, autism resources, homeless, battling sexual assault and domestic violence.
- Children and/or health.
- Women's issues. Poverty/economic justice. Youth engagement.
- Youth, my university, state pride.
- Human service, evangelistic organizations, outdoors.
- Kids.

- Refugees, Human Rights, Animal rights, Multicultural Education.
- Health, education, development.
- Anything that makes the world a better place—I give to a variety of organizations (Woman's Rights, Human Rights, Animal Rights) though my environmental choices tend to be more focused on things like clean water for villages.
- Educational and economic/job-development programs, including "the arts."
- Higher Education.
- Social justice.
- Civil rights, arts and culture, HIV\AIDS.
- Youth sports.
- Environmental sustainability, human rights, peace.
- Children's issues, diversity.
- Human rights, women's rights, international issues, health care, environmental—all of them!
- Disability awareness.
- Anything to do with children (I've cared for children in one form or another for most of my life), the environment, animals (my husbands' cause) and organizations that focus on improving communities (such as homeless shelters).
- Conservation and environment.
- Education, women and girls empowerment.
- Human services.
- Education, particularly early care and education.
- The Arts and human rights.
- Women's Issues.
- Education, Professional Dev.
- Human rights, the arts, environmental.
- Education in inner-city schools. I was a 2006 Teach For America corps member, so I have an appreciation for and want to support urban schools that are doing good things.

- Human rights, human trafficking, emergency relief, Buddhism, international development.
- Capacity building efforts, women's issues.
- Children Education.
- Youth initiatives (especially those geared towards the inner-city), poverty issues, social justice issues, gang violence prevention, women's rights, etc.
- Leadership, education, aids/HIV research, LGBT & human rights.

Question 18: Do you plan on continuing your philanthropy in the future?

- **Yes (99.2%)**
- No (0.4%)
- Maybe (0.4%)
- Other (please specify):
  - I plan on working with a nonprofit once I graduate from college.
  - Depends on my financial situation.
  - I hope to give more in future.

Question 19: Do you plan to increase your total value of your annual financial contributions in the future?

- **Yes (85.5%)**
- No (3.7%)
- Not sure (10.8%)
- Other (please specify):
  - Work hard to make more so I can give more.
  - Yes—I have not yet inherited my wealth, so when I do, my giving will greatly increase.
  - I am currently unemployed, but once I am gainfully employed again I plan to increase my contributions.
  - Long term.
  - To the extent that I plan to be (hopefully!) in a better financial position in the future, I plan to give more.
  - Once I make more money.

- If I can.
- Depends on my financial situation.
- I increase my giving every year 1% of my gross salary. This year I am up to 13% of my gross salary[, which] is the minimum that I will give in 2011.
- I hope so!

Question 20: Do you plan to increase the number of nonprofits that you donate to in future?

- Yes (35.0%)
- No (17.7%)
- **Not sure (47.3%)**
- Other (please specify):
  - Depends on how I feel about the org.'s and causes my family and friends become or stay involved with.
  - I will likely shift the organizations I support based on where I am living but will continue to concentrate on a smaller number.
  - If giving at same level, want to focus the impact of my donations.
  - I would like my gifts to make a difference, so I try to support a few charities rather than throwing small amounts of money at many organizations.
  - Will probably donate to a small number with more significant gifts but attend more nonprofit events where I give small gifts.
  - May just give more to the same charities I current contribute to.
  - Depends on my financial situation[;] don't want to spread my giving too thin.
  - I hope so, but . . .

Question 21: What do you think restricts your philanthropic contributions the most? Mark up to three options.

- Economic climate (38.1%)
- **Salary/wages (89.4%)**
- Family (0.8%)
- My age (8.9%)
- Understanding about philanthropy (3.0%)

- Lack of outreach from nonprofit organizations (5.1%)
- Lack of causes in which I am connected to (6.8%)
- Family dynamics (2.5%)
- Access to family wealth (14.8%)
- Other (please specify) (9.7%)
  - Being in law school limits my involvement with organizations, and I try to match my financial contributions with contributions of time or service.
  - Want to make sure my family is settled and long-term comfortable first (home ownership, college fund, etc.).
  - The fact that donations inevitably lead to my mailbox being SPAM-ed by other organizations with similar missions. I'm tired of junk mail.
  - The mentality of "I'll give when I have more money." People don't start giving when they are young or just start working, so they don't build it as part of their lives.
  - I already give a lot.
  - Lack of information about how my contribution is being spent and/or which causes I can make most impact with through financial contributions.
  - It takes a lot of time to find, research, and feel comfortable about giving to a new organization.
  - Because I work at a non-profit I feel as though my work is my philanthropic contribution!
  - Understanding of organizations' effectiveness relative to others in industry; concern that robust nonprofit sector provision of basic services allows government to step away from responsibilities I believe to be its.
  - Too many to choose from—hard to determine who REALLY needs the monies and will use them most responsibly.
  - Learning curve.
  - Learning curve.
  - Insane daycare costs.
  - I work for a nonprofit, and live in Southern CA—I'm on a VERY limited budget.
  - Financial debt from school.

- Lack of transparency from organizations on how funds are spent and impact achieved.
- My age because I don't have a credit card yet; salary/wages because I'm a college student, so I need my money to go toward tuition.
- Lack of confidence that donations will be used effectively.
- Not getting a personal ask.
- If I had more, I would likely give more.
- Nothing restricts my contributions.
- I give as much as I can, but as a professional making the transition from my 20s to my 30s my expenses have grown. Now I look to ways I can help that are not solely financial.
- A lack of stewardship on the part of the nonprofit.
- Nothing.

Question 22: Have you considered leaving money to a charity or charities after you die?

- **Yes (67.1%)**
- No (19.4%)
- Not sure (13.5%)
- Other (please specify):
  - Not there yet. College fund and something for offspring is bigger priority.
  - No, but only because I've never thought of that before. Sounds like a good idea.
  - Will not do this until after my children are out of the house (now they are 2 and 4—all monies will go to them and their caretakers).
  - My goal is to spend out before I die.
  - Would spend it during my lifetime.
  - If possible, after my family is taken care of.
  - I probably will consider it at some point, but since I'm not expecting to die anytime soon, I haven't considered it or made a plan.
  - I would rather endow a place like a library . . .
  - Not there yet. . . .
  - Already written into our plans.

Question 23: How would you MOST like to see nonprofit organizations contact you about donating to their organization? Select up to three options.

- In person solicitation (20.3%)
- Direct mail (19.5%)
- Phone call (8.7%)
- **Email (50.2%)**
- E-newsletter (32.4%)
- Facebook Page or Cause (25.7%)
- Twitter (6.6%)
- Blog (11.6%)
- Other social media: please describe in comments (3.3%)
- Fundraising event (46.1%)
- Networking event (24.9%)
- Board of Directors (19.1%)
- Advisory Board (9.5%)
- Workplace giving (12.0%)
- Other (please specify) (12.4%)
  - Concentrate on their mission (the work) and communicate about it in all circles. If you build it, and especially are remarkable about how you communicate it and build word of mouth, THEY will come.
  - Solicitation by close friend, not an acquaintance. I need to trust the solicitor and see them as also having made a commitment (their employment by the org doesn't count, I want to see their personal commitment). Also, an e-mail from a close friend, not a generic one from the org.
  - I know it's old school, but it's the one that gets me hooked most often.
  - Engage via social vehicles: YouTube, Twitter, Facebook, Linkedin, Blogging, Video, Email Marketing, it's all about integrated communication.
  - Friends.

- This is an odd question because it's not frame[d] as what is the MOST effective,
- Which I would have to say is a personal ask, but how I MOST like . . .
- Through friends.
- Not Facebook.
- Their own sites. I recently made a donation through Donors-Choose.org and I'm a member of Kiva.org helps others via micro lending.
- Some kind of creative fundraising event and/or campaign that incorporates online donations with tangible way to see impact of cause.
- I don't want to be contacted—but I want to easily find organizations that I hear about, so having a website and Facebook page are the most convenient.
- Text.
- Banner ads on the organization's website.
- Email newsletters with links to articles.
- I don't want them to contact me. I'll contact them, end of story.
- We're not currently looking for unsolicited proposals.
- I don't know. I don't pay much attention when organizations I don't know contact me out of the blue. It's better if it comes through a channel I'm already familiar with and believe in.
- I don't want nonprofits to solicit me.
- Solicitations do not influence my giving. So, it's really a waste of time and resources for organizations to contact me.
- Through methods that are low cost.
- I would prefer that they not contact me. I donate to local charities or when friends ask me to sponsor them. I don't like being called, mailed, solicited, etc. from strangers.
- I don't care.
- Not sure. So tired of marketing calls and Facebook is ok but not enough. Mail is expensive and ineffective. So not sure.
- I prefer to not be contacted about donating. Rather, I enjoy receiving newsletters about how funds are being used to expand programs/services.

- Stayclassy.org.
- Mostly I like to find them rather than have them ask me for money.
- I'd like to see more place-based use of social media.
- I prefer to not be solicited, in fact when I get mailers, it makes me not want to donate.
- I want a relationship with them first or at least some regular understanding of what services they provide. I prefer to receive that information via Internet (all channels acceptable to me) and events.
- Other social media: I consider event sites (walks, rides, auctions, etc.) to be a form of social media—or at least an online option, which is not mentioned above. Those sites are incredibly effective because they are generally shared with me by a close friend, there are personal stories and I get to learn more about the cause. Once I've read up on things—it's incredibly easy to donate right from the page.

Question 24: How would you MOST like organizations to recognize your charitable donations (this does not include IRS requirements to recognize a financial contribution)? Select up to three options.

- Phone call (11.6%)
- Hand-written thank you letter (38.6%)
- Printed thank you letter (21.2%)
- Emailed thank you letter (33.2%)
- Printed recognition (annual report, program, newsletter) (14.1%)
- Event recognition (6.2%)
- Online recognition (website, blog, social media) (14.9%)
- Newsletter (printed or electronic) (12.0%)
- Annual report (10%)
- Naming opportunity (plaque, building, etc.) (6.2%)
- **No recognition needed (41.1%)**
- Other (please specify) (8.7%)
  - Concentrate on the work. And build a personal relationship between me & the organization.

- Printed letter with real signature.
- I feel so traditional clicking those—but they still feel more important than the quick and easy online thanks or the overly stilted "big" thank you's.
- Good solid relationship moving forward (knowing the organization and the organization knowing me).
- Use my company for their fundraising needs.
- Updates on what the organization is up to.
- To me the most meaningful recognition would be to be given the opportunity to become involved in the organization beyond just the role of a funder.
- Thank you's are the least important aspect, however, it's always nice to get a postcard or a nice letter about how my money will be used and what will help. It's not necessary, but I probably enjoy receiving the postcards or pictures of the people/causes I'm helping so I can have it hanging up somewhere as a reminder that I need to be conscious about giving.
- I generally prefer that most of my money go to supporting the organization's work, but a small, attractive, postcard is always appreciated. Particularly from art or environmental organizations, who have access to lots of nice images. IRS stuff is best through email, because I won't lose it!!!
- I think recognition is important in order to encourage other people to donate. However, I really don't care how I am recognized.
- Invitation to a donor appreciation/fundraising event to act as an ambassador for them.
- Being personally named in a public setting would make me very uncomfortable.
- I really am turned off by offers of naming opportunities.
- I really like the DonorsChoose model, where we hear back directly from the teachers . . . it makes me feel as though my donation matters and makes a difference.
- Some confirmation that the donation arrived if it was not given in person.
- I prefer NOT to get an ask included with a thank you note!

- Just send an annual report or information about the organization progress.
- I don't care much about which medium the thank you comes in, but I've had some organization barely recognize what was a meaningful gift, which is hard to believe.
- "Thank you" Networking Events with other volunteers & donors with shared time and money with NPO personalized emailed thank you note with an offer to see the program in action.
- The school I donate to sends thank you notes from the kids who participated in the field trip that I donated towards. Amazing!

Question 25: Are your financial donations affected by where you volunteer?

- **Yes (62.7%)**
- No (30.0%)
- Not sure (7.3%)
- Other (please specify):
  - Not at this time, but I believe they will be in the future.
  - In some cases.
  - I usually volunteer at places where I have donated in the past. One-time donation of money is easier than donating time. As I learn about more opportunities and what that organization has to offer, I get more involved personally.
  - Personal involvement, as well as volunteering.
  - Absolutely!
  - A significant number of organizations that I support are either my alma maters (undergraduate & graduate) or organizations where I have worked in the past. Most others are one-time gifts as a result of being asked by close friends & colleagues or orgs that I intend to support throughout my life.
  - What does this question mean?
  - Actually, the organizations that I donate the most to are nowhere near my current city.
  - Mostly, perhaps half.

Section 2: Volunteer Time Contributions

Question 1: If you have volunteered, at what age did you begin volunteering with nonprofit organizations?

- 0–5 years old (3.7%)
- 6–10 years old (28.4%)
- **11–15 years old (31.2%)**
- 16–20 years old (20.6%)
- 21–30 years old (14.7%)
- 31–40 years old (1.4%)
- Other (please specify):
  - Family volunteering is key.
  - My volunteer time has not been through nonprofit organizations but rather directly in communities that I have been involved in.
  - Unknown. I probably started volunteering through things like Earth Day, but that was just picking up trash with my family, not through a nonprofit.

Question 2: How did you first learn about volunteering? Select up to two options.

- **Family (63.6%)**
- Elementary School (16.8%)
- Middle School/Junior High School (10.0%)
- High School (21.4%)
- College (10.0%)
- Graduate school (0.9%)
- Financial institution (0.0%)
- Foundation (2.3%)
- Nonprofit organization (15.9%)
- Other (please specify) (18.6%):
  - Church.
  - Church.
  - Church.

- Family, School/Church, Family Friends.
- I helped start the organization.
- Church.

Question 3: Do you volunteer at this time?

- **Yes (71.9%)**
- No (8.9%)
- Sometimes (19.2%)
- Other (please specify):
  - Depends on your definition. Does committee member (and meetings, etc.) count?
  - Just moved—figuring it out.
  - Not too often, but here and there. This is something I would like to get better at.
  - Surprisingly hard to find opportunities.
  - Yes, in the manner described above.
  - Work too long hours—no time that is reliable to volunteer.

Question 4: How often would you say you volunteer?

- Daily (7.1%)
- Weekly (30.0%)
- **Monthly (37.6%)**
- Annually (25.2%)
- Other (please specify):
  - Working full time limits my ability at this time.
  - To some capacity I do something for some type of non-profit almost daily.
  - I used to volunteer weekly, but have recently become employed with a non-profit myself so my time has cut down.
  - Every 3–4 mths on average.
  - I hold volunteer positions through my church on an ongoing basis. I also volunteer at events periodically.
  - I pick a major event to volunteer with each year, so my volunteering is usually concentrated into a 3-month period. Sporadically. Sometimes I volunteered weekly when it was organized and

facilitated through school. Other times I went off and on when it wasn't as coordinated (and I was younger). Now I volunteer regularly as a nonprofit board member.
- 1–2 times a month.

Question 5: Approximately how many hours annually do you think you contribute volunteer time to nonprofit organizations?

- **1–25 hours (22.6%)**
- 25–50 hours (21.7%)
- 50–75 hours (10.4%)
- 75–100 hours (12.3%)
- 200–300 hours (7.1%)
- 300–400 hours (2.8%)
- 400–500 hours (1.9%)
- More than 500 hours (4.7%)
- Other (please specify):
  - About 10 hours per week on average, so about 520 hours a year.
  - Around 25 hours a month, 300 hours a year.
  - As mentioned above, I do not currently volunteer through nonprofit organizations.
  - For the past two years I was on a conference planning committee, which was very time-intensive, but now I'm volunteering much less.
  - Varies significantly from year to year depending on my job (I was in AmeriCorps NCCC and VISTA).
  - Much more if you count the time I work at my non profit without being paid (i.e., uncompensated overtime).
  - A lot right now!

Question 6: Approximately how many organizations do you volunteer with annually?

- **1–5 (94.3%)**
- 6–10 (4.3%)
- 11–15 (1.4%)

- 15–20 (0%)
- 21–25 (0%)
- 26–30 (0%)
- More than 30 (0%)
- Other (please specify):
  - 0–1.
  - I serve on five boards and do occasional volunteering with a couple others.
  - Most of my time is with a service club, so there can be many nonprofits.
  - As mentioned above, I do not currently volunteer through nonprofit organizations.
  - One board, one weekly commitment, and various one-time opportunities through friends.

Question 7: In what ways do you donate your time? Mark all that apply.

- Staff member (30.4%)
- Skilled volunteering (i.e., consulting, accounting, fundraising, marketing) (66.4%)
- **Event volunteer (67.8%)**
- Administrative (filing, paperwork, answering phones, etc.) (14.5%)
- Board member (38.3%)
- Committee member (39.3%)
- Advisory board member (19.2%)
- Other (please specify) (10.7%)
  - Social media outreach.
  - Work at food pantry.
  - Online contributions.
  - Girl Scout leader.
  - Direct service—Big Sister.
  - Working at nonprofit events to raise money via silent auctions.
  - Volunteer event manager (managing volunteers for various events with different local orgs.)

- Funder organizing and I also sell jewelry for women in the Ecuadorian amazon and send the profits back to them.
- Pro bono technical work.
- Mentoring staff.
- I get out of it what I put into it . . . by leading a [G]irl [S]cout troop I have developed relationships with girls and moms. I'm not just an occasional event staffer. Leading a troop is a much more gratifying role. I also advise my former sorority and have developed friendships with other alumni, while watching/helping college women blossom as leaders. This is what life is about!
- Mentoring.
- Whatever needs to be done.
- Volunteer mentor.
- Girl Guide leader (Sparks).
- Search and rescue group.
- Various positions at church including leadership roles, teaching etc.
- Phone canvassing.
- Labor.
- Cooking for food kitchen.
- Manual Labor.
- Logistics.
- I am a mentor with Big Brothers Big Sisters.

Question 8: How do you learn about volunteer opportunities? Mark all that apply.

- **Word of mouth (Friend, family, colleague) (87.5%)**
- Print publication (12.1%)
- Organizational website (45.5%)
- Volunteer management origination (i.e., Hands On Network) (16.1%)
- United Way (4.0%)
- School (11.6%)
- Religious institution (18.3%)
- Sorority or fraternity (4.5%)
- Online search (18.8%)
- Facebook, LinkedIn, Twitter, etc.) (26.8%)

- E-newsletter (19.6%)
- Email (30.8%)
- Listserv (12.9%)
- Phone call (6.7%)
- Other (please specify):
  - Events.
  - Idealist.org.
  - They call me.
  - Through organizing training I'm involved with and through my travels/work abroad.
  - Areas of impact I want to make.
  - I don't know (and it made me check a box above).
  - Boards or orgs I am familiar with.
  - Independent research (again, without an "other" box to check, my response to this question is corrupted).
  - I seek out groups that have impacted me and choose to give back to them.
  - Work.
  - Television campaign.
  - People have approached me.
  - Alumni Network.

Question 9: What inspires you to volunteer?

- Make the world a better place. Maintain my rights.
- The fact that it can make a difference to someone's life.
- Connection to the organization's mission.
- Helping others, making a difference, giving back.
- Cause I believe in and a friend or family member invites me to volunteer.
- Mission.
- It gives me an opportunity to do a different type of work, meet new/ interesting people, and it makes me feel good to make a difference I can see. I want to help the community and the people. If what a non-profit is doing moves me, then I will try to help them as much as I can.

- Making a difference. Being asked.
- It's a way to give back and make a difference when you don't necessarily have the funds to do so.
- I feel good seeing the direct impact of my efforts. Frankly, I'm also inspired to volunteer because my job gives me 8 hours of PTO to volunteer each year . . .
- Active participation in a cause I donate money to.
- Sound management; use my time wisely; passion for the cause.
- Making a difference, personally.
- Passion.
- Showing God's love to others. Personal commitment.
- Cause I believe in.
- Causes I care about; I want to create positive change in our world.
- Amazing groups that can make use of my skills/networks to accelerate their work.
- Opportunities to meet people, contribute time and energy and build community.
- Wanting to give back.
- Give back and a desire to help organizations I believe in.
- Feeling of connection and contribution.
- The people and the cause.
- Desire to be part of an organization that I care about.
- Usually just being asked, sometimes I reach out to the organization.
- I am inspired by the same factors that motivate donations—the cause and the organization's ability to fulfill its mission effectively.
- Believing I can make a difference; share my skills/knowledge with someone who needs it.
- The work is infinitely fun and rewarding.
- Having that direct connection to the organization, using my non-profit experience & skills to help the organization advance its mission.

- I feel like it makes a difference and I like being able to be part of an organization which I think is doing good things.
- Knowing I can make a difference.
- Utilizing my time in a good way. Making a difference when I am not able to contribute financially.
- Ability to see how my investment of time will support someone.
- It is the right thing to do. We need to learn and teach to pass it forward.
- 1. I can help do something positive. 2. It gives me insight to the organization and personal contact with the staff.
- I should give back. It's pretty simple.
- Being able to see impact of the volunteer work *meeting and interacting with inspiring people doing important work *when there is great need for volunteers.
- My passion for the cause—recruiting bone marrow donors to the national registry and raising money to support the cause. Compassion, we engage in philanthropy in order to create a more thoughtful, welcoming and just world.
- At the time I wanted to do use my talents/expertise to help, in the end I just made it my fulltime job.
- Organizations that provide evidence of tangible, real-world change. Also, the chance to connect with like-minded people who envision a more just and less polluted world.
- Sense of privilege and civic responsibility.
- Relationships.
- Now I'm confused because staff member was considered as volunteering . . . is my work all volunteering? I like sharing with people who I think will be personally affected.
- God and the people that need it—giving back for what I have been given.
- The mission of the organization and its need for my skill set.
- Makes me feel good.
- I like skills based volunteering, particularly when I can use a skill that I don't use much in my job.

- Organizations that have meaningful, often short term opportunities. I am too busy working for a nonprofit to volunteer extensively for others.

- If I believe in the organization, I want to do my part to make a difference.

- Causes, impact.

- Impact on the land and smiling faces.

- Close personal association with the cause—or if a friend is doing it and asks me to join.

- I like being involved.

- I love meeting other people passionate about helping others, I know it's good for my résumé and career/skill development, I like saving organizations money (particularly if I'm donating to them . . . knowing more money can go directly towards the need), etc.

- Better than working.

- Knowing I'm helping do something good for our community.

- Helping organizations that do direct service or social justice work.

- The desire to help others with what skills I have.

- Knowing that I cannot contribute financially at the level I would like, feeling like I am making a 'hands-on' difference, having worked in non-profit and understanding the needs.

- More effective way to give back than writing a check, I enjoy seeing the impact.

- Knowledge that my service can be of assistance to the mission of organization.

- Being personally affected by a cause.

- Personal connections to the organization and the cause.

- I believe in the cause and want to give back.

- I was always taught that giving back to the community (whether it was with time, money, or both) was really important.

- Faith.

- A group that I care about + a need for my skill set.

- Desire to share my skills and time with organizations understaffed.

- Wanting to give to those who need a voice.
- Need.
- My connection with the cause.
- They need help.
- To reduce the overhead costs to the organization—usually I do this by volunteering at fundraising events.
- I seek out groups that have impacted me and choose to give back to them.
- I desire to give back and an awareness that nonprofit organizations thrive with the use of volunteers.
- A desire to contribute directly to my community. We don't have much money, so volunteering is a good way to give locally.
- The energy of the people at the organization I volunteer with.
- Finding a cure for breast cancer.
- Other people's need.
- Don't volunteer at this time.
- I am currently home raising kids and volunteering is my "adult time" outlet so I can use my brain and skills on a regular basis.
- Making a direct impact to improve someone's situation.
- Want to help and teach my child to help. Even if I don't have a lot of money to donate, I can still give back.
- The desire to give back. It was instilled in me from a young age by my parents that I should give back regardless of circumstances and in any way I can.
- Want to make a difference. Know that communities are built by volunteers.
- The people you meet.
- The same things that inspire me to give—I feel that we are called—as Christians and community members. I also enjoy volunteering and wish that more people my age did volunteer.
- I volunteer for a local neighborhood group. I'm inspired to volunteer to make my neighborhood a better place and to be involved in the political decisions affecting my neighborhood.

- The asker.
- I'm inspired to volunteer for the same reasons I donate: cause, mission, sustainability.
- Causes about which I am passionate and those who ask me to do specific jobs/tasks.
- I want to make a difference in my community through Girl Guides. I want to support philanthropy and AFP through my involvement on committees.
- Want to make the world a better place.
- That my time is meaningful to the organization.
- Personal connection to the cause.
- A desire to feel a stronger connection to helping animals than I get from only donating financially. Also, a desire to help improve the efficiency and success of the organization in support of its mission.
- Working with people who appreciate what I have to give.
- Wanting to help others, benefits for me.
- To give back to the community.
- People.
- Believe in the organization, cause and when my friends are involved with a specific cause/organization.
- Feeling connected to the organization, feeling that my volunteer work is helpful and useful.
- I approach organizations I have a personal connection to, but I enjoy volunteering almost anytime I'm asked.
- If you care about an issue and you want to be change you need to be willing to give your time and be a part of the movement. Personal connection to people in organization and/or cause.
- Being involved hands on with the population I care about.
- I do not have a lot of money to donate and I feel that volunteering your time is more rewarding as it's more tangible.
- Nothing[.] I really do not like to volunteer[.] it is only when I feel guilty.
- Personal interest, networking opportunity, professional development.

- Probably same reason I give, to be a part of something bigger than I am individually.
- Giving back to the community.
- Wanting to give back to society and help organizations I believe in.
- Desire to get more deeply involved with an organization and see more directly the impact that is made. It's an opportunity for me to share some of my talents & skills that I don't get to utilize in my current job.
- I don't earn enough to donate much financially but I can contribute with time. And also the fun of attending events.
- I generally volunteer when I can't give financially.
- The role the organization is playing in the community to strengthen the community and break down stereotypes.
- I enjoy it. It is important to be civically engaged. I like to meet new people. It has also been helpful professionally (learning new skills etc.).
- Face to face connection.
- If we wait for other people to step up, nothing will ever get done. Or it will only be done for self-promotion.
- Friends.
- Knowing that I've made a difference.
- If it fits skills that I have.
- Where I think I can add unique value to an organization based on my skills.
- The cause.
- Direct impact on local community, and the other volunteers.
- Since I lack passion for the work I do for a living, I need another outlet.
- Mission and the ability for my skills to have an impact.
- Events that fit into my schedule, the opportunity to connect with others that I see only through volunteering, meaningful work that incorporates my strengths as well as organizational needs (Shakti Rising's Transformation Through Service model is the best I've ever seen for inspiring volunteers).
- Give back.
- Making a difference . . . feeling like life has meaning and purpose.

- Similar to giving money, was brought up volunteering.
- I like to reinvest my talents and gifts into various communities to improve the lives of others.
- Civic engagement; passion about mission.
- I am able to support an organization even though I cannot contribute financially. Also, it is usually a good time.
- I love my community and being able to connect with people and give back what I can.
- Knowing that funds are limited and my experience can help.
- Service to others.
- It's my responsibility to give back when I can.
- Cause that is aligned with my values. NPO staff & volunteers that are similar to me.
- Helping people! It's great to see that I can do something with my day that makes life a little better for someone else.
- Internal obligation.
- Special, focused events usually.
- Great groups!
- Belief in organization.
- Needs of organization. Feels good to volunteer!
- The importance of volunteering was something that was deeply ingrained in me as a child and it is a way that I can invest in my community and work to make it better.
- Feels good to help engaging with organizations and causes I care about.
- Opportunity to make a difference in my community.
- I want to help but cannot give $.
- The mission of the organization initially and then the actual "volunteer job description." Is it interesting? Will it have a "real" impact? Does it connect me to key people in my community?
- Belief in the cause, skills the organization is looking for, effectiveness of the program, organizational dynamics.
- I've never understood that there is an option not to volunteer. Service is central to why we are all here.

- Contributing to my community in order to help others.
- If the cause is something I care deeply about.
- Helping others.

Question 10: What types of volunteer activities are most rewarding? Mark all that apply.

- Staff member (18.8%)
- **Skilled volunteering (i.e., consulting, accounting, fundraising, marketing) (67.1%)**
- Event volunteer (54.5%)
- Administrative (filing, paperwork, answering phones, etc.) (4.2%)
- Board member (36.2%)
- Committee member (28.2%)
- Advisory board member (18.3%)
- Other (please specify) (11.3%)
  - Outdoor work.
  - Anything.
  - Extra hands when really needed!
  - Working with the kids.
  - Working hands-on with those in need.
  - Direct service provided to a community member.
  - Hands on, physical work, working with the individuals the org serves.
  - Engaging with clients.
  - Direct service.
  - Group volunteering events that have social aspect of it as well.
  - Pro bono technical work.
  - Camp Counselor, being with the kids.
  - Working directly with people who need the support (whether it's tutoring in a shelter, playing at a community center, or helping to plant a garden).
  - All. I don't mind doing the little jobs.
  - Mentoring.
  - Participating in athletic events that raise money for a cause.
  - Girl Guide leader (Sparks).

- None of them really.
- Church positions.
- Manual Labor.
- Being a one on one mentor.
- Mentoring at-risk individuals
- Hands on! I love getting out there and doing something. Many of the orgs. I have volunteered with need a lot of people for a handful of days each year. It's great to know.

Question 11: How would you like most nonprofit organizations to contact you about volunteering? Select three.

- In person (23.0%)
- **E-mail (65.7%)**
- Phone call (22.1%)
- Word of mouth (friend, family, colleague) (47.9%)
- Print publication (8.5%)
- Organizational website (25.8%)
- Social media (Facebook, Twitter, etc.) (31.9%)
- E-newsletter (26.8%)
- Listserv (8.9%)
- Other (please specify) (4.2%)
  - None, I'll seek it when I have the time to donate my time.
  - I'm not looking for any organizations to contact me at this time.
  - It depends on the relationship that I have with that nonprofit.
  - I don't want to be contacted.
  - Church.
  - Never.
  - Affiliated organizations.
  - Volunteer fairs.

Question 12: Does your volunteer work impact your financial contributions?

- **Yes (63.1%)**
- No (26.6%)
- Not sure (10.3%)

- Other (please specify)
  - I assume you mean for that organization? Somewhat.
  - Less likely to give cash when I volunteer locally. For some charities, money is the best gift I can provide.
  - In some cases.
  - In a way . . . I often justify my lesser financial contributions because I give so much time. I believe everyone has to give one or the other.
  - Mentoring involves me spending money on my mentees so I contribute less.
  - Would probably give either way.
  - I often volunteer in lieu of giving $.

Section 3: Closing Thoughts and Thank You

Question 1: Additional Comments or Questions

- Great work! As Chairman of the Gordian Fund, a giving circle to educate and encourage the next generation of philanthropists, I am fully supportive of this survey. I hope it shows some discrete trends about how our colleagues give. Good luck!

- I do not have time for in-person interviews, but I would appreciate receiving a copy of the survey results and sub sequential report.

- Survey included very few options about faith based giving. The only one that came close to that idea is the option of religious institution. Good luck on your survey. I hope you get a great response!

- I would be interested in receiving the survey results.

- What a wonderful questionnaire and idea to study our philanthropic habits. I am interested in learning about the outcomes of your study! Feel free to contact me if you have additional questions!

- Looking forward to the results!

- I don't really think of myself as a philanthropist. I just do social justice work and put my money where my mouth is.

- Please ask before quoting me? I am always happy to talk about my experiences, but I don't want to end up defined by something I dashed off quickly on a web form!!!

- So glad you are doing this. As a young development officer and philanthropist, I am interested in learning what others my age are thinking about their own giving, since it is so ingrained in me through my work!

- I liked this survey—I volunteered for over a year with a hunger relief organization, Numana, Inc., before taking on the paid freelance/ contract marketing & editing work that I do for them now.

- I may not be able to give now while I'm in the midst of raising my children, but I believe in the power of leaving a legacy by giving a specific cash amount from their estate or designating even a small portion of a life insurance policy to a charity.

- This seems like little more than a market research tool for develop- ment professionals seeking to micro-target their solicitations, rather than serious research that's seeking to change the field of philan- thropy for serious social and environmental change. RG is not a good forum for such blasé, plain vanilla surveys. As indicated above in my responses, the survey tool was also sloppily designed and the questions suggest a lack of informed understanding of the issues that are of real concern to RG members and the tools we use—such as investing our assets and leveraging our giving for systemic social im- pact. This is a "Philanthropy as usual" questionnaire. Disappointing.

- I'm very interested in the results of this survey.

- I look forward to reading/seeing your final product. Would love to see if there is a way to do some presentations to various groups and industry organizations where this information is important. This could be vital information to the future of philanthropy. Good luck!!!

- I still do not think that the third sector has enough of a profile within communities. More people would Volunteer and donate if they know how easy it was and also if not for profit organizations told the general public "Honestly" where the donations went.

- I'd love to find out more about how our generation responded to the survey.

- A major organization I am involved with is internationally based (in Portugal) and therefore this may provide another aspect for you to report on.

- Working in non-profit has a Catch-22 effect on giving. I am more aware of the needs of nonprofits and want to give, yet I'm also bitter about how little I earn and am appreciated, so I sometimes resist giving.

- I have little time but love helping out alums. My donations are small to nonexistent and my volunteering is well above par, I believe or at least relatively.

- I realize "church" could fit under nonprofit, but you may want to separate out "religious institution."

- I've only worked for non-profit organizations as a Development Director, so my perspective is different.

About the Author

Emily Davis has been working in the nonprofit sector as an executive director, staff member, consultant, founder, board member, adjunct professor, and volunteer for more than 15 years. She currently serves as President of EDA Consulting, training and consulting in a number of different areas including board development, online communications, multigenerational philanthropy, and fundraising.

Emily serves in a number of board and advisory roles in Colorado and nationally including as a Partner at Social Venture Partners of Boulder County; an Advisory Board Member at Nonprofit Cultivation Center; and an Editorial Advisory Board Member for *Nonprofit World* magazine. Emily is the co-founder of Young Nonprofit Professionals Network in San Diego and the Metro Chapter of Resources Generation. Emily is a member of multiple giving circles including The Gordian Fund and Women Give San Diego.

Her passion for effective leadership has garnered numerous awards and nominations. Emily has her Masters in Nonprofit Management from Regis University. Emily lives with her two Labrador retrievers in Boulder, Colorado.

Index

A

Abrams, Brian, 197

Academic learning, experiential knowledge (combination), 25

Adultism, 104

Advancement opportunities, Next Gen development staff (impact), 25f

AFP Fundraising Dictionary
Online, usage, 8
stewardship definition, 155

AmeriCorps, involvement, 27

Andrea and Charles Bronfman Philanthropies (ACBP), 105, 184

Annie E. Casey Foundation, 22
leaders identification, 13

Annual giving, college degree (impact), 44

Arbogash, Jennie, 5
interview, 202

Associate, status, 203

Association of Fundraising Professionals (AFP), mentorship program provision, 30

B

Baby Boomers, 9, 10–11
change, 118
characteristics, 11
charitable trusts, establishment, 59

directors/boards, leader perspectives, 22

executives/leaders, experiential learning, 13

fundraising professional search, 11–12

leadership transition/values, 13

multigenerational office survey, 19f

nonprofit leadership, 37–38

research, 10

retirement, 16

summary, 16t

Ballard, Amanda, 34, 36

Blogs
direct mail appeal, contrast, 124–125
posts
sharing, 123
template, 171–172
usage, 121

Boards
buddies, usage, 86
description, creation, 88
development, components, 86
diversity, tokenism (relationship), 83–85
dues, fundraising, 87
giving (100 percent), 86–87
involvement, 84
leadership, investment, 85–86

Boards (*continued*)
  members
    discovery. *See* Next Generation
      (Next Gen).
    diversity, 84
    responsibility, 78
  new board members, welcoming,
    163–164
  recruitment plan
    application process, 163
    new board members, welcoming,
      163–164
    orientation, 164
    preplanning, 162
    sample, 162–164
  service, 82–90
  trainings, provision, 85
  usage. *See* Junior boards.
  younger members
    addition, 89
    interaction, 90
BoardSource
  board matrices, availability, 84
  interviewees, young board member
    addition (barriers), 89
  Nonprofit Governance Index 2007
    survey, 82
Bolder Giving, Franklin interview, 179
Boomers. *See* Baby Boomers
Boulder 2140, young professional
  creation, 54
Boushey, Heather, 36
Building Movement Project, 22

C
Carrot Mob, 191–192
Case Foundation, social media (usage),
  101
Cause on Facebook, advocacy, 57
Center on Philanthropy (Indiana
  University), 44–45, 96

Challenges for Nonprofits and Philanthropy
  (Eisenberg), 27
Charitable trust, establishment, 59
Charities
  communication
    process, preference, 177, 181, 199
    satisfaction, 182
  support
    process, 176
    time/length, 181, 198–199
Chartered Advisors in Philanthropy, 179
Chicano Movement, experiences, 10
Chronicle of Philanthropy (Thurman), 15,
  22
Civil Rights Movement
  experiences, 10
  principles, unity, 19–20
Coaching, 29–30
  consideration, 24
Colorado College
  internship programs (development),
    29–30
  Public Interest Fellowship Program,
    54–55
Committees
  experiences, 178
  participation, 80–82
Communications
  challenges, 25
  channels, usage, 121
  gap, 33–34
  questions/results, 225
Community Foundation Market
  Research study, 43
Community foundations, youth
  philanthropy groups, 54
Community Shares, 148
Consultants, hiring, 131–132
Continuing education, 30–31
Convio, 14, 44, 62
Cooper, Ellen, 64

Council on Foundations (COF),
Annual Conference, 98
Coupland, Douglas, 12–13
*Creating Change Through Family
Philanthropy* (Goldberg/Pittelman/
Resource Generation), 104
Creating Change Through Family
Philanthropy (retreat), 110
Cultivation strategies, 62

D
Daniels Young Leaders Circle (Daniels
Legacy Circle), 197, 199
Daring to Lead (nonprofit research), 11
Debt Explosion Among College Graduates
(Boushey), 36
Decision making, generational leadership
(contrast), 28
Del.i.cious, tools (usage), 124
Development departments, leaders
(goals), 24–25
Development professionals
balance, promotion, 31–33
multigenerational issues, 24
next generation, investment, 31
Development staff, cause/job
commitment, 36–37
Dialogue, transparency, 27
Diggs, usage, 125–126
Direct mail appeal, blogs (contrast), 124–125
Donors
appropriation, NPO determination, 62
communications channels, usage, 121
engagement, 60
entry point, 56
listening, rule, 111
Next Generation, cultivation, 45–60
relationships
cultivation, 111
stability, 60–63
trends/changes, 186

E
Education debt, young professionals
(management), 36
Eisenberg, Pablo, 27, 37
Electronic communications, user access,
121
El Pomar Fellowship Alumni Advisory
Board, 199
El Pomar Foundation, 197
Emerging Practitioners in Philanthropy
(EPIP)
awareness, value, 113–114
conversations, 97
creation, 96
Impact Assessment, 96–97
multigenerationalism conversations,
97
networking connections, 100
organizational spotlight, 98–100
partnerships, 100
E-newsletters, usage, 128
"Engaging Tomorrow's Donors Today"
(Community Shares), 148
Enterprise Foundations, subsidiary, 185
Enthusiasm, opportunities, 26–27
Entry-level opportunities, avoidance, 27
EPIP. *See* Emerging Practitioners in
Philanthropy
Events, 51–53. *See also* Networking
coordination, planning, 52
creation, 55–56
development, advice, 53
donor entry point, 56
holding, fundraising professionals
(time commitment), 51–52
organization hosting, 52–53
planning, 78–79
Executive transition, challenges, 25
Experiential knowledge
academic learning, combination, 25
importance, 30–31

Experiential learning, Baby Boomer
valuation, 13

F

Facebook
blockage, 130
Page, responses, 136–137
questions, usage, 122
usage, 62
percentages, 118
Face-to-dace connections, opportunity,
124
Family Circle Advisors, Parker interview,
190
Family dynamics, shift, 104–106
Family foundations
decision-making process, college-age
family members (inclusion), 105
Galeti interview, 193
leadership, 108
Family foundations, youth philanthropy
groups, 54
Family fund, perception, 113
Family hierarchies, 104
Family legacy, maintenance, 103
Family members, NPO (relationship),
186
Family philanthropists
dynamics, awareness, 185
engagement, 110–113
Family philanthropy
engagement, 95
generational involvement, 188
Next Gen donor involvement, 108
understanding, 102–113
wealth, transfer, 103
"Family Philanthropy and the
Intergenerational Transfer of
Wealth" (Community Foundation
Market Research study), 43–44
Family Quest Giving Deck, usage, 106

Fans, listening, 120–122
Fellowship, status, 203–204
Financial contributions, recognition, 62
IRS requirements, 63f
Financial support/flexibility, provision, 24
Fine, Allison, 119
Fischler, Sarah, 148
Followers, listening, 120–122
Foundation Center
family foundation contribution,
102–103
social media, usage, 101
Foundations
impact, 95
infrastructure, development, 194
junior boards, usage, 82–83
staff, training, 97
Franklin, Jason, 5
interview, 179
Frosh, Alan H., 5
interview, 196
Full Circle Advisors, 102
Full partner, status, 203
Funders, financial solutions, 34–37
Fundraising
approaches, 1–3
inspiration, 1–2
art/science, 6
event
building/faltering, 79
development, advice, 53
future, 141–142
generational dynamics, understanding,
16–17
Next Generation worksheet, 146–147
professionals, events time
commitment, 51–52
resources, 142–143
social media
incorporation, 5
usage, 120

staff, stereotype awareness, 31
success, sharing, 123

G
Galeti, Mary, 5, 103, 193
Gary, Tracy, 112
Gast, Mike, 5, 83, 97, 110
  interview, 174
Gates, Bill (Generation X), 12
Gender dynamics, 104
Generational Changes and Leadership
      (Kunreuther), 28
Generational changing work styles,
      recognition, 24
"Generational Difference in Charitable
      Giving and in Motivations for
      Giving" (Campbell and
      Company study), 46
Generational dynamics, understanding,
      16–17
Generational leadership, decision making
      (contrast), 28
Generational qualities, understanding, 24
Generations
  characteristics, 7–8
  communication styles, 187
  definitions, 7, 8–16
  fundraising, 8
    communications, 9t
  gap, strategic solutions, 17
  invitations, 112
  philanthropic communications, 35t
  summary, 16t
  survey, 17f, 18f
  types, 8–9
  values/work styles, tensions, 7
Generation X, 9, 12–14
  charitable trust, establishment, 59
  communication styles, 45
  contributions, 78–79
  donors, giving, 44

Facebook usage, percentage, 118
  frustration, 13
  fundraising, 1
  generational challenges, 20–21
  leadership positioning, 109
  multigenerational office survey, 20f
  nonprofit cultivation, 44
  perspectives, diversity, 18
  recruitment, 2
  summary, 16t
  values/work style, 12
Generation Y (Millennials), 9, 14–15
  communication styles, 45
  contributions, 78–79
  Facebook usage, percentage, 118
  fundraising, 1
  generational challenges, 20–21
  leadership positioning, 109
  multigenerational office survey, 20f
  nonprofit cultivation, 44
  number, 44
  perspectives, diversity (benefits), 18
  power, 15
  questions/challenges, 15
  recruitment, 2
  summary, 16t
  work style/communications, 14
GenNext, 4, 64–68
  communications, 67–68
  launch, 64–66
  program, uniqueness, 65
Gifts, young participants solicitation, 56
Giving. *See* Planned giving
  amount/frequency, limitations, 181,
      199
Giving circles, 49–51
  creation process, advice, 50
  Frosh interview, 196
  Next Gen donor philanthropy, 50
  popularity, increase (strategy), 50–51
  young philanthropist involvement, 49

Goldseker, Sharna, 5, 105
  interview, 184
Gonzalez, David, 64
Google Alerts, setup, 124
Gordian Fund
  focus, 198
  Frosh interview, 196
"Grandparent Legacy Project" (21/64),
    184
Grand Street
  facilitation, 184
  peer group, goals, 112
Grant makers
  Next Generation, 95
  nonprofit professionals, challenges, 112
  print resources, 114
  resources, 114
  websites, 114
Grant making (change), 105
  social media, impact, 101–102

H
Hands On Network, 88
Hare, Carly, 100
Harris, Trista, 52
Headwaters Foundation, 52

I
IdeaEncore, 137
Idealist website, volunteer opportunities
    platform, 88
Inclusiveness, Gen X/Millennial value, 80
Inclusive organizational cultures/
    dynamics, shift, 25
Indiana University, Center on
    Philanthropy, 44–45, 96
Individuals, recruitment, 205
Influencers, impact, 57–58
Innovation, opportunities, 26–27
In-person connections, importance,
    61–62

Inspired Philanthropy (Gary), 112
Internal Revenue Service (IRS)
    requirements, 62
Internet, tools, 62
Internships, 29–30
  consideration, 24
  involvement, 27
Interviews, 173
Invisible Children, 119

J
Jewish Community Endowment Fund
    (JCEF), Peninsula Community
    Jewish Teen Foundation, 49
Jordan, Michael (Generation X), 12
Jumo (nonprofit organization website),
    51
Junior boards, usage, 82–83

K
Kanter, Beth, 119
Kennedy, John F. (assassination), 10
Kim, Helen, 22
King, Jr., Martin Luther (assassination),
    10
Kopf, Alyssa, 148
Kunreuther, Frances, 22, 28

L
Lawrence Welk Family Foundation,
    generational philanthropy, 111
Leadership
  age, impact (perception), 25f
  assumptions, challenge, 26–27
  capacity, growth, 33f
  challenges. *See* Shared leadership.
  gaps, challenges, 21–29
  investment, 28. *See also* Boards.
  models, change, 27–29
  New Structures and Practices Theory,
    23–24

Next Gen development staff, impact (perception), 25f
Next Gen fundraising survey participants, tools, 32f
opportunities, 81
    creation. *See* Volunteers.
    generation, 25
    positioning, 109
    qualitative gaps, 23–24
    Recognition Problem Theory, 23
    Redefining the Position Theory, 23
    Replacement Theory, 23
    roles, nonprofit professionals (interest), 28–29
    Staying on Top Theory, 23
    team, homogeneity, 83
    transition/values, 13
Learning organization
    becoming, 143–144
    qualities, usage, 25
Liquid Leaders, laws, 27
Liquid Leadership (Szollose), 27
Listservs, usage, 88, 128
Lymphoma Society, 55

M
Make Money Make Change (MMMC) retreat, 110, 174–175
Marketing, social media (usage), 120
Mashable, 137
MediaMasters, message map (usage), 78
Memorandum of Understanding (MOU)
    sample, 160–161
    usage, 55
Mentoring, 29–30
Mentorships
    consideration, 24
    opportunities, YNPN provision, 30
    program, AFP provision, 30
Millennials. *See* Generation Y
Moore, Cassie J., 28

interviews, 30–31
Motivational Values, cards (usage), 106
Movement Generation Support Committee, coordination, 174
Moving to End Sexual Assault (MESA), recognition event, 134
Multichannel communications plan, social media (usage), 117–118
Multigenerational (multigen) communications, nonprofit struggle, 102
Multigenerational (multigen) conversation, 21/64 approach, 188
Multigenerational (multigen) development department, challenges, 20
Multigenerational (multigen) development offices
    challenges, 33–34
    participants, survey, 17
    survey, 2
        results, 6
Multigenerational Development Office Survey
    communications, questions/results, 225
    fundraising office, 208
    overview, 208
    results, 208
Multigenerational (multigen) Development Office survey, 81
Multigenerational (multigen) family philanthropy, 184
Multigenerational (multigen) fundraising efforts, leading, 16–37
Multigenerational (multigen) issues, 24
Multigenerational (multigen) office, working (benefits)
    Baby Boomer/Traditionalist survey, 19f
    Generation X/Generation Y survey, 20f

Multigenerational (multigen) office, working (challenges) Baby Boomers/Traditionalists survey, 22f

Multigenerational (multigen) office, working (challenges) Baby Boomer/Traditionalist survey, 21f, 22f

Multigenerational (multigen) staff interaction, benefits, 18 members, recruitment/retention, 3

N

National Hemophilia Foundation, Colorado Chapter activities/news, mixture, 124 blog posts, 123

Negative feedback, personal opinion, 144

Networked Nonprofit, The (Fine/Kanter), 119–120

Networking events, 66–67 opportunities, sharing, 25 resources, 100–101

Networks expansion, 88 young people access, 57

New board members, welcoming, 163–164

New Structures and Practices Theory, 23–24

New York University, grant-making certificate, 96

Next Generation (Next Gen) annual giving, 47f board members, discovery, 87–89 causes, attraction, 46, 48 contact methods, 61 development staff, impact, 25f donation age, 47f

fundraising survey participants leadership capacity tools, 33f tools, importance, 32f

giving, philanthropic influences, 57f

grant maker, Franklin interview, 179

intention, philanthropy continuation, 58f

organization research process, 48f

philanthropy clarity, 7–8 engagement, 43 planned giving, interest, 59f print resources, 69 resources, 69 volunteering, NPO contact method, 77f

volunteers leadership opportunities, creation, 75 opportunities, knowledge, 77f

websites, 69

worksheet, 146–147

Next Generation (Next Gen) donors cultivation, 45–60 engagement, 60 family philanthropy involvement, 108 organization preference, 61f philanthropy, 50 preferred recognition types, 63f

"Next Generation of American Giving, The" (Convio), 14, 44, 117

Next Generation (Next Gen) philanthropists charity considerations, 59 development, 112 engagement, 205–206 Gast interview, 174

Nonprofit associations, networks (expansion), 88

Nonprofit boards recommendation, 177–178 service, 177, 199

young professionals recruitment,
200–201
Nonprofit communities, change, 15
Nonprofit development department,
generations (survey), 17f
Nonprofit development staff, generations
survey, 18f
Nonprofit Governance Index 2007 survey
(BoardSource), 82
Nonprofit Law Blog, 137
Nonprofit leaders, policies (institution),
37
Nonprofit missions, long-term health
(support), 90
Nonprofit organizations (NPOs)
abilities, 113–114
age, assumptions, 26
Baby Boomers, founding, 11
boards, service, 182–183
donor appropriation strategies, 62
family member, relationship, 186
junior boards, usage, 82–83
leaders, goals, 24–25
Next Gen contact methods, 61
tools, leverage, 119
volunteers, usage, 133
Nonprofit practices, Generation X
challenge, 13
Nonprofit professionals
challenge, 112
leadership role interest, 28–29
Nonprofit professionals, recruitment/
retention, 24
Nonprofit staff, communication, 9
Nonprofit Technology Network
(NTEN), 119, 137
North Star Fund, 179, 183

O
Older generations, Generation X
frustration, 13

Older leaders, nonprofit professionals
(perspective), 22
Onboarding, 89–90
100% board giving, 86–87
One-on-one interactions, 76
importance, 61–62
One-time donation, solicitation, 52
Online communications
foundations management, 102
goals/purpose, consultant review, 131
Organizational Readiness Assessment,
152–153
power, harnessing, 117
print resources, 138
resources, 138–139
websites, 138–139
Online resources, sharing, 112–113
Online sharing policy, elements, 136
Organizational history, 155–156
Organizational Readiness Assessment,
148–154
online communications, 152–153
planning, 151–152
score, evaluation, 153–154
Organizations
board, involvement. *See* Boards.
branding, 131
changes, 38
Generation X contributions, 78–79
global focus, donors (characteristics),
45
improvement, 178
Millennials, contributions, 78–79
Next Gen donors
contact method preference, 61f
research, 48f
online communications, goals/
purpose (consultant review), 131
policy, website placement, 136
ROI evaluation, 62
social media plan, 127

Organizations (*continued*)
  stories (sharing), social media (usage), 121
  strengths/weaknesses, evaluation, 84
  Traditionalists, loyalty, 45
  value (addition), social media (usage), 124
  volunteers, experience, 76
Outreach, 75–78

P
Parker, Lisa, 5, 102, 107
  interview, 190
Partnerships
  donor alternative, 55
  options, 203–204
  tiers, description, 202–203
Payton, Robert, 98–100
Peace Corps, involvement, 27
Peer-to-peer networks, 56–58
Perspectives, diversity, 18
Philanthropic communications, generational examination, 35t
Philanthropic communities, change, 15
Philanthropic influences (Next Gen giving), 57f
Philanthropic practices, Generation X challenge, 13
Philanthropic status quo, Millennial questions, 15
Philanthropists
  charity, considerations, 59
  relationships, cultivation, 103
Philanthropy
  Association of Fundraising Professionals definition, 73
  career, consideration, 99
  continuation, Next Gen intention, 58f
  donor perspective, 4
  engagement
    opportunities, 191

process, 175–176, 180
  generations, 7
  involvement story, 179–180, 196–198
  issues/activities, connection, 107
  learning, 107–108
  multigenerationalism, EPIP conversations, 97
  Next Generation
    engagement, 43
    resources, 69
    survey, 61
  print publications, 39
  resources, 39–40
  usage, 97
  volunteering, comparison, 73
  volunteerism, usage (advice), 91–92
  websites, 40
Philanthropy Advisors, 184
Philanthropy's Next Generation
  charitable organizations, financial contributions, 230
  closing thoughts, 286
  survey, 2–3, 62
    results, 6, 230
  volunteer time contributions, 271
"Picture Your Legacy" (21/64), 184
Picture Your Legacy cards, usage, 106
Pioneer Leadership Program Alumni Advisory Board, 199
Planned giving, 58–60
  Next Gen donor interest, 59f
Planning, 151–152
Plans, 145
Playbooks, usage, 132
Power struggles, 104
Princeton University, internship programs (development), 29–30
Professional development, 66
  investment, 96–97
Prospective donors (increase), volunteer opportunities (impact), 74–79

Proteus Fund, 179
Public Interest Fellowship Program
    (Colorado College), 54
Public philanthropy, burden, 105

R
Ratliff, Jasmine Hall, 97
Razoo, 79
    nonprofit organization website, 51
    usage, 62
Ready to Lead (nonprofit research), 11
Recognition Problem Theory, 23
Recruitment plan, 162–164
Redefining the Position Theory, 23
Relationships
    building, 187
    stability, 60–63
Replacement Theory, 23
Resource Generation (RG), 97
    EPIP partnerships, 100
    Gast interview, 174
    importance, 110
Return on investment (ROI),
        organization evaluation, 62
Risks, calculation, 144
Robert Wood Johnson Foundation, 97
Rodriguez, Robby, 22–23
RSS feed, usage, 126

S
Service learning, 66
Sexism, impact, 104
Shared leadership, challenges, 25
Shultz, Molly Hafid, 113
Sibling rivalries, 104
Silent Generation (Traditionalists), 9
    charitable trust establishment, 59
Social change (support), philanthropy
        (usage), 97
Social Justice Philanthropy Collaborative,
    179

Social media
    appreciation, problems, 125–126
    consultant, contracting, 131–132
    cross-promotion, 126
    efforts, control, 130
    expense, 126
    feedback, 125
    goals/objectives
        clarification, 127–128
        suggestions, 128
    growth, 122–123
    impact, 101–102
    importance, 117–118
    incorporation, 5
    networks, usage, 101
    outlets, 168–169
    policies, 135–137
        feedback, 137
        resources, 137
    posts/comments, inappropriateness,
        135–136
    purpose, 127
    quickness/access, 119
    staff, hiring, 130–131
    stewardship, 123
    strategies, 124, 168–169
        evaluation, 135
    tool, 119–120
    two-way street, 124–125
    usage, 61–62
    volunteers, impact, 132–134
Social Media Examiner, 137
Social Media Governance, 137
Social media plan
    advice, 129
    building, 126–129
    evaluation, 170
    goals/objectives, 167
    implementation, 129–134, 169–170
    metrics, 170
    outline, 167–170

Social media plan (*continued*)
  purpose, 167
  target audiences, 167–168
  worksheet, 165–166
Social networking sites, usage, 130
Social networks, identification, 128–129
Social Venture Partners (SVP), Arbogash
    interview, 202
Staff
  balance, 32
  hiring, 130–131
  nonprofit leader encouragement, 81
Stahl, Rusty, 96, 98–99
Stakeholders (reaching), social media
    (usage), 120
StayClassy
  nonprofit organization website, 51
  organizational spotlight, 79–80
Staying on Top Theory, 23
Stereotypes, fundraising staff awareness,
    31
Stewardship
  activities, 157
    list, 158t
  AFP definition, 155
  communications, examples, 159t
  development, social media (usage),
    61–62
  strategies, 62
Stewardship Plan Worksheet, 155–157
  implementation, assumptions,
    156–157
  organizational history, 155–156
Students for a Free Tibet, 54
Surveys, summaries, 207
Susan G. Komen Walk for a Cure, 55
Szollose, Brad, 27

T
Team in Training for Leukemia, 55
Tecovas Foundation, 193

Templates, 145
Thurman, Rosetta, 15
Tiered partnership program, success, 204
Tokenism, board diversity (relationship),
    83–85
Touchpoint, 155
Traditionalists, 8, 9–10
  loyalty, 45
  major donation candidate, 10
  multigenerational office survey, 19f
  names, alternatives, 9
  philanthropy/volunteerism,
    retirement, 185
  planned giving candidate, 10
  summary, 16t
  work styles, 9–10
Turnover
  rates, reduction, 31–33
  reduction, 38
21st Century School Fund, 179
21/64
  EPIP partnership, 100
  Goldseker interview, 184
  mission, description, 105
  multigenerational conversation, 188
  organizational spotlight, 106
Twitter
  followers, 132
  questions, 122
  usage, 62

U
"Understanding the Next Generation of
    Nonprofit Employees" (Ballard),
    34, 36
Unitarian Universalist Veatch Program,
    113
United Way of Greater St. Louis (UW),
    4, 81
  GenNext, organizational spotlight,
    64–68

networking events, 66–67
professional development, 66
service learning, 66
staff support, 68

V

Value (addition), social media (usage), 124
V-Day Global, 54–55
Veterans (Traditionalists), 9
Vietnam War, experiences, 10
Volunteering
  age group, committee creation, 82
  committee participation, 80–82
  NPO contact method, Next Gen preference, 77f
  orientation process, 78
  philanthropy, comparison, 73
  print resources, 93
  resources, 93
  skill, provision, 82
  strategy, 74
  websites, 93
Volunteerism, advice, 91–92
Volunteers
  activities, types, 74f
  committee, launching/recruitment (considerations), 80–81
  development, challenge, 190
  development program, design, 134
  impact, 132–134
  intentions, 133
  interaction, 134
  job description, 133–134
  leadership opportunities, creation, 75
  management, challenge, 190
  opportunities
    Next Gen individuals, knowledge, 77f
    survey respondents, knowledge, 76

opportunities, creation, 74–79
outreach, 75–78
progress, evaluation/conversations, 134
prospective donor status, 75
time, contributions, 271
usage, NPO option, 133

W

Walk-a-Thons, 55–56
Wealth, transfer, 44, 103
Wealth for the Common Good, 179
Web 1.0 technology, usage, 128
Websites, usage, 128
Wild Apricot, 137
Women Give San Diego, 50–51
Women's Foundation of California, donor circle, 51
Women's Movement, experiences, 10
Word-of-mouth marketing, 57
Working Across Generations (Kunreuther/ Kim/Rodriguez), 22–23, 37
  nonprofit research, 11
Working environments, encouragement, 31–33
Work models, change, 27–29
Worksheets, 145
World War II Generation (Traditionalists), 9

Y

Young Americans Bank, involvement, 196–197
Young board members, addition (barriers), 89
Young donors
  interaction, 148–151
  monetary/physical goals, setting, 55–56
  responsibility, struggle, 109
Young Leaders Giving Society, 64

Young Nonprofit Professionals Network
 (YNPN), 54
 board members, responsibility, 78
 chapter, boards recruitment, 88
 EPIP, comparison, 96–97
 mentorship opportunities, 30
 volunteer-led organization, 132
Young participants, gifts solicitation,
 56

Young philanthropists
 donation levels, 46
 funds appropriations, opportunities,
 43–45
 giving circle, 49
Young professionals
 education debt management, 36
 groups, partnerships, 54–55
Youth philanthropy groups, 54